CREATING

Keepsakes

SCRAPBOOK | MAGAZINE

A TREASURY OF FAVORITES

Scrapbooking
Family Heritage

Presenting over 800 of the best designs and ideas
from *Creating Keepsakes* publications, devoted to
creating unique family heritage scrapbooks.

PRODUCED EXCLUSIVELY FOR LEISURE ARTS

Founding Editor	Lisa Bearnson
Co-founder	Don Lambson
Editor-in-Chief	Tracy White
Special Projects Editor	Leslie Miller
Copy Editor	Kim Sandoval
Editorial Assistants	Joannie McBride, Fred Brewer
Administrative Assistant	Michelle Bradshaw
Art Director	Brian Tippetts
Designer	Blue Sky Studios
Production Designers	Just Scan Me!, Exposure Graphics
Publisher	Mark Seastrand
Media Relations	Alicia Bremer, 801/364-2030
Web Site Manager	Emily Johnson
Assistant Web Site Editor	Sarah Wilcox
Production Manager	Gary Whitehead
Business Sales Manager	Tara Schofield
Business Sales Assistants	Jacque Jensen, Melanie Cain
Advertising Sales Manager	Becky Lowder
Wholesale Accounts	800/815-3538

Donna Hair, stores A–G,
and outside of U.S., ext. 235

Victoria James, stores H–R, ext. 226

Kristin Schaefer, stores S–Z
(except "Scr"), ext. 250

Sherrie Burt, stores starting with "Scr,"
ext. 244

Kim Biehn, distributor accounts, ext. 251

PRIMEDIA
Consumer Magazine & Internet Group

Vice President, Group Publisher	David O'Neil
Circulation Director	Lisa Harris
Associate Circulation Director	Darcy Cruwys
Circulation Manager	Sara Gunn
Promotions Manager	Stephanie Michas
Business Manager	Laurie Halvorsen

PRIMEDIA, Inc.

Chairman	Dean Nelson
President & CEO	Kelly Conlin
Vice-Chairman	Beverly C. Chell

PRIMEDIA Enthusiast Media

EVP Consumer Marketing/Circulation	Steve Aster
SVP/Chief Financial Officer	Kevin Neary
SVP, Mfg., Production & Distribution	Kevin Mullan
SVP/Chief Information Officer	Debra C. Robinson
VP, Consumer Marketing	Bobbi Gutman
VP, Manufacturing	Gregory A. Catsaros
VP, Single Copy Sales	Thomas L. Fogarty
VP, Manufacturing Budgets & Operations	Lilia Golia
VP, Human Resources	Kathleen P. Malinowski
VP, Business Development	Albert Messina
VP, Database / e-Commerce	Suti Prakash

PRIMEDIA Outdoor Recreation and Enthusiast Group

SVP, Group Publishing Director	Brent Diamond
SVP, Marketing and Internet Operations	Stephen H. Bender
VP, Marketing and Internet Operations	Dave Evans

SUBSCRIPTIONS

To subscribe to *Creating Keepsakes* magazine or to change the address of your current subscription, call or write:

Phone: 888/247-5282

International: 760/745-2809

Fax: 760/745-7200

Subscriber Services
Creating Keepsakes
P.O. Box 469007
Escondido, CA 92046-9007

Some back issues of *Creating Keepsakes* magazine are available for $5 each, payable in advance.

CORPORATE OFFICES

Creating Keepsakes is located at 14901 Heritagecrest Way, Bluffdale, UT 84065. Phone: 801/984-2070. Fax: 801/984-2080. Home page: *www.creatingkeepsakes.com*.

Scrapbooking Family Heritage
Hardcover ISBN 1-57486-462-9
Softcover ISBN 1-57486-463-7
Library of Congress Control Number 2004113014

Published by Leisure Arts, Inc., 5701 Ranch Drive, Little Rock, Arkansas 72223. 501-868-8800. *www.leisurearts.com*. Printed in the United States of America.

Special Projects Director: Susan Frantz Wiles
Vice President and Editor-in-Chief: Sandra Graham Case
Executive Director of Publications: Cheryl Nodine Gunnells
Senior Publications Director: Susan White Sullivan
Senior Design Director: Cyndi Hansen
Senior Art Operations Director: Jeff Curtis
Art Imaging Director: Mark Hawkins
Director of Retail Marketing: Stephen Wilson
Director of Designer Relations: Debra Nettles
Graphic Design Supervisor: Amy Vaughn
Graphic Artist: Katherine Atchison
Associate Editor: Susan McManus Johnson
Editorial Assistants: JoAnn Forrest, Merrilee Gasaway, Amy Hansen, April Hansen, and Janie Wright
Imaging Technicians: Stephanie Johnson and Mark Potter
Publishing Systems Administrator: Becky Riddle
Publishing Systems Assistants: Clint Hanson, John Rose, and Chris Wertenberger

Publisher: Rick Barton
Vice President, Finance: Tom Siebenmorgen
Director of Corporate Planning and Development: Laticia Mull Dittrich
Vice President, Retail Marketing: Bob Humphrey
Vice President, Sales: Ray Shelgosh
Vice President, National Accounts: Pam Stebbins
Director of Sales and Services: Margaret Reinold
Vice President, Operations: Jim Dittrich
Comptroller, Operations: Rob Thieme
Retail Customer Service Manager: Stan Raynor
Print Production Manager: Fred F. Pruss

you are your family's historian

Recently, I came across an envelope containing some old photos. Although I recognized a few of the faces peering out at me from across the years, I realized that I knew very little about the events and people in the photos. Curious, I took the photos to my mom and asked her for some details. As it happens, the photos were of my grandparents during the early years of their marriage. My mom related some of the memories triggered by the photos. As she shared her memories, I realized that it was up to me to make sure that these heart-touching stories did not disappear.

You have the same charge: You can begin today to capture all of those memories that will soon fade away if not otherwise recorded. To help spur creative ideas for scrapbooking the memories behind your old family photos, we've gathered our favorite heritage articles and scrapbook pages from the past five years of *Creating Keepsakes* Magazine. In this volume, you'll find an enormous collection of great design ideas, journaling jumpstarts that will help you uncover stories that may otherwise be lost, and terrific tips for restoring damaged photos and capturing tomorrow's heritage photos today.

During my more than seven years at *Creating Keepsakes* Magazine, I have seen countless scrapbook pages from all over the world. One thing strikes me every time I see another scrapbook page: Your family's stories are important, heart touching and worth remembering. Don't waste another minute. Become your family's historian today. You'll be creating heirlooms that will be treasured for generations to come. ❤

Sincerely,

Tracy

Editor-in-Chief
Creating Keepsakes Magazine

207

DENISE PAULEY

Grandma Mar was a traveler even as a teenager. Seen here with her friend Charlotte in 1953, she was already drawn to the relaxation and thrill of discovery while exploring new places — a fascination that has since taken her across the country and around the globe.

80

MARILYN HEALEY

Glen Alfred Openshaw
My Grandfather

Billings, Montana about 1938
Blanche, Carl Eugene (back) Darlene, Glen (front)

![Creating Keepsakes logo]

contents

SCRAPBOOKING FAMILY HERITAGE

LEE ANNE RUSSELL

31

ASHKEY GULL

244

Articles

Page Ideas

Tips and Accents

WENDY SUE ANDERSON

54

MICHELLE TARDIE

149

NOW'S THE TIME

Gather the memories of older relatives

When's the last time you sat down with an older relative and talked about his or her life? If you're like me, I've always been interested, but I've put it off again and again. Why? I've been waiting for a time I'm not so busy. I've felt it important to focus on completing my children's album and my theme albums first. I've always thought I had plenty of time to capture the memories of older family members. I was wrong.

I'm here to tell you that time is running out. The time to capture details is not when your parents or other loved ones are in their 80s or their health begins to decline. It's now, while they're still active and able to share the stories of their childhoods, lives and ancestors.

BY MARY LARSON
ILLUSTRATION
BY JOHN REES

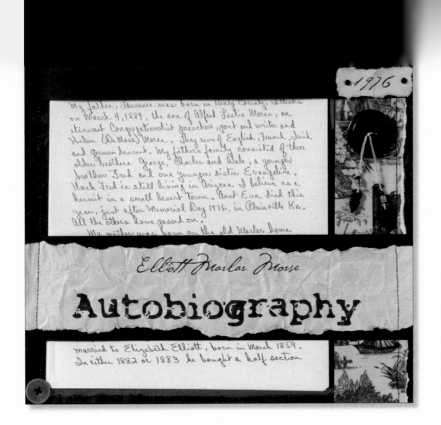

My father, Laurence was born in Henry County, Illinois on March 4, 1889, the son of Alfred Leslie Morse, an itinerant Congregationalist preacher, poet and writer and Helen (DeMoss) Morse. They were of English, French, Irish and German descent. My father's family consisted of three older brothers George, Charles and Dale, a younger brother Fred and one younger sister Evangeline. Uncle Fred is still living in Arizona I believe as a hermit in a small desert town. Aunt Eva died this year, just after Memorial Day 1976, in Plainville Ka. All the others have passed on.
My mother was born on the old Marlar home

Elliott Marlar Morse

Autobiography

married to Elizabeth Elliott, born in March 1859.
In either 1882 or 1883 he bought a half section

Figure 1. Make a large pocket with a page protector and a sewing machine to save a special document. *Page by Mary Larson.* **Supplies** *Patterned paper and embossed paper:* K & Company; *Computer fonts:* Smash, downloaded from the Internet; Cézanne, P22 Type Foundry; Stitches, Making Memories; *Other:* Beads, brads and antique buttons.

A Little Background

My parents aren't young, but to me they've always seemed invincible, even immortal. They've enjoyed great physical health. They still golf and garden and volunteer. They live life to its fullest. As the family's "designated historian," I've always thought I have plenty of time to capture their stories.

I've since learned I'm wrong. My parents may be healthy, but they're not young. Another complication? I've learned they're not invincible. My father is having trouble with his memory. He gets a bit confused at times, and his short-term memory is much weaker than his long-term memory. My father's recollections are getting foggy. We all know where this could be leading.

My Efforts

I realized I needed to hurry and capture my father's memories while I still could. My first dilemma was figuring out where to start. I knew I wanted to ask Dad a lot of questions, but he doesn't live near me, and I worried I wouldn't get all the information I needed or wanted.

Fortunately, I got a head start when I came across a hand-written autobiography my father had created for a time capsule in 1976. My father had forgotten about the document, and I was ecstatic to discover it in a box of his papers.

As I read the autobiography, I cried. It contained more information than I could ever have dreamed of getting now. I felt incredibly lucky, although I knew I still had more work to do to record the rest of Dad's life.

The Autobiography

My father's autobiography gave me numerous ideas of what to record (Figure 1). You can use the following as a guide:

• **Family Members.** Record all family members, plus any ancestors you know about. Include as many names and dates as possible, such as birth, death or marriage.

• **Earliest Memories as a Child.** My dad has these recollections, and so do I. Write them down,

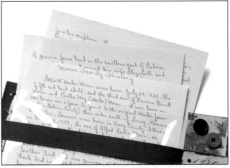

Figure 2. List heirlooms and belongings in notepad fashion. *Page by Mary Larson.* **Supplies** *Patterned paper:* K & Company; *Corrugated cardstock:* DMD Inc.; *Computer font:* Cooper MD BT, downloaded from the Internet, *Alphabet stamps:* Barnes & Noble; *Chalk:* Craf-T Products; *Other:* Ribbon and brads.

as sometimes they're the funniest and most memorable moments of childhood. (Otherwise we wouldn't remember them!)

- **A Typical Day as a Child.** My parents' background is very different from how I grew up and how my children are growing up. I want my children to know how times change and what life was like for those before them.

- **Memories of Their Parents.** This was difficult for my father since his mother died when he was seven and his father died four years later. Still, he wrote down the memories he did have.

- **Education and Careers.** Record dates and schools. Ask about careers or work history, including military careers. My dad even wrote down what his brothers and sisters ended up doing with their lives.

- **Personalities of Family Members.** Record how they would describe their spouse and children. What goals or expectations do they have for them? I didn't realize until I read Dad's autobiography that he thought I was the most outgoing of his children.

- **Description of Self.** This may be more difficult, but it's interesting to read how one describes one's personality.

- **Religious and Personal Beliefs.** Record a person's religious or personal beliefs.

- **Political Beliefs.** Share your loved one's political beliefs if any. What's important to them? Do they still vote? Why do they vote the way they do? My dad had a very lengthy explanation of his political beliefs and why he thought the way he did.

- **Views of the World.** What do they think of the way the world is today? Do they see things as good or wish for the days of old?

- **Predictions for the Future.** Since my father's autobiography was in a time capsule that wasn't to be opened until 2076, he took some guesses as to what the future could hold. Wouldn't it be fun to have your parents or grandparents predict what the world will be like when you are a grandparent or your children are grandparents?

My Additions

Once you've considered the ideas above, here are four more suggestions of my own:

- **Heirlooms in Their Possession.** As shown in Figure 2, my parents have an antique china cabinet filled with heirlooms. The last time I was in my hometown,

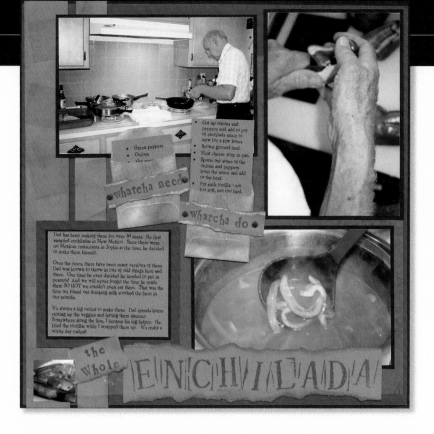

Figure 3. Put recipe ingredients and instructions on pullout cards for convenience. *Page by Mary Larson.* **Supplies** *Handmade paper:* ArtisticScrapper.com; *Stamps:* Ma Vinci (large alphabet), PSX Design (small alphabet) and Stampin' Up! (square); *Computer font:* CK Constitution, "Fresh Fonts" CD, *Creating Keepsakes; Envelopes:* Coffee Break Design; *Stamping inks:* Clearsnap; *Brads:* GoneScrappin.com.

I sat down with my parents and went through these items one by one, starting with the cabinet itself.

I recorded which side of the family each heirloom came from, who owned it originally, how my parents came to own it, and any memories associated with it. I also went through the house and documented other antiques passed down to my parents.

- **Recipes.** We've all seen scrapbooks done with family recipes. Don't forget the unwritten recipes. While my father is known for his famous enchiladas, the recipe existed only in his head. Luckily, I asked him a few years ago why he even started making the enchiladas in the first place. Although I've helped Dad make the enchiladas over the years, it was important to

document the history and recipe, which I did in Figure 3.

- **Parent/Child Photo.** When's the last time you had a picture taken with your parents? I

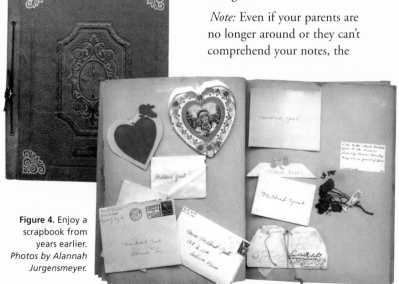

Figure 4. Enjoy a scrapbook from years earlier. *Photos by Alannah Jurgensmeyer.*

hadn't really considered it, but the last time I was with my parents, I made a point of having my friend Alannah take our picture. I tucked thoughts about my parents in small envelopes and included them on my page in Figure 5.

Note: Even if your parents are no longer around or they can't comprehend your notes, the

Figure 5. Use envelopes to hide personal notes and letters on a heartfelt layout. *Page by Mary Larson, photograph by Alannah Jurgensmeyer.* **Supplies** *Patterned paper:* Anna Griffin; *Envelope templates:* ScrapPagerz.com; *Ribbon:* C.M. Offray & Son; *Computer font:* CK Elegant, "Fresh Fonts" CD, *Creating Keepsakes; Beads:* Westrim Crafts (hearts) and Magnetic Poetry (words). *Idea to note:* Mary sanded some patterned paper for a worn look, then used it for the frame and envelope accents.

notes are a great way to let your children know your feelings.

- **Scrapbooks.** Do your parents have scrapbooks of their own? In the summer of 2002, I discovered my mother had a scrapbook from her senior year in high school (more than 60 years ago). I was surprised to learn it even existed. (See Figure 4.)

While saving an old scrapbook can be a daunting, time-consuming task, be sure to talk with the owner about it so you can capture those memories now.

Other Ideas

Here are four other ways to capture the past:

- **Buy or borrow a handheld, sound-activated tape recorder.** The family member can carry it around and record memories as he or she thinks of them.

- **Set up a video camera and "interview" your family member.** Provide the questions beforehand, then let the conversation take its own course.

- **Create a journal jar.** Fill a jar with questions written on individual pieces of paper. Each day or week, a family member draws a question, writes down the answer, then stores it for safekeeping.

- **Take notes while the relative is reminiscing.** This is most ideal when your relative is reminiscing with another person from the same generation. The common ground makes a terrific starting point for sharing memories and history.

Now's the time to record the memories of your older relatives. I promise you won't be sorry!

P.S. Right after I finished writing this article, my mother-in-law died unexpectedly. I'd planned to sit down with her and record her story. Unfortunately, I hadn't heeded my own advice yet and didn't get it done. I thought I had more time. ♥

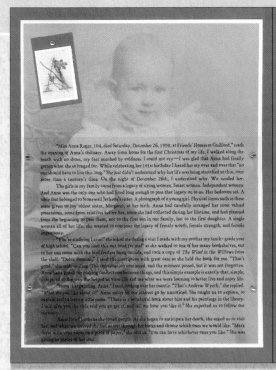
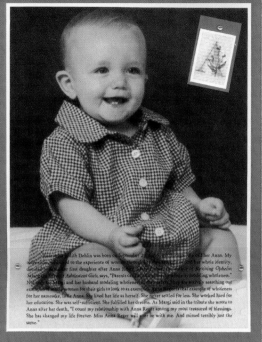

"Anna's Tribute"

by Catherine Scott
Salt Lake City, UT
S U P P L I E S
Computer font: Garamouche,
Impress Rubber Stamps
Stickers: K & Company
Brads: HyGlo

Transparency film: 3M
Idea to note: Catherine used Adobe
Photo Deluxe to turn a modern-day
photograph into an aged, sepia-tone
photograph to match the heritage
photograph included on the layout.

Border Ideas: Tag Title
by Lori Houk

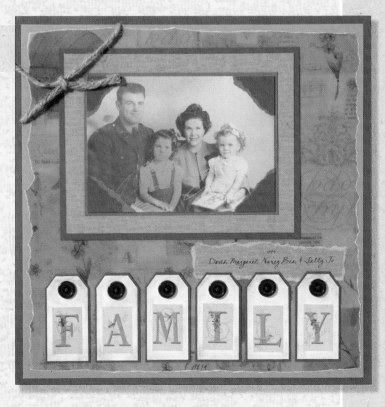

This simple, clean tag border is perfect for heritage photographs. The tags "ground" the letter stickers and add a framing effect that adds a fancy touch to the border. Creating this look is simple:

❶ Age the tags by chalking them with brown chalk.

❷ Adhere letter stickers to the tags to spell out the title of your layout.

❸ Mat each tag with a thin border of cardstock. Adhere the tags to your page.

❹ Adhere buttons to the tags, then sew them onto your layout with embroidery floss.

The simplicity of this tag title border is perfect for heritage photos—and it's simple to create!
Page by Lori Houk. **Supplies** *Patterned vellum:* Autumn Leaves; *Handmade paper:* Paper Source; *Alphabet stickers:* K & Company; *Computer font:* CK Bella, "The Best of Creative Lettering" CD Vol. 4, *Creating Keepsakes; Tags:* Office Max; *Buttons:* Button Boutique; *Chalks:* Craf-T Products; *Other:* Twine and embroidery floss.

in the beginning

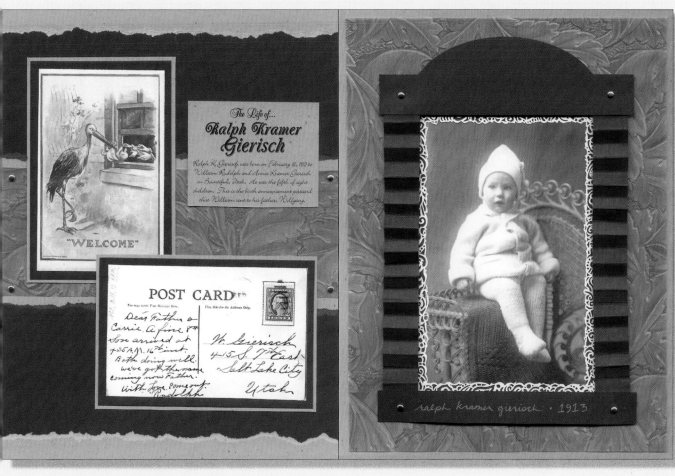

"Ralph Kramer Gierisch"
by Kerri Bradford
Orem, UT
SUPPLIES
Embossed vellum: K & Company
Computer fonts: Balmoral, Oberon
and Bickley Script, downloaded
from the Internet
Pen: Gelly Roll, Sakura
Brads: American Pin & Fastener
Laser-cut frame: Provo Craft
Idea to note: To create the frame,
Kerri folded two strips of cardstock
like a fan and adhered them to
the page.

QUOTABLE QUOTE:

"What we call the beginning
is often the end. And to make
an end is to make a beginning.
The end is where we start from."

—T.S. ELIOT

"Zelma Neal"
by Lana Rickabaugh
Maryville, MO
SUPPLIES
Computer font: ChaseCallasSH,
package unknown
Ribbon: Offray
Corner punch: Memories Forever
Photo corners: Canson
Other: Silk flowers, fabric, and a glove

Accent Idea:
Ribbons and Lace

❖ ❖ ❖

Finding accents appropriate for the time period you're scrapbooking can be challenging. A solution? Look directly to your photographs for inspiration—more specifically, the clothing the subject in the photograph is wearing. Not only does clothing give specific hints as to the era in which the photo was taken, it also gives great ideas for the perfect accents to use on your page.

Lee Anne Russell, of Brownsville, Tennessee, discovered how helpful this is. For her page "Carrie C. Siler Haynes," she used scraps of lace that looked similar to the lace on the dress in the picture to create a border for her page and journaling block.

Create accents, borders and backgrounds with scraps of fabric, lace, ribbon, buttons, handkerchiefs or swatches of old tablecloths or upholstery that are true to the time period you're capturing. You'll be surprised at how much the symmetry between clothing and accents brings your page together!

"Carrie C. Siler Haynes"
by Lee Anne Russell
Brownsville, TN
SUPPLIES
Computer fonts: Calligrapher, Microsoft
Word; CK Journaling, "The Best of
Creative Lettering" CD Vol. 2,
Creating Keepsakes
Punches: The Punch Bunch (fern),
McGill (circle), EK Success (flower)
Photo corners: Canson
Chalks: Craf-T Products
Other: Lace

"Morgan Children"
by Cheryl Sumner
Nevada City, CA
SUPPLIES
Embossed paper: K & Company
Computer font: Edwardian Script
ITC, downloaded from the Internet
Stickers: Classic Images
Punches: McGill (corner slot),
Family Treasures (square)

Edith Mary Morgan
Clarence James Morgan
July 5, 1910

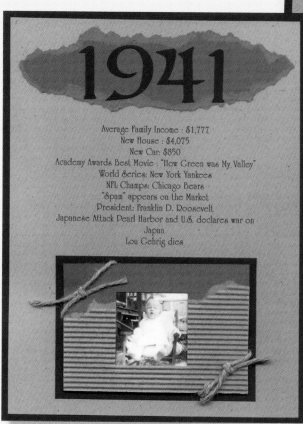

1941

Average Family Income : $1,777
New House : $4,075
New Car: $850
Academy Awards Best Movie : "How Green was My Valley"
World Series: New York Yankees
NFL Champs: Chicago Bears
"Spam" appears on the Market
President: Franklin D. Roosevelt
Japanese Attack Pearl Harbor and U.S. declares war on
Japan
Lou Gehrig dies

"1941"
by Lori Houk
Lawrence, KS
SUPPLIES
Corrugated paper: DMD Industries
Computer font: Source unknown
Other: Twine

"Christmas 1942"
by Dayna Gilbert
McMinnville, OR
SUPPLIES
Patterned paper: K & Company
Velvet paper: Paper Adventures
Pen: Zig Writer, EK Success
Christmas tree and holly: K & Company

Dad's Baby Book

"Where did you come from, Baby dear?"
"Out of the Everywhere into the Here."
George MacDonald

For
William Farnsworth Weber

Presented by
Grandmother Lawson
June 9-1937

"Where did you come from, Baby dear?" the poem by George MacDonald begins. Well, to tell the truth, I hadn't really thought of this question in relation to my dad until I was sitting in his home office during my first summer home from college and my eyes rested on a pile of boxes under a table. Curious, I opened the lids and found that the boxes were full of little treasures. Inside were stacks of photographs I had never seen, bundles of letters my dad had written to his mom and dad through his years of boarding school, summer camp and college, and mementos of his growing-up years.

At the bottom of the box, I pulled out a book and realized it was a baby book my dad's mom had created for him. I was amazed to see what his birth announcement looked like, and how tiny his first footprints were. There were pictures of every house he lived in, and of his dog, Honey Boy, and of his mother and father cradling him in their arms in the front yard. His mom kept notes of his progress—when he spoke his first word, what his first foods were, and the funny things he did and said at a young age. She collected poetry about motherhood and sons and pasted the clippings into his album. And, the most emotional thing captured in the book are her personal notes to my dad through the pages. Some are short, and some are longer, but all of them express her feelings for him and her love of being a mother.

The book is aged, the pages are yellowed, and the paste is starting to lose its stick. Yet, I couldn't even imagine removing these items from the book to put them in a safer environment because it is so sacred to me that this book was created by my dad's mother's hands. Instead, I have scrapbooked some of my favorite things in the book using copies, and behind these scrapbook pages is a color copy of each page of the baby book.

Pictured at right (clockwise, starting at top right): William Farnsworth Weber at age one; Footprints taken at the hospital; A handwritten birth announcement; Charles Swan Weber holding William (who is yawning, not screaming, according to the note above the picture!); and Mary Helen Lawson Weber holding three-week-old William.

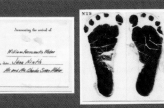

"Rights of Children"
From the White House Conference on Children

From your earliest infancy we give you our love, so that you may grow with trust in yourself and others.

We will recognize your worth as a person and we will help you to strengthen your sense of belonging.

We ... lp you to understand the

From The Prophet
by Kahlil Gibran
(Alfred A. Knopf, Inc. 1923)

And he said:
Your children are not your children.
They are the sons and daughters of

They come through you but not fr

My First Son
By Elsie McKinnon Strachan

thank you, God, for this most gracious gift:
This tender life intrusted to my care,
This baby boy to gladden and uplift
My days. Joy fills my humble prayer.
thank you, God, for sending me a son
perfect as the purest bud-wrapped rose,
inute hand that clings to my strong one,
ell-pink ears, these petal-sculptured
me be worthy

First-Born
By Beulah Fenderson Smith

Petals of fingers
Softly unfold;

Poems and Notes
Collected and written by Dad's Mom
and included in his baby book

Why It All Matters

When I found this baby book, I spent the whole day turning the pages, reading the information, and looking at the photographs. I couldn't help but cry when I realized what a tender, precious possession this baby book must be for my dad. His mother died very young, so I never had the chance to meet her, but he always speaks of her with incredible love and emotion. This book is a witness of her love for him, a documentation of her thoughts, wishes and feelings for him. Her voice speaks to him from the pages and her face shines from the photographs. He can look to this book and feel her presence in his life. I vowed at the moment I had this realization that I would do the same for my family and loved ones so they would always remember how I cherish them. Included in these envelopes are my dad's feelings about the baby book his mother created for him and my feelings on having this lasting record of my father's childhood, created with such loving care.

MOTHER'S NOTES 1937

When Dad's mom found out she was sick, she wrote a note in dad's baby book about her wishes and hopes for him. The text of the note is included in this envelope.

Mrs. C. S. Weber, Amateur Poet

Mrs Helen L. Weber of 1037 McCamy avenue, Burnt Mills Hills, died Saturday night in Johns Hopkins Hospital in Baltimore after a lengthy illness.

A native of Ravenswood, W. Va., she was an amateur poet who had had several poems published in the New York Times.

Mrs. Weber leaves her husband, C. Swan Weber, two sons, William F. and Charles S. Jr.; a daughter, Miss Diana, all of the home address; a sister, Mrs. Frank B. Moore, Clarksburg, W. Va.; and a brother, James Lawson, Kansas City, Mo.

Services and burial will be private.

Dad's Reflections

My Reflections

"Dad's Baby Book"
by Catherine Scott
Salt Lake City, UT
SUPPLIES
Computer fonts: CaslonOpenFace BT
and BernhardMod BT, WordPerfect

"Kathleen Ann"
by Amy Grendell
Silverdale, WA
SUPPLIES
Patterned paper: Colors By Design
Computer font: Carpenter ICG,
downloaded from the Internet
String: On the Surface Fibers
Other: Brads
Idea to note: Amy adapted the idea
for the crumpled paper from Rebecca
Sower's article "Roughing It" in the
September 2001 issue of
Creating Keepsakes magazine.

Kathleen Ann Murphy - age 1, 1951

Preservation 101: Restoring Photographs

❖ ❖ ❖ ❖ ❖

As you're working with heritage photographs, you'll no doubt come across some in need of repair. Whether your photos are faded, stained or even torn, you can get picture-perfect prints to use in your scrapbooks. Here are three practical options:

• **Use digital photo restoration.** Some basic digital restoration can be performed on a home computer with photo-editing software. Simply scan your photograph, use the software to remove stains or enhance the color, and print out the image to use in your scrapbook. If your photograph has more serious problems, like cracks, tears or large areas of damage, check your yellow pages for a photo processor near you that offers digital restoration.

• **Have a new negative made.** Professional photography labs often have special camera equipment that allows them to take a picture of your photograph, then create a new negative. While creating the print from the new negative, the technician should be able to lighten stains or add contrast to faded areas. This method is preferred for important photographs because the new negative will be available if additional prints are needed in the future.

• **Find an airbrush artist.** Many photography studios and developers use an airbrush artist to touch up photographs. After making a copy of the photo, the artist uses a tool that sprays paint onto the print to cover stains, add color or even change the appearance of a photo

graph. Before choosing this option, however, remember that the more work required to correct the photo, the more the photo will look like a painting.

Ask for an estimate before you agree to any type of photo restoration, since costs will vary according to the amount of work needed. Remember never to alter an original photograph—these three processes use a copy of the photo, leaving the original intact. If you're working with particularly valuable photographs, you may want to seek the advice of a professional conservator (check with a local university or museum for more information).

Philip Richard Brenton
1948

Daniel Anthony
Caligiuri
1958

Daniel Barret
Caligiuri
1988

"In the Beginning"
by Andrea Reid
St. George, UT
SUPPLIES
Lettering template: Block, ABC Tracers,
Pebbles for EK Success
Computer font: CK Cursive, "The Best
of Creative Lettering" CD Vol. 2,
Creating Keepsakes
Baby buggy paper-piecing: Downloaded
from *www.twopeasinabucket.com*
Chalk: Craf-T Products

"Father and Son"
by Melissa Caligiuri
Winter Park, FL
SUPPLIES
Patterned paper: Crafter's
Workshop
Computer fonts: CK Flair
and CK Primary, "The Art
of Creative Lettering" CD,
Creating Keepsakes
Chalk: Craf-T Products
Colored pencils:
Prismacolor, Sanford
Pop dots: All Night Media

"Philip Richard Brenton"
by Amy Brenton
Tucson, AZ
SUPPLIES
Patterned paper:
Keeping Memories Alive
*Rubber stamp and stamping
ink:* Susan Branch, Colorbök
Computer font:
Garamouche, Fontographer
Colored pencils:
Prismacolor, Sanford
Buttons: Jesse James Company
Embroidery floss:
Coats and Clark

"The Red Purse"
by Catherine Scott
Salt Lake City, UT
SUPPLIES
Patterned paper: Susan Branch, Colorbök
Vellum: Paper Cuts
Rubber stamp: Stampin' Up!
Stamping ink: Fiskars
Photo corners: Canson
Pen: G-2, Pilot

Page Idea: Create a Collage

❖   ❖   ❖

Struggling to come up with a cover or title page for your heritage album? Creating a sophisticated, timeless photo collage is a terrific way to introduce viewers to the subject matter of your album. Here are two great photo-collage ideas:

Title Page
Laura McGrover of Clearwater, Florida, created a strikingly simple title page for one of her heritage albums using a photo-collage technique. First, Laura looked through the scrapbook pages she had created for the album and chose photographs to feature on the title page. She scanned the photographs (color or black-and-white photocopies will also work), resizing them so they created a square when pieced together. Laura then cut out the photographs and pieced them together, slightly overlapping the photos where necessary, to create a collage that covers her entire 12" x 12" page. In the middle of the collage, she included a title with information about the album, including when and by whom it was created.

Album Cover
Julie Williams of Sunnyvale, California, created a beautiful collage to adhere to her heritage album cover. First, she scanned the photographs she wanted to include in the collage. Then, using photo-editing software (Julie used Adobe Photoshop), she sized, shaped, layered and faded the photographs into each other. Once the collage was complete, Julie printed it onto transfer paper, ironed the image onto muslin and adhered the finished artwork to her album cover using fabric adhesive.

"Heritage Album Cover"
by Julie Williams
Sunnyvale, CA
SUPPLIES
Computer software:
Photoshop, Adobe
Album cover: Close To My Heart
Ribbon: Offray
Buttons: LaMode
Other: Transfer paper, muslin and fabric adhesive

"Charles F. Brooks"
by Laura McGrover
Clearwater, FL
SUPPLIES
Computer fonts: CK Script, "The Best of Creative Lettering" CD Vol. 1; CK Journaling and CK Wedding, "The Best of Creative Lettering" CD Vol. 2, *Creating Keepsakes*
Stickers: me & my BIG ideas
Pen: Pigma Micron, Sakura

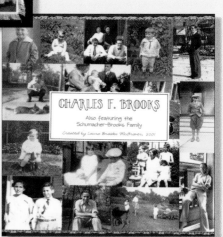

"Turning Two"

by Lisa Brown
Berkeley, CA
SUPPLIES
Patterned paper: Paper Patch
Title and balloons: Lisa's own
designs

Pen: Zig Writer, EK Success
Chalk: Craf-T Products
String: On the Surface Fibers

"3 Generations"

by Alexandria Bishop
Honolulu, HI
SUPPLIES
Embossed paper: Making Memories
Pens: Zig Writer and Zig Calligraphy, EK Success
Mom and baby die cut: Alexandria's own design

"The Little Things"
by Catherine Scott
Salt Lake City, UT
SUPPLIES
Patterned paper:
Lasting Impressions for Paper
Computer fonts: Monotype Corsiva
and Book Antiqua, WordPerfect
Stickers: K & Company

"It's the little things that make up the richest part of the tapestry of our lives."

I love seeing pictures of my mom as a little girl. This is one of my favorites because it shows, even at her early age, so many of the qualities I love about my mom, including:

Pure Joy

Enthusiasm

Gentleness

Sensitivity

Curiosity

Elaine Margaret
Comi Weber, age 2

Journaling Starter: Reflecting on a Photograph

❖   ❖   ❖   ❖   ❖

One of the most common struggles of heritage scrapbooking is the lack of information or resources to provide details about the photographs you're working with. But don't let this keep you from creating meaningful pages about your ancestors. If you find all you have to go along with a photograph is a name and date, or perhaps less, consider including the following information in your journaling:

* What strikes you about the photograph? Did you immediately connect with the subject because of a certain feature, such as his or her eyes or smile, or did you have strong feelings in reaction to viewing the photograph?
* Did you have the chance to meet the person pictured? Can you record personality traits or characteristics you learned about the person by meeting him or her? Are any of these personality traits apparent in the photograph?
* Is the person in the picture still alive? If so, can he or she share stories or insights, even if he or she doesn't remember dates or events? Is the person willing to view the picture, then share any memories, reflections or feelings triggered by the photograph? Include this information on your layout, whether it's directly related to the photograph or not.
* Is there anyone in your family (perhaps an older relative) who can tell you anything about the person in the photograph? Even if the information isn't factual (like names or dates), can he or she relate any stories connected to the photograph or the subject of the photo?

Even if you can't provide a complete life history for every person you have a photograph for, you can add meaning to your heritage album by including honest commentary about why heritage photographs have meaning to you. Don't be afraid to say something like, "I'm not sure who this person is, but he bears a strong resemblance to my father. His warm eyes and gentle face struck me the moment I picked up the photograph, and I knew I had to include it in an album about my heritage." In years to come, this information will be more valuable than nothing at all!

the beauty of youth

Elizabeth Ann Williams
(Born November 26, 1936)

Elizabeth says that this is her favorite photograph.

Viewing it evokes memories of an
adorable three-year-old
who didn't want her photo taken.

Elizabeth remembers that she hated
the bow in her hair.

Not even the baby-doll could produce a smile.
She has memories of
throwing the doll-baby to the floor.

And look at her left hand ...
She says that her fingers are obviously
ready to "thump" the photographer.

Isn't it wonderful what emotions
a priceless photograph can
preserve?

QUOTABLE QUOTE:

"A life-long blessing for children

is to fill them with warm

memories of times together.

Happy memories become treasures

in the heart to pull out on the

tough days of adulthood."

—CHARLOTTE DAVIS KASL

"Elizabeth Ann Williams"
by Joyce Schweitzer
Greensboro, NC
SUPPLIES
Patterned paper: Minigraphics
Vellum: Paper Adventures
Stickers: Paper Whispers, Mrs. Grossman's
Computer font: Harrington, Microsoft Word
Rubber stamp: Stampington & Company
Other: Ribbon

"Beth and Wayne"
by Elza Marshall
Orem, UT
SUPPLIES
Vellum: Autumn Leaves (patterned),
Frances Meyer
Mulberry paper: PSX Design
Computer font: CK Cursive, "The Best of Creative
Lettering" CD Vol. 2, *Creating Keepsakes*
Brads: American Pin & Fastener
Embroidery floss: DMC

"Portrait Day"
by Emily Zimmer
Spanish Fork, UT
SUPPLIES
Patterned paper: Ever After
Scrapbook Company
Vellum: Source unknown
Border stickers: me & my BIG ideas
Computer fonts: CK Grapevine (title),
"The Best of Creative Lettering" CD
Vol. 1, *Creating Keepsakes*;
Invitation (journaling), WordPerfect

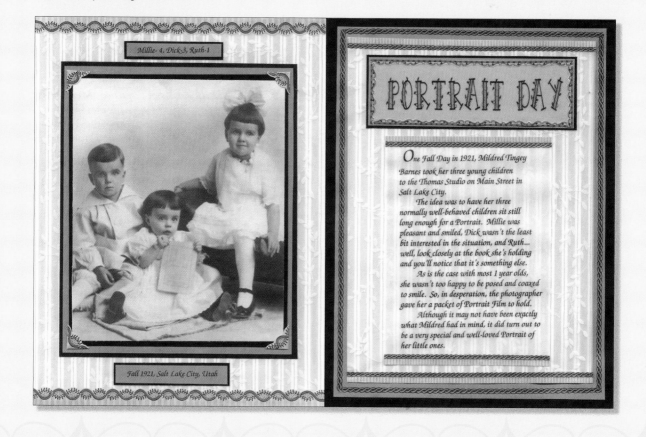

Millie- 4, Dick-3, Ruth-1

Fall 1921, Salt Lake City, Utah

PORTRAIT DAY

One Fall Day in 1921, Mildred Tingey
Barnes took her three young children
to the Thomas Studio on Main Street in
Salt Lake City.
The idea was to have her three
normally well-behaved children sit still
long enough for a Portrait. Millie was
pleasant and smiled, Dick wasn't the least
bit interested in the situation, and Ruth...
well, look closely at the book she's holding
and you'll notice that it's something else.
As is the case with most 1 year olds,
she wasn't too happy to be posed and coaxed
to smile. So, in desperation, the photographer
gave her a packet of Portrait Film to hold.
Although it may not have been exactly
what Mildred had in mind, it did turn out to
be a very special and well-loved Portrait of
her little ones.

This picture of Barbara was probably taken when she was around 3 or 4 years old in 1926 or 1927. Barbara was raised by her Granny, Verna (York) Westervelt. Her Granny made all the clothes that she wore, including the one she has on here.

Barbara June Steenblock

"Barbara June Steenblock"
by Amy Brenton
Tucson, AZ
SUPPLIES
Patterned paper: Making Memories
Computer font: Unknown
Rubber stamp: Ann-ticipations
Stamping ink: Close To My Heart
Embroidery floss: DMC

STAR *of the Family*

Darlene Joyce Braswell

"Star of the Family"
by Carolyn Gray
Shawnee, KS
SUPPLIES
Patterned paper: Debbie Mumm, Creative Imaginations
Lettering template: Party, ScrapPagerz.com
Computer font: CK Bella, "The Best of Creative Lettering" CD Vol. 3, *Creating Keepsakes*
Punches: Emagination Crafts (star), Family Treasures (square), Fiskars (rectangle)
Chalk: Craf-T Products
Ribbon: Sheer Creations
Pop dots: All Night Media

Who is this Little Girl?

Who is this little girl?
What happened on this day?
Did she grow up to be a Mom?
No one can hardly say.

Such a pretty little picture
And its condition is quite good.
But no one ever placed it in
The place they really should.

How proud and honored you'd be
To look at yourself someday,
But nothing ever happened
For it to be viewed today.

Forgotten in an old box
Exposed to heat and cold and danger.
The box was sold at auction
To a complete and total stranger.

So when I came across your picture
It made me sad to see.
For it meant your story's meaning
Had been lost in history.

"Who Is This Little Girl?"
by Nikki Krueger
Liberty, MD
SUPPLIES
Patterned paper: Anna Griffin
Embossed vellum: K & Company
Computer font: PC Script, "For Font Sakes" HugWare CD, Provo Craft
Antique shoe accent: Wallies, McCall's
Scissors: Arabian edge, Provo Craft
Embroidery floss: DMC
Other: Buttons

"Eric Allen Grendell"
by Amy Grendell
Silverdale, WA
SUPPLIES
Patterned paper:
Karen Foster Design
Computer font: CK
Journaling, "The Best of
Creative Lettering" CD Vol. 2,
Creating Keepsakes
Boat paper-piecing:
BumperCrops
Star template: Provo Craft
Chalks: Craf-T Products

**"Life on the
Chicken Farm"**
by Karen Burniston
Littleton, CO
SUPPLIES
Denim paper: Frances Meyer
White pen: The Ultimate
Gel Pen, American Crafts
Lettering: Karen's own design
Other: Karen scanned chicken
wire and feathers to create
the border for her layout.

Problem Solving:
Adding Dimension without Bulk

❖   ❖   ❖   ❖   ❖

Q: **I love the look of non-traditional scrapbooking materials, but I'm worried about adding extra thickness to my pages, especially in my heritage albums. Are there any "substitutes" that will add dimension and texture without the bulk?**

A: If you love the old-fashioned look of dimensional accents but not the added bulk, you can substitute other items and still get the same homemade look you love. A suggestion? Take advantage of technology. Many scrapbookers have scanners as part of their everyday computer equipment, and those who don't most likely have access to a copy shop with a color-copy machine. Karen Burniston of Littleton, Colorado, wanted the look of chicken wire on her layout but hesitated to use the real thing. Instead, she put the chicken wire on her home scanner, arranged feathers on top of the chicken wire, and placed a sheet of denim patterned paper on top of the arrangement. Then she printed the scanned image onto acid-free cardstock and included it as a border on her layout. You can use this technique with a variety of items, such as wire, screen, buttons, memorabilia, coins and more.

"Tricycle Built for Two"

by Dayna Gilbert
McMinnville, OR
SUPPLIES
Patterned paper: Scrap-Ease
Computer fonts: Papyrus,
Microsoft Word; CK Bella,
"The Best of Creative
Lettering" CD Vol. 3,

Creating Keepsakes
Stickers: NRN Designs
Idea to note: To resize the
stickers, Dayna placed them
on white paper, scanned
them and printed them on
cardstock in black ink.

"Blowing in the Wind"

by Dayna Gilbert
McMinnville, OR
SUPPLIES
Patterned paper: Hot Off The Press
Vellum: The Paper Company
Computer font: Fine Hand,
WordPerfect
Hemp: Darice
Clothespins: Dayna's own design

Colored pencils: Prismacolor,
Sanford
Idea to note: To create a "just
washed" look, Dayna wrinkled
the blue vellum before printing
on it. Then she placed it over
white cardstock to lighten up
the color.

Quick Tip: Duplicate Pages

❖ ❖ ❖ ❖ ❖

If you're working on a heritage album for a family
member, make duplicate photos and create
pages for yourself at the same time. While scrapbooking her grandmother's photographs to give as a
gift, Dayna Gilbert of McMinnville, Oregon, used the
same supplies and design elements to create pages
for her own album.

"Flying High"

by Carolyn Gray

Shawnee, KS

SUPPLIES

Patterned papers: Bo-Bunny Press
(blue spatter),
Paper Adventures (wood)

Airplane accent: Wallies, McCall's

Clouds, sun and fence:
Carolyn's own designs

Computer font: Doodle Cursive,
"PagePrintables" CD Vol. 1,
Cock-A-Doodle Design, Inc.

Punches: EK Success ("F," "H" and
grass), Fiskars (flower and oval)

Craft wire: Artistic Wire Ltd.

Chalk: Craf-T Products

Pop dots: All Night Media

"Simple Times"

by Gwyn Calvetti

West Salem, WI

SUPPLIES

Computer font: Unknown

Rubber stamp: Judikins

Stamping ink: Close To My Heart

Embossing powder: Mark Enterprises

Chalk: Craf-T Products

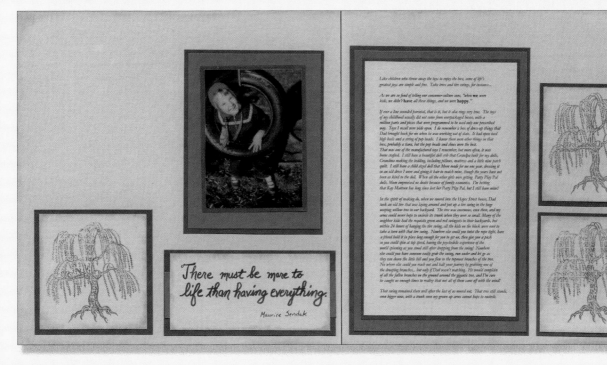

"I'm a Little Teapot"
by Lee Anne Russell
Brownsville, TN
SUPPLIES
Computer font: CK Jot, "The Art of Creative Lettering" CD, *Creating Keepsakes*
Teapot buttons: Hillcreek Design
Leaf punch: The Punch Bunch
Embroidery floss: DMC
Ribbon: Stampendous!
Photo corners: Canson
Chalk: Craf-T Products
Idea to note: Lee Anne pieced her cardstock together using embroidery floss. She also chalked and crinkled the photo mat to give it an aged look.

Getting Organized:
Choosing a Storage System

❖ ❖ ❖ ❖ ❖

If you're like most people, your heritage photographs were passed along to you piled in shoeboxes or stuffed into large manila envelopes. Before you begin sorting these snapshots, visualize what type of organizational system you'd like to use. Consider all the options, such as acid-free photo boxes with divider tabs, archival hanging file folders, divided sheet protectors or acid-free envelopes. Make sure you have all the materials you need on hand before you start sorting your photographs. This simple step will help alleviate a lot of headaches and prevent a bigger mess!

"Joan"
by Amy Brenton
Tucson, AZ
SUPPLIES
Patterned paper: Loves Me Paper
Computer fonts: DJ Fancy, "Fontastic!" CD Vol. 1, D.J. Inkers; BC Merced, Microsoft Word
Punches: EK Success (flower and grass), Marvy Uchida (sun), McGill (hole)
Fence stickers: Mrs. Grossman's
Clear photo corners: Canson

My grandfather, Harold Osborn Stewart was born in Rochester New York in 1885. He loved cameras, taking pictures, and anything else remotely to do with the art of photography. I don't know if it was because Rochester is home to Kodak or if he just had "developer and fixer" in his blood. He had a "brownie" camera and at one time, even had a darkroom in his attic. In 1986, when he passed away, my mother and my aunt cleaned out his attic and found about 60 boxes of very old glass slide negatives (before the film negatives were around). These boxes contained photos of my dad and his siblings when they were growing up in the 1920's and beyond, and are absolutely priceless. Some of them have shown the "wear and tear" of the ages, with the emulsion actually flaking off the slide. I think it adds to the authenticity of these beautiful photos. They are so special to me. So next time you have to clean out an attic, stop and look in every box. You never know what treasures you will find up there.

"Treasures in the Attic"
by Mary Cowan
Sandy, UT
SUPPLIES
Vellum: Paper Adventures
Computer font: Papyrus, Microsoft Word
Photo oils: Marshall's Oils,
Marshall's/Brandess-Kalt-Aetna
Idea to note: Mary created an overlay
that lifts to reveal journaling.

"Jerry Schadegg"
by Shannon Wolz
Salt Lake City, UT
SUPPLIES
Patterned papers: Magenta
Rubber Stamps (red), Provo
Craft (blue and green)
Clip art: "Remember When"
HugWare CD, Provo Craft

Computer font: Bernard
Fashion BT, downloaded from
the Internet
Stars: Westrim Crafts
Chalk: Craf-T Products
Idea to note: Shannon crumpled the patterned paper to
give her layout an aged look.

EVERY SUMMER ALVIN AND PALMER OVERBYE WOULD RIDE THE TRAIN TO RUSSELL, N.D. TO VISIT THEIR MATERNAL GRANDPARENTS. THEY HAD LOTS OF FUN PLAYING WITH THEIR COUSINS. BEING LITTLE BOYS THEY LIKED TO TEASE THE GIRL COUSINS AND EVEN SLIPPED FROGS IN THEIR POCKETS. JULY 1937

COUSINS ...

PALMER OVERBYE • MORRIS ANDERSON • ALVIN OVERBYE

"Cousins"

by Lisa Brown
Berkeley, CA
SUPPLIES
Patterned papers: Crafter's Workshop (tan swirl), Mustard Moon (green striped), Ever After Scrapbook Company (tan plaid)
Frog vellum: Source unknown
Raffia: Plaid Enterprises
Brads: American Pin & Fastener
Title: Lisa's own design

"Overbye Boys"

by Lisa Brown
Berkeley, CA
SUPPLIES
Patterned paper: Keeping Memories Alive (green speckled), Mustard Moon (green striped)
Velveteen paper: Paper Adventures
Lettering template: Script, ScrapPagerz.com
Pen: Zig Writer, EK Success
Idea to note: Lisa added overall clasps from a doll's outfit to her layout to match the overalls and suspenders her grandfather and his brothers are wearing in the photos.

OVERBYE BOYS

ALVIN
PALMER
GEORGE
ART

JUNE 1939

"First Grade"
by Lee Anne Russell
Brownsville, TN
SUPPLIES
Lettering templates: Grade School (title),
ScrapPagerz.com; Block ("A"), ABC Tracers,
Pebbles for EK Success
Pencils and apples: Lee Anne's own designs
Chalk: Craf-T Products
Envelope: Source unknown
Pen: Zig Writer, EK Sucess
Photo corners: Canson

"The Great 48"
by Torrey Miller
Lafayette, CO
SUPPLIES
Patterned paper: Hot Off The Press
Wooden stars: Darice
Computer fonts: Currency and Harrington,
downloaded from the Internet
Corner punch and pop dots: All Night Media

Journaling Starter:
Including History

❖ ❖ ❖ ❖

As you scrapbook your heritage photographs, you may marvel at the history represented in some of your snapshots. Torrey Miller of Lafayette, Colorado, found a picture of a little girl holding an American flag with 48 stars instead of the current 50. Photographs like this provide a terrific opportunity to include historical facts—and remember the past in a fun, personal way—on your layouts.

By performing a simple search on the Internet or making a trip to the library, you can find endless facts, stories, trivia and historic data. Adding information like this to your layouts will give friends and family members valuable details about their heritage and the history of their country!

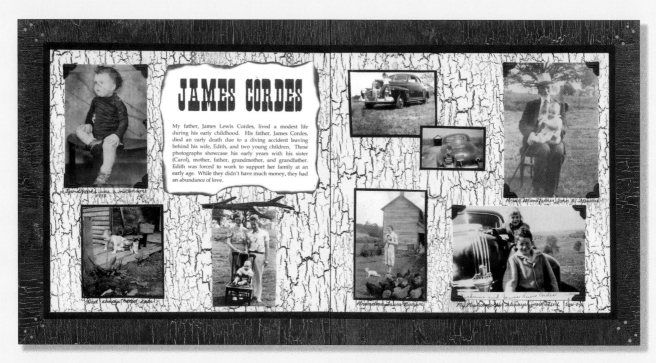

"James Cordes"

by Pamela Kopka
New Galilee, PA
SUPPLIES
Patterned paper: Stamping Station
Computer fonts: Book Antiqua and Fisticuffs, downloaded from the Internet
Pens: Pigma Micron, Sakura; Metallic Gel Roller, Marvy Uchida
Idea to note: Pamela created an antique look on her layout by burning the edges of her journaling block.

"Blumenthall Children"

by Elza Marshall
Orem, UT
SUPPLIES
Stickers: Provo Craft
Computer font: CK Calligraphy, "The Best of Creative Lettering" CD Vol. 1, *Creating Keepsakes*
Brads: American Pin & Fastener
Oval templates: Coluzzle, Provo Craft
Frames and photo mats: Accu-Cut Systems
Photo corners: Canson
Scissors: Deckle edge, Family Treasures

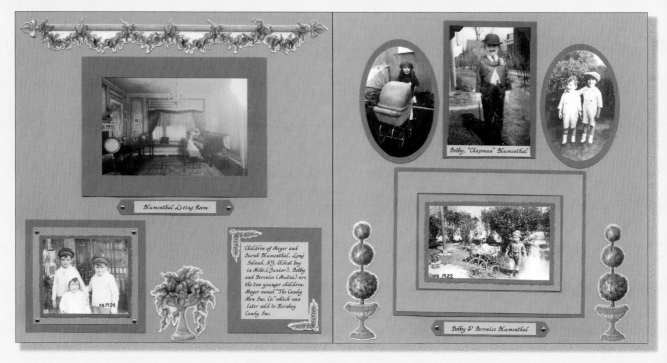

"Girl on the Bench"

by Elza Marshall
Orem, UT
SUPPLIES
Patterned papers: Autumn Leaves (banner and rod), Black Ink (green speckled)
Gold metallic paper: Paper Adventures
Embroidery floss: DMC
Computer font: DJ Calli, "Fontastic!" CD Vol. 1, D.J. Inkers
Brads: American Pin & Fastener
Eyelets: Stamp Studio, Inc.
Pens: Metallic Gel Roller, Marvy Uchida; Photosafe Marker, Pilot
Chalk: Craf-T Products
Button chain and tassel: Elza's own designs
Photo corners: Canson
Idea to note: To create the rod for the banner, Elza rolled the paper left over from the banner into a rod shape.

"Brothers, Sisters"

by Elaine Schwertner
Lubbock, TX
SUPPLIES
Patterned paper: Family Archives
Computer fonts: Flemish Script BT (title) and Nuptial Script (journaling), downloaded from the Internet
Punches: Marvy Uchida (photo corner and accent), Emagination Crafts (corner), McGill (hole)

"Sisters"
by Elaine Schwertner
Lubbock, TX
SUPPLIES
Border stickers: me & my BIG ideas
Computer fonts: Flemish Script BT (title) and Nuptial
Script (journaling), downloaded from the Internet
Photo corner punch: Marvy Uchida

"Sisters"
by Shannon Wolz
Salt Lake City, UT
SUPPLIES
Patterned paper: Deborah Designs
Specialty paper and vellum: Solum World Paper
Computer fonts: CK Leafy Capitals, "The Art of Creative
Lettering" CD, *Creating Keepsakes*; Invitation, Fontography
Flower accents: Deborah Designs
Studs: Be-Dazzler
Pens: Zig Writer, EK Success
Pencil: Metallic Pencil, Pentel
Idea to note: Shannon adapted the idea for her torn frame
from a layout by Heidi Swapp featured in the Dec 2000/Jan
2001 issue of *Creating Keepsakes*.

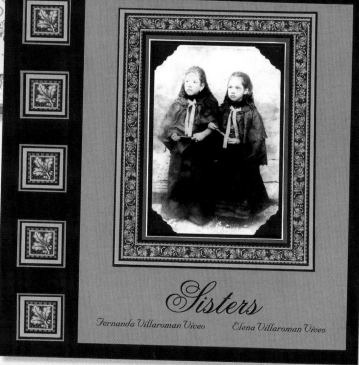

Preservation 101: A Necessary Precaution

❖　❖　❖　❖　❖

Creating a scrapbook is the perfect way to make sure your heritage photos are available for future generations to enjoy. Once they're placed on a page with journaling and carefully selected archival materials, your snapshots are pretty safe behind sheet protectors. But, if the photographs you're working with are truly one of a kind, consider making copies to work with. You can store the original photographs in acid-free, archival envelopes or photo holders in a dark place with a cool, even temperature. The less the originals are handled, the longer they'll be preserved—and scrapbooking with duplicate photographs opens the door to limitless creativity!

sweet sixteen

A
Portrait
for Daddy

I cherish these pictures
because of the story my Mother
has told me about them.

"When I was eleven years old,
Mother curled my hair, had me
wear my brown velvet dress
with the gold buttons and took
me into Lethbridge on the bus
to have my portrait taken.
Daddy said that he wanted
a picture of me while I still
thought that he was the best
and smartest man in the world.
He was worried that when I
became a teenager my opinion
of him would change.
I was determined from that
day on that I would never become
that kind of teenager.
I would always love and respect
my Daddy and cherish the
relationship I had with him."

Verda

"A Portrait for Daddy"
by Cheryl McMurray
Cardston, AB, Canada
SUPPLIES
Patterned paper: Hot Off The Press
Vellum: Paper Adventures
Computer fonts: Daresiel Demo,
WordPerfect; CK Penman, "The Best
of Creative Lettering" CD Vol. 3,
Creating Keepsakes
Punches: EK Success (flower, small hole),
Family Treasures (leaf), Darice
(mini flower)
Oval template: Frances Meyer
Scissors: Deckle edge, Fiskars
Pen: Zig Writer, EK Success

QUOTABLE QUOTE:

"Woe to the man whose heart has
not learned while young to hope,
to love—and to put its trust in life."

—JOSEPH CONRAD

Taken for Sunny's graduation from
Indianola Junior High School
Columbus, Ohio - Circa 1922

Sunny died when he was sixteen while
playing baseball. From acute
endocarditis, a result of childhood
rheumatic fever.

"He loved playing sports of all kinds"

Howard Culbertson Hoeflich
November 13, 1909 - August 23, 1926

Days fly by quickly
and children move on
Before we know it
the "old times" are gone
But as we look back
at generations gone by
we reflect on the memories
that serve as a tie
Binding us together
with future and the past,
and building a story
that forever will last
--- Sharon Fashoe ---
Happy Father's Day!
Kent, Lori, Coleman & Chase

"Sunny"
by Carolyn Hassall
Bradenton, FL
SUPPLIES
Patterned paper: Gibson's Greetings
Border stickers: me & my BIG ideas
Computer fonts: CAC Shishoni Brush, package unknown,
American Greetings; Scrap Katie and Scrap Calligraphy,
"Lettering Delights" CD Vol. 2, Inspire Graphics
Embossed frames: K & Company

Page Idea: Heritage Poems and Quotes

❖ ❖ ❖ ❖ ❖

"Days Fly By"
by Lori Houk
Lawrence, KS
SUPPLIES
Patterned paper:
Source unknown
Vellum: Paper Adventures
Computer font: CK Bella,
"The Best of Creative Lettering"
CD Vol. 3, *Creating Keepsakes*
Other: Raffia

Poems and quotes add a fun twist to scrapbook pages, but have you ever considered creating a scrapbook page that features just a poem or quote? Lori Houk, of Lawrence, Kansas, created a beautiful title page for a heritage album using a poem she found on the Internet. The poem sets the tone for the rest of the album and helps communicate her motivation for creating it.

Another way to incorporate poem or quote pages in your heritage album is to place them next to one-page layouts. Instead of rushing right into an unrelated layout on the opposite side of a page, the viewer can pause and read the poem or quotation before going on to the next spread.

You'll find hundreds of poems and quotations on the Internet. The web sites below have offerings that are perfect for heritage albums:

- *http://www.wildheartcreations.com/poems/ heritage.html*
- *http://genealogy.about.com/cs/scrapbooks/*
- *http://www.scraplink.com/heritage.htm*

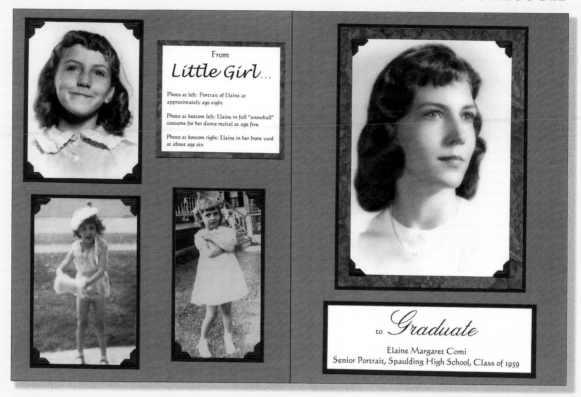

From
Little Girl...

Photo at left: Portrait of Elaine at
approximately age eight

Photo at bottom left: Elaine in full "snowball"
costume for her dance recital at age five

Photo at bottom right: Elaine in her front yard
at about age six

to *Graduate*

Elaine Margaret Comi
Senior Portrait, Spaulding High School, Class of 1959

"From Little Girl to Graduate"
by Catherine Scott
Salt Lake City, UT
SUPPLIES
Patterned paper: Hot Off The Press
Computer fonts: Calligraph421BT, Lucida Handwriting
and Lucia BT, WordPerfect
Photo corners: Canson

"Ardell Ripley"
by Lisa Brown
Berkeley, CA
SUPPLIES
Patterned paper: K & Company
Vellum: K & Company

Mulberry paper: PrintWorks
Title: Lisa's own design
Pen: Zig Writer, EK Success

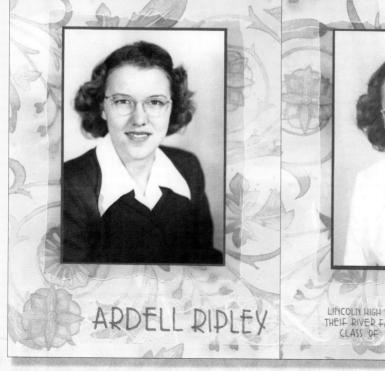

ARDELL RIPLEY

LINCOLN HIGH SCHOOL
THEIF RIVER FALLS, MN.
CLASS OF 1949

"Neighbors of Woodcraft"
by Amy Williams
Old Town, ME
SUPPLIES
Patterned paper: K & Company
Computer fonts: CK Bella and CK Penman,
"The Best of Creative Lettering" CD Vol. 3,
Creating Keepsakes
Stickers: K & Company
Chalk: Craf-T Products

"Her Teacher's Footsteps"
by Julie Turner
Gilbert, AZ
SUPPLIES
Embossed paper: K & Company
Vellum: Paper Cuts
Computer font: Dearest Script, IHOF
Ribbon corners: Anna Griffin
Other: Ribbon
Ideas to note: Julie included a framed
photo and an original document on her
layout.

Neighbors of Woodcraft was an insurance company but also a sorority. You could be a member just by paying your insurance or be a social member by paying $2 a year. In Utah it was really big in the 1940's. My great grandmother, Martha B. Lindstrom, was the clerk in the Ogden, Utah area and enrolled 8 of her grandchildren in group. My grandmother, Marion Lindstrom Lewis, was also pretty active in the group. She was president of the local chapter and would have meetings at her home once a month. My aunt Georgia remembers that they would rig colored lights in the backyard and put up chairs around a fake fire and wooden teepee. She remembers it being very ritualistic but a fun social get together. By the 1950's things were winding down and by 1960 the group no longer had monthly meetings or big social gatherings. This picture was taken in 1947 and we think it was from a big Neighbors of Woodcraft gathering. My aunt remembers my Grandma talking about all the area chapters getting together. Even chapters from Southern Utah and parts of Wyoming came together. This picture was published in a local newspaper sometime in November of 1947, but we don't know which one.

Very front – Sherrie Lindstrom
First row, from left – #2 Edith Doyle, #3 Hedy Doyle, #4 Layle Lindstrom, #6 Janie Lewis (my aunt), #9 Beatrice Lewis (my mom)
Second row, from left – #1 Martha B. Lindstrom (My great grandmother), #2 Marty Lewis (my aunt), #4 ? Doyle, #9 Marion Lewis (my grandmother)

My mother and her twin sister wear matching dresses as they stand in front of their school.

After graduating from high school in 1941, mom completed a one year program at the teachers college. This photo is from her teaching application.

Circa 1930

Following in her teacher's footsteps.

State of North Dakota
Department of Public Instruction

This is to Certify, That   Mrs. Melvin Zimmerman

has complied with the requirements of the law for the certification of teachers of North Dakota and is, therefore, granted this

First Grade Elementary Certificate

VALIDITY: This certificate is valid for three years from the date of issuance and quali-fies the holder to teach in the public schools of North Dakota up to and including the eighth grade except in such schools which under rules of standardization require higher qualifications.

This certificate must be recorded in the office of the County Superintendent of Schools, of the County in which the holder teaches.

BASIS for GRANTING:
Graduation from a high school doing four years of standard work and completion of the one-year teacher training course at a State Teachers College or Normal School or an equivalent course.

RENEWAL: This certificate may be renewed by offering twelve quarter-hour credits earned in residence at a State Teachers College or Normal School.

Issued at Bismarck, North Dakota, this 28th.
day of September 1945 as No. 867-H
of Cass County.
This certificate expires September 28, 1948.

(SEAL)

Lorene York
DIRECTOR OF CERTIFICATION

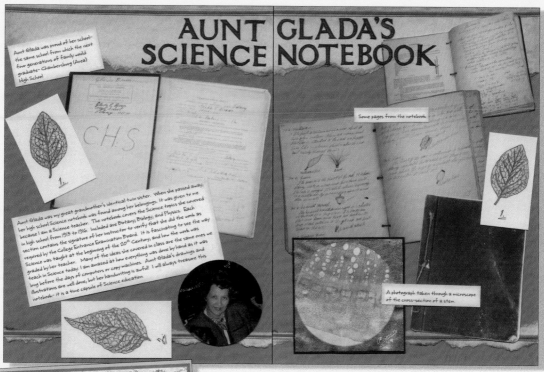

AUNT GLADA'S SCIENCE NOTEBOOK

Aunt Glada was proud of her school—the same school from which the next four generations of family would graduate—Chambersburg (Area) High School

Some pages from the notebook

Aunt Glada was my great-grandmother's identical twin sister. When she passed away, her high school Science notebook was found among her belongings. It was given to me because I am a Science teacher. The notebook covers the Science topics she covered in high school from 1915 to 1916. Included are Botany, Biology, and Physics. Each section contains the signature of her instructor to verify that she did the work as required by the College Entrance Examination Board. It is fascinating to see the way Science was taught at the beginning of the 20th Century, and how the work was graded by her teacher. Many of the ideas she covered in class are the same ones we teach in Science today. I am amazed at how everything was done by hand as it was long before the days of computers or copy machines. Aunt Glada's drawings and illustrations are well done, but her handwriting is awful! I will always treasure this notebook—it is a time capsule of Science education.

A photograph taken through a microscope of the cross-section of a stem

"Aunt Glada's Science Notebook"

by Nicole Keller
Rio Hondo, TX
SUPPLIES
Computer fonts: Intimacy, downloaded from the Internet; CK Sketch, "The Art of Creative Lettering" CD, *Creating Keepsakes*
Pen: Pigma Micron, Sakura
Colored pencils: Prismacolor, Sanford
Chalks: Craf-T Products

Childhood Memories

Grandmother

Mother

"Childhood Memories"
by Barbara Gardner
Scottsdale, AZ
SUPPLIES
Patterned paper: Minigraphics
Vellum paper and envelopes: The Paper Company
Computer font: Monotype Corsiva, Microsoft Word
Chalks: Craf-T Products
Other: Ribbon
Idea to note: Barbara wrapped acid-free matting board with the patterned paper, then mounted her photographs on the board to add dimension.

Problem Solving: Discreet Journaling

❖   ❖   ❖   ❖   ❖

Q: As I've started interviewing family members for information to include in our family's heritage album, I'm struck by the tender memories and stories they're willing to share with me. How can I include these personal reflections in a more discreet or private way on my layouts?

A: If you come across stories, feelings or memories that are too tender to leave out in the open on your pages, here are some options for including them in more subtle journaling:

◆ **Include them in an envelope.** Barbara Gardner of Scottsdale, Arizona, agonized for days wondering what she should write about the two women who had the most influence on her life—her mother and her grandmother. After deciding to write some of her most personal thoughts in her journal, she wrote "letters" to include in envelopes on her layout. The envelopes keep the information from the casual viewer's eye but make it available for future generations to enjoy.

◆ **Create a photo flap.** Instead of just matting your photograph and adhering it to your page, mat the photo as if it were being placed on the cover of a card. Use the inside of the card to journal reflections and feelings, then adhere the card to the layout.

◆ **Include information on the back of the layout.** This guarantees the journaling will be readily available for the people you'd like to share it with.

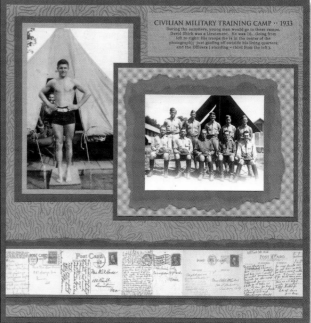

CIVILIAN MILITARY TRAINING CAMP · · 1933
During the summers, young men would go to these camps. David Shirk was a Lieutenant. He was 16. Going from left to right: His troops (he is in the center of the photograph); just goofing off outside his living quarters; and the Officers (standing - third from the left).

"C.M.T.C"

by Lori Houk
Lawrence, KS
SUPPLIES
Patterned papers: Carolee's Creations, Design Originals
Handmade paper: Art Cornerstone
Computer fonts: Unknown
Dog tags: Paper Source
Pop dots: Stampa Rosa

"Summer Camp Blues"

by Katherine Brooks
Gilbert, AZ
SUPPLIES
Computer fonts: CK Script, "The Best of Creative Lettering" CD Vol. 1 and CK Journaling, "The Best of Creative Lettering" CD Vol. 2, *Creating Keepsakes*

Lettering template: Script, ScrapPagerz.com
Handmade paper: Ink It!
Pen: Milky Gel Roller, Pentel
Chalks: Craf-T Products
Other: String, beads and plastic screening

My mother's (Judy McKay-Harker) first trip away from home was in 1954, when she attended summer camp for the first time. My mother loves to tell me how much she hated summer camp, and how homesick she was during that summer. This was also her first time to learn how to swim, which she disliked even more than camp. She says she still remembers how cold the water was, and she didn't like the fish swimming around her. I think these pictures of my mom tell it all. She looked as if she was having the worst time of her life. I asked my mom if she had any good memories of summer camp, and she told me that she loved art class and being with her cousin Sandy. The summer camp was located in Grass Lake, Michigan.

In the picture to the left my mother is the third girl from the left (her cousin Sandy is the second girl from the left). In the picture above my mother is the second girl from the left (Sandy is behind her to the right).

"1920's Kansas"
by Therese Boyd
Merriam, KS
SUPPLIES
Patterned paper: Scrap-Ease
Heritage vellum and antique car: Hot Off The Press
Computer font: Caslon Regular, package unknown
Idea to note: Therese enlarged a wallet-sized photo that belonged to her father and used it as the focal point of her layout.

"The Fastest Horse"
by Marsha Hudson
Seattle, WA
SUPPLIES
Patterned paper: Scrap-Ease
Velveteen paper: Paper Adventures
Computer fonts: Alleycat ICG (title) and Book Antiqua (journaling), downloaded from the Internet
Laser-cut accent: Deluxecuts.com
Wire: Darice
Photo corners: 3L
Stamping ink: ColorBox, Clearsnap, Inc.
Idea to note: Marsha "aged" the wire by attaching the ends to the negative and positive ends of a battery.

Ora Mae Crossland,
Charles Fredrick Demo
&
Hattie Belle Crossland Demo

Kansas
in the 1920's

"Love"

by Lori Houk

Lawrence, KS

SUPPLIES

Heart punch: Emagination Crafts

Computer font: Lucida Hand, Microsoft Word;
CK Bella, "The Best of Creative Lettering" CD
Vol. 3, *Creating Keepsakes*

Accent Idea:
Vintage Cards and Stationery

❖ ❖ ❖ ❖ ❖

Finding page accents that reflect the era of your photographs can prove to be quite a challenge! Instead of limiting yourself to the products available today, use your scrapbooker's resourcefulness. You might have access to cards, postcards, letters and stationery hidden away in boxes of memorabilia that would make charming accents for your pages.

While shopping at a discount store, Trice Boerens of Ogden, Utah, found a pack of vintage cards with images that were perfect complements for some of her old photographs. Ask your older relatives if they've saved items such as this, visit antique and discount stores, and keep an eye out at craft fairs and flea markets. (Once you have the items, you'll need to deacidify them before including them on your pages. You can also make a color copy or color scan to include on your layouts.) The whimsical artwork you'll discover will add authenticity and an appropriate feel to your scrapbook pages.

"How They Met"

by Amy Williams

Old Town, ME

SUPPLIES

Patterned paper: Keeping Memories Alive

Computer fonts: CK Shadowed Block, "The Best of Creative Lettering" CD Vol. 3 and CK Journaling, "The Best of Creative Lettering" CD Vol. 2, *Creating Keepsakes*

Heart and arrow: Amy's own designs

Chalk: Craf-T Products

Pen: Zig Writer, EK Success

Other: Twine

"David and Margaret"

by Lori Houk

Lawrence, KS

SUPPLIES

Patterned paper: Scrap-Ease

Handmade paper: Art Cornerstone

Computer font: Dobkin, downloaded from the Internet

Corrugated frame: Hobby Lobby

Fern: USArt

Fiber: Yarn Barn

"Sports Legend"

by Lori Houk
Lawrence, KS
SUPPLIES
Patterned paper and gold paper: The Family Archives
Leather paper: Paper Source
Computer font: College-condensed, downloaded from the Internet
Fibers: Yarn Barn
Brads: Source unknown
Chalk: Craf-T Products
Pop dots: Stampa Rosa
Idea to note: Lori included newspaper clippings on her layout.

"Crimson and the Blue"

by Lori Houk
Lawrence, KS
SUPPLIES
Corrugated paper: DMD Industries
Computer fonts: Amazon and Roman University, downloaded from the Internet
Buttons: Button Boutique
Embroidery floss: DMC

"A Classical Education"

by Noralee Peterson
Orem, UT
SUPPLIES
Patterned papers: Anna Griffin (beige),
Rocky Mountain Scrapbook Company
(dark red)
Pillars: Noralee's own designs
Wire ribbon: Offray
Computer fonts: Times New Roman,
Microsoft Word; CK Bella,
"The Best of Creative Lettering"
CD Combo, *Creating Keepsakes*
Swirl punch: EK Success
Chalk: Craf-T Products
Idea to note: Noralee used photos
from several college yearbooks on
her layout. She colored in the photo
on the right page with chalk.

Organization: Beginning the Sorting Process

❖ ❖ ❖ ❖ ❖

Sorting unlabeled photographs is a daunting task—especially when you didn't even take the pictures in the first place! When you're ready to tackle the task, try breaking it up into a series of smaller "projects." This way, you'll walk away from each organizational "project" feeling a sense of accomplishment instead of frustration. Here's a series of smaller organizational goals to help you get started:

◆ **Project 1.** Sort your heritage photographs into three main piles: your mother's family, your father's family and unknown subjects.

◆ **Project 2.** Using the organizational system of your choice, store the "unknown subject" photographs in a safe place until you can gather more information about them.

◆ **Project 3.** Sort your mother's family photos into generations, then repeat the process for your father's family photos.

◆ **Project 4.** Store the photographs by generation (still keeping your mother's family photos and your father's family photos separate) until you decide how you want to scrapbook your heritage photographs (chronologically, by memory, etc.).

Once you have a better idea of the pages you'll be creating, you can break the piles down into even smaller groups according to your needs.

The advantages of this system are numerous. Storing all of your unknown photographs together makes them easily accessible in case the opportunity to ask questions about them arises unexpectedly. It also leaves the photos you do know about handy for scrapbooking right away—while you're excited about the project. And, although you may have piles of photographs spread on the floor for a few days, incorporating them into your organizational system as you go will help you clean up the clutter while protecting your priceless pictures from damage.

ANTIQUE Elegance

Products your ancestors

would love—and you will, too

LET ME INTRODUCE YOU to my third great-grandparents, Michael and Marianne Beus. In the mid-1800s, they and their nine children immigrated to America from Italy. The youngest, still an infant, couldn't handle the rigors of the journey and died along the way.

After months of difficult travel across an ocean and two continents, the Beus family finally reached their destination. Their struggles weren't over. In an unfamiliar country and speaking only a French-Italian dialect, Michael found it difficult to get work. The family spent their first winter in America in a dugout cut into the side of a mountain.

Knowing the struggles of my ancestors has made me want to honor their memories in a respectful, especially memorable way. I've discovered wonderful products (showcased here) that can help. Create a little "antique elegance" today!

BY KAREN GLENN

Page by Mary Larson.
Supplies *Paper, mesh, pewter heart sticker, frame and corner stickers:* Magenta; *Sheer ribbon:* Magic Scraps; *Chalk:* Craf-T Products; *Computer fonts:* CK Smokey and CK Sketch, "CK Fresh Fonts" CD and "The Best of Creative Lettering" Super CD Combo, *Creating Keepsakes; Other:* Velvet ribbon.

Magenta

With their rich, lovely tones and textures, Magenta papers, albums and Maruyama meshes provide elegant settings for vintage pictures. Want to "adorn" your layout with antiqued, artsy accents? Check out Magenta's fine pewter stickers—they're self-adhesive, soft, pliable and paintable. And don't miss the company's fine pewter ChicCharms. They're enchanting and another great fit for Magenta's theme: "Where Remembering Becomes Art."

Web site: . . . . www.magentastyle.com

Check your local scrapbook store.

Page by Trudy Sigurdson. **Supplies** *Patterned paper and cardstock:* The Family Archives; *Fiber:* On The Surface; *Letter stickers:* Flavia, Colorbök; *Computer font:* Wedding, PrintMaster Platinum, The Learning Company.

The Family Archives

Next time you need a sumptuous set of paper in nostalgic colors and patterns, check out the offerings from The Family Archives. Printed on acid-free paper, the designs are available separately or coordinated with the company's heritage kits for easy themed pages.

Choose from heritage papers (with coordinating cardstock), old-fashioned florals, and decorative papers designed to work beautifully with black-and-white or sepia photos.

The Family Archives also offers distinctive corners, stickers and frames.

Web site: . . . . www.heritagescrapbooks.com
Phone: 888/622-6556

Page by Amy Yingling.
Supplies *Patterned paper, fiber and stickers: All My Memories; Mulberry paper: PrintWorks.*

All My Memories

Your memories from days past deserve extra-special treatment, and All My Memories offers vintage touches you'll treasure. Choose from delicately patterned paper in muted colors carefully selected for use with heritage photos. Add a nostalgic touch with understated fibers in vintage colors, plus new typewriter-key stickers that are stand-outs for elegant titles.

Web site: . . . . www.allmymemories.com
Phone: 888/553-1998

Check your local scrapbook store.

Page by Wendy Sue Anderson. **Supplies** *Patterned paper and tags:* Rusty Pickle; *Computer font:* 2Peas Evergreen, downloaded from *www.twopeasina-bucket.com; Ribbon:* C.M. Offray & Son; *Chalk:* EK Success; *Other:* Vellum and antique brass brads. *Idea to note:* Wendy removed the lock and key charms from an extra tag and tied them across her photo with ribbon.

Thomas William
&
Ellen Caroline Selin

RHOADES

October 9, 1912
Wedding Day
Salt Lake Temple

the
heart
has
reasons
that
reason
knows
nothing
of

Rusty Pickle

Vintage is all the rage in scrap-booking, and Rusty Pickle offers delicious solutions you'll savor. Choose from memorable 12" x 12" papers in themes like Vintage Collage, Western Union, Vintage Atlas and Vintage Music. Whip up creations from scratch with the company's walnut-inked or leather tags. Add extra spice with dimensional, hand-made tags that you and others will relish!

Web site: . . . . www.RustyPickle.com
Online suppliers: . www.LifetimeMoments.com
. . . . and www.Embellish-This.com

Page and book sample by Lori Pieper. **Supplies** *Patterned paper and book photo accent:* Time & Again, Déjà Views, The C-Thru Ruler Co.

The C-Thru Ruler Co.

Want a classic, coordinated look for your vintage pages? Consider the Déjà Views Time & Again kits by The C-Ruler Ruler Company! Available in themes such as The Early Days, Through the Years, Military & Career, Portraits, Wedding and Seasons, each kit contains patterned paper, cardstock, vellum, a plastic template, title frame sheets and more. Create multiple pages per kit.

Another hot item? The company's TidBits Story Books. Whether used separately or on a layout, they present photos and journaling in a powerful and memorable way.

Web site: . . . . www.cthruruler.com

Phone: 800/243-8419

Check your local scrapbook store.

Page by Karen Russell.
Supplies *Patterned paper and postage embellishments, circle letters and tag:* K & Company; *Computer fonts:* CK Typewriter, "Fresh Fonts" CD, *Creating Keepsakes;* GF Halda Normal, downloaded from the Internet; *Other:* Transparencies, screen, watch heads, eyelets and ribbon.

K & Company

Life's Journey, a new line by K & Company, is filled with distinctive products—everything from beautiful papers and embossed stickers to metal accents and albums—that will delight any vintage scrapbooker.

The line's heirloom look is perfect for highlighting your sepia photos and treasured memorabilia. Life's Journey is designed to coordinate with your favorite K & Company products.

Web site: . . . . www.kandcompany.com

Page by Wendy Sue Anderson.
Supplies *Typewriter key letters,
ribbon, conchos, transparency
envelopes and documents:*
ARTchix Studio; *Patterned
papers:* Daisy D's (green stripe),
K & Company (brown),
The C-Thru Ruler Co. (red);
Stamping ink: Hero Arts; *Chalk:*
Stampin' Up!; *Other:* Antique
brass brads. *Idea to note:*
Using a tip from designer Kristy
Banks, Wendy sewed on her
layout with white thread, then
chalked over the thread with
brown chalk. She erased the
brown chalk from the paper
with a chalk eraser (the chalk
stays on the thread).

ARTchix Studio

Transform your scrapbook pages into works of art with
antique ribbons, beads, charms and other pieces by
ARTchix Studio. You can be an "art chick," too! Add a
classy, keepsake touch by layering transparencies, fabrics, collage sheets and more. ARTchix offers a variety
of intriguing items, including brass oval lockets,
word pebble charms, vintage ledger pages, envelope charms and velvet leaves.

Web site: . . . . www.artchixstudio.com
Phone: 250/370-9985

Page by Mary Larson.
Supplies *Watch pieces, letters, postcard and clock transparencies:* Limited Edition Rubber Stamps; *Patterned paper:* K & Company and Mustard Moon; *Mesh paper:* Magenta; *Small brads:* GoneScrappin.com; *Metal tag:* Hot Off The Press; *Embossing powder:* Suze Weinberg; *Computer font:* CK Ranch, "Fresh Fonts" CD, *Creating Keepsakes*; *Chalk:* Craf-T Products; *Fiber:* Magic Scraps; *Photo corners:* Canson; *Other:* Beads.

Limited Edition Rubber Stamps

From vintage postcards to letter tiles, Limited Edition Rubber Stamps offers an intriguing array of distinctive accents. Choose from watch pieces, transparencies, labels, miniature postcards and more. Use the accents separately, or group them for a memorable collage. Create a classic, "limited edition" look today!

Web site: . . . . www.limitededitionrs.com
Phone: 877/9-STAMPS (877/978-2677)

Check your local scrapbook store.

Page by Wendy Sue Anderson.
Supplies *Metal frame and accent piece:* JewelCraft; *Mesh eyelets:* Making Memories; *Patterned paper:* K & Company; *Ribbon:* C.M. Offray & Son; *Letter stickers:* Sonnets, Creative Imaginations; *Computer font:* CK Tea Party, "Fresh Fonts" CD, *Creating Keepsakes;* *Chalk:* EK Success; *Glue dots:* Glue Dots International.

Border design by Deb Ringquist.
Supplies *Nailheads, findings, drops, charms, and Preciosa stones:* JewelCraft; *Craft wire:* Artistic Wire Ltd.

JewelCraft

Add a touch of brilliance and "charm" to your most cherished pages and cards with filigree nailheads, drops and charms by JewelCraft. Intricately crafted, the accents come in a variety of colors and sizes. They're lightweight and easy to apply for instant elegance. Mix them for a sparkle all your own!

Web site: . . . . www.jewelcraft.biz
Phone: 201/223-0804

Check your local scrapbook store.

it's all a
mAtteR *of* tIMe

William Randolph & Annie Cheriel came to the farm in Burley, Idaho (the Pella area) on December 26, 1918 from Bountiful, Utah. They had been married on June 10, 1903.

It is absolutely amazing to think what years of growing, caring and nurturing can do to a place. The way the farm used to be and the way it is now are like night and day. I can't even imagine what must have been in great grandpa and grandma Cheriel's minds when they settled here. Nothing but sage brush and dirt. They put in so much hard work to make a beautiful place to live. The way life used to be back then, the equipment they had to use, it must have taken so long to get anything done. Even as they still managed to have their fun, as you can see from photo to the right. The top left photo is of William milking a cow in the early 1920's. The top right photo is of William and Annie's kids, Gladys, Honer, Ralph, Wyendzel, and Anta taking a break, dangling their feet in the ditch in 1925. This is something all "us kids" still do today. The bottom left photo is of William and Annie being "serenaded" by Dick and Joe to the tune of "While You Were Young" in the early 1920's. And the bottom right photo is of William working in the field with the old power Lorie in the late 1930's.

Now, there are so many different kinds of flowers, raspberries, vegetables, apple trees, pine trees, willow trees, and many other kinds of trees. The pine trees near the Lower Lawn have been growing for almost one hundred years. It's hard to imagine how they've stood the test of time. Well, most of them. The farm Lorie definitely seen it's share of changes over the years. Barns, cellars, homes, they've come and gone as was needed. But what a beautiful place Lorie has become. Not only did Lorie bring many years growth, and life in the way of plants, flowers, and trees, but also in the wildlife that took up residence here. So many birds, including owls and mourning doves, squirrels, rabbits, and even the occasional skunk. The photos on this page were taken in April 2003. The old power Lorie it's mostly in the grass, grandpa's dowel is there as a memory to the time when he would take care of the gardens and whistle while he worked, and you still hear the sound of the tin can on top of the pump when it runs to water the gardens. What a legacy that Lorie has left for our family.

Pages by Kerri Bradford. **Supplies** *Stickers:* Tumblebeasts (pump and hoe), Colorbök (letters); *Patterned paper:* Karen Foster Design; *Mesh paper:* Magenta; *Eyelets and metal glue:* Making Memories; *Fibers:* On The Surface; *Key, key hole and watch parts:* Ink It!; *Computer fonts:* CK Extra (title), "Fresh Fonts" CD; CK Artisan (journaling), Becky Higgins "Creative Clips & Fonts" CD, *Creating Keepsakes.*

Farm Fresh **EGGS** FOR SALE

Classic Cars

Tumblebeasts

With the vintage stickers by Tumblebeasts, you can mentally take a ride back in time in a classic car, or hop on an antique tractor for a spin around the old homestead. Think of the weathered tools you've seen lying around the farm. Reflect on sweet-scented roses resting against a white-picket fence. It's never been easier to revisit the "good old days" than with the charm of stickers from Tumblebeasts.

Web site: . . . . www.tumblebeasts.com
Phone: 505/232-5554

Check your local scrapbook store.

Family Cars

As best we can tell, this car is a 1914 Ford Model T. The people in the photo, which includes my great grand-rents, Engebret and Guri were leaving their North Dakota to a ship that to Norway. We think my

Pages by Julie Turner. **Supplies** *Decoupage paper:* Artifacts; *Adhesive:* Perfect Paper Adhesive, USArtQuest; *Fabric:* Jo-Ann's; *Snaps, eyelets and letter charms:* Making Memories; *Fiber:* DMC; *Letter stamps:* PSX Design; *Stamping ink:* Ranger Industries; *Tag:* American Tag Company; *Computer fonts:* Zapf Ellipt, Microsoft Word; Typewriter, P22 Type Foundry; *Other:* Key and envelope.

Artifacts, Inc.

Looking for the romance of the Victorian era? Consider indulging in decoupage papers (20" x 28" sheets) or paper scraps from Artifacts. Their Golden Series line of beautiful, authentic Edwardian and Victorian paper accents is suitable for embellishing scrapbook pages and many other items. Decoupage a picture frame, hatbox, or anything you want to give a genuine vintage feel.

MSRP: . . . . Varies

Web site: . . . . www.maryjeanonline.com

Phone: 903/729-4178

"The Marlar Girl"
by Mary Larson
Chandler, AZ
SUPPLIES
Patterned paper: Hot Off The Press
Vellum: PrintWorks
Lettering template: Calligraphy,
ScrapPagerz.com
Computer font: Flat Brush,
downloaded from the Internet

QUOTABLE QUOTE:

"A family with an old
person has a living
treasure of gold."

—Chinese Proverb

Success

To **laugh** often and much;
to win the **respect** of intelligent
people and the **affection** of children;
to earn the **appreciation** of honest
critics and **endure** the betrayal
of false friends; to appreciate
beauty; to find the best in others;
to leave the world a bit **better**,
a **garden** patch or redeemed social
condition; to know even **one life**
has breathed **easier** because you
have lived. **This is to have succeeded.**

RALPH WALDO EMERSON

HCH and Carolyn - 1939

318 Orchard Lane
Columbus, Ohio
1938

Taken Fall of 1953
for 50th Wedding Anniversary

Howard C. Hoeflich
November 8, 1881—March 3, 1984
My Grandpa!

July 28, 1940

May 1942

Grandpa taking a snooze—Alliance, OH

"Howard C. Hoeflich"

by Carolyn Hassall
Bradenton, FL
SUPPLIES
Patterned paper: Gibson Greetings
for Kinko's
Computer fonts: CAC Shishoni, package unknown, American Greetings;

Scrap Calligraphy, "Lettering
Delights" CD Vol. 2, Inspire Graphics
Stickers: me & my BIG ideas
Embossed frames: K & Company
Idea to note: Carolyn color-copied
her grandfather's watch and included
the copy on her layout.

Accent Idea: Photographs of Actual Items

❖   ❖   ❖   ❖   ❖

Looking for page accents that match the time period you're scrapbooking? Try taking photographs or making color copies or scans of actual items from that time period and using them on your layouts. On a layout about her grandfather's life, Carolyn Hassall of Bradenton, Florida, included a color copy of his pocket watch as the perfect finishing touch. Other heirloom items that would make interesting accents include jewelry, china, book covers, picture frames, pottery, bags or briefcases, medals and badges.

To photograph these items, place them on a neutral background in even lighting (direct sunlight will cause a glare in your photos). Turn off the flash on your camera, stand directly over the item (you may need a chair), and snap the picture. Remember, the size of the item in your viewfinder will be proportional to the size of the item on your developed print. Keep the scale in mind as you zoom in or out on the object.

ANDREW LOCY ROGERS

(handwritten journaling block, partially legible)

This picture
was taken in Belfast, Ireland
in 1910
Andrew Locy Rogers
lived from
1854-1943

"Andrew Locy Rogers"
by Eva Flake
Tucson, AZ
SUPPLIES
Computer fonts: St. Charles Thin, downloaded from the Internet;
CK Penman, "The Best of Creative Lettering" CD Combo, *Creating
Keepsakes*
Chalk: Craf-T Products
Photo corners: Canson
Embroidery floss: DMC
Other: Buttons and twine

My Grandmother's
Motorcycle Boots
Sybil Stewart (1930)

My grandparents met when my grandfather got a job with the
Westmount Police force where my grandmother's brother,
Clifford, also worked. Soon after, my grandparents, Clifford
and his girlfriend began double dating- motorcycling around
town. My grandfather had the motorcycle boots, shown in this
picture, especially made for my grandmother.

"Motorcycle Boots"
by Janet MacLeod
Dundas, ON, Canada
SUPPLIES
Patterned paper: K & Company
Vellum: Paper Adventures
Computer fonts: Garamouche Regular and
Macromedia, Fontographer;
Lucida Handwriting, Microsoft Word
Charms: Source unknown
Eyelets: Impress Rubber Stamps
Laces: Tana

"Mazel Alma Nielson"
by Marci Tribe
Bountiful, UT
Photo by Jed Clark
SUPPLIES
Computer font: Stilted Man,
downloaded from the Internet
Song lyrics: Eddie Noak, c. 1955,
Highland Range Songs, Inc.
Corner punch: Family Treasures

These hands ain't the hands of a gentleman,
These hands are calloused and old,
These hands raised a family,
These hands raise to praise the Lord.

These hands won the heart of my loved one,
And with hers they were never alone.
If these hands filled their task,
Then what more could one ask?
For these fingers have worked to the bone.

Now don't try to judge me by what you'd like to be,
For my life ain't been much success.
While some people have power, still they grieve,
While these hands brought me happiness.

Now I'm tired and I'm old and I ain't got much gold.
Maybe things ain't been all that I planned.
God above, hear my plea,
When it's time to judge me,
Take a look at these hard workin' hands.

Mazel Alma Nielson
October 19, 1911 ~ December 26, 2000

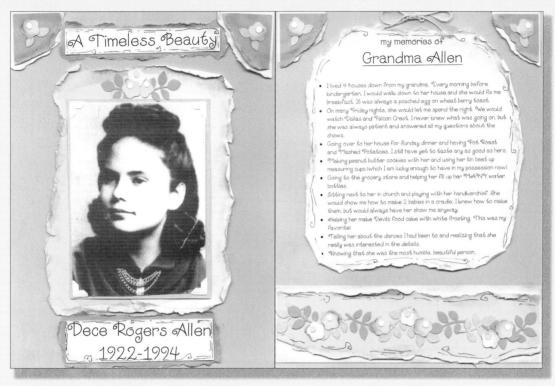

A Timeless Beauty

my memories of
Grandma Allen

- I lived 4 houses down from my grandma. Every morning before kindergarten, I would walk down to her house and she would fix me breakfast. It was always a poached egg on wheat berry toast.
- On many Friday nights, she would let me spend the night. We would watch "Dallas" and "Falcon Crest." I never knew what was going on, but she was always patient and answered all my questions about the shows.
- Going over to her house for Sunday dinner and having "Pot Roast and Mashed Potatoes. I still have yet to taste any as good as hers.
- Making peanut butter cookies with her and using her tin beat up measuring cups (which I am lucky enough to have in my possession now)
- Going to the grocery store and helping her fill up her "MaANy water bottles.
- Sitting next to her in church and playing with her handkerchief. She would show me how to make 2 babies in a cradle. I knew how to make them, but would always have her show me anyway.
- Helping her make "Devils food cake with white frosting. This was my favorite!
- Telling her about the dances I had been to and realizing that she really was interested in the details.
- Knowing that she was the most humble, beautiful person.

Dece Rogers Allen
1922-1994

"A Timeless Beauty"

by Eva Flake
Tucson, AZ
SUPPLIES
Computer font: CK Curly, "The Best of Creative Lettering" CD Combo, *Creating Keepsakes*
Punches: The Punch Bunch (ash leaf), EK Success (flower), McGill (hole)
Chalk: Craf-T Products
Eyelets: Coffee Break Design
Photo corners: Canson
Pen: Zig Writer, EK Success
Other: Twine
Idea to note: Eva created an aged look for her layout by curling the cardstock on her title and journaling blocks, borders and photo mat.

"Fond Memories"

by Carolyn Hassall
Bradenton, FL
SUPPLIES
Patterned paper: Hot Off The Press
Computer fonts: Scrap Calligraphy and Scrap Katie, "Lettering Delights" CD Vol. 2, Inspire Graphics
Basket stamp and stamping ink: PSX Design
Frame: Keeping Memories Alive

Fond Memories

When I was young, Grandma Gayer lived in Columbus, Ohio in a brick row house just off High Street across from the Ohio State Campus and right across from the Ohio State Museum. That was my very favorite place to go and she would take me there so that I could spend the day looking at the different exhibits, especially the stuffed birds and animals and the working model of a mill and water wheel, the antique bicycle and dresser and a panorama in miniature of an Indian village.

Grandma made a lot of quilts and it was fascinating to watch her load all those stitches onto the needle and to work the treadle sewing machine. I also loved watching her do her hair. She would roll it on a curling iron that she heated on the stove. Then after it was all in long curls, she would roll it up in a bun — I couldn't understand why she wouldn't wear it long!

Grandma at the Country Church of Hollywood

Aunt Marguerite and Grandma with Ruth, Paul, Carolyn, Keith Circa 1942

When I was in the sixth grade, I could ride the trolley to her house and stay for the weekend. She would take me to the museum and sometimes to a nearby movie theater. After the movie, we would go into the dime store that was next door — that's where I saw the first Barbie doll!

Grandma was supposedly born at midnight on September 12-13th, and she always celebrated both days! She was born and grew up in Columbus, Ohio. At a time when few young women worked outside of the home, she worked as a bookkeeper for five years previous to her marriage. In her youth, everyone called her "Frankie", but later she became "Polly", and still later, Aunt Polly, to everyone. She enjoyed music of all kinds, sang well, liked dancing and bridge. She loved making scrapbooks for everyone that came into her life - they were filled with comments, newspaper clippings, poems, songs, and whatever else she could think of.

Grandma as a little girl in 1880

Frances Inez Culbertson Hoeflich
September 12, 1879 - January 10, 1970
My Maternal Grandmother

"Frances Inez Culbertson Hoeflich"

by Carolyn Hassall
Bradenton, FL
SUPPLIES
Alphabet stickers: K & Company
Computer fonts: CAC Shishoni, package unknown, American Greetings; Scrap Calligraphy, "Lettering Delights" CD Vol. 2, Inspire Graphics

Rubber stamp: Stampin' Up!
Stamping ink: Source unknown
Embossed frames: K & Company
Corner punches: Emagination Crafts, Hyglo
Idea to note: Carolyn created the border corners by combining two different corner punches.

"Great-grandma Culbertson"

by Carolyn Hassall
Bradenton, FL
SUPPLIES
Computer fonts: CAC Shishoni, package unknown, American Greetings; Scrap Calligraphy, "Lettering Delights" CD Vol. 2, Inspire Graphics
Stickers: me & my BIG ideas
Corner punches: Emagination Crafts, Family Treasures

Great Grandma Culbertson
circa 1930 . . . 78 years old

Great Grandma Culbertson, holding Carolyn at 12 weeks old in 1938. Four Generations are Anna Leonard Culbertson, Frances Culbertson Hoeflich, Miriam Hoeflich Gayer, and Carolyn Louise Gayer.
1939

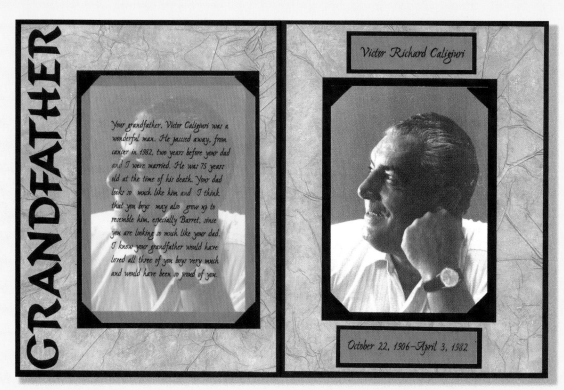

"Grandfather"

by Melissa Caligiuri
Winter Park, FL
SUPPLIES
Patterned paper: Scrap-Ease
Vellum: Paper Adventures
Lettering template: Calligraphy, ScrapPagerz.com
Computer font: PC Stone Script, "Little Images"
HugWare CD, Provo Craft

"James Bryan Sullivan"

by Dece Gherardini
Mesa, AZ
SUPPLIES
Computer fonts: CK Classic
(title), "The Art of Creative
Lettering" CD, *Creating
Keepsakes*; CK Bella (journaling),
"The Best of Creative Lettering"

CD Vol. 3, *Creating Keepsakes*
Star Template: Block, ABC
Tracers, EK Success
Paper crimper: 'Lil Boss
Hole punch: Fiskars
Photo corners: Fiskars
Other: Buttons and hemp cord

"Allene Pace Cole"
by Lisa Pallipaden
San Jose, CA
SUPPLIES
Vellum: K & Company (embossed),
Paper Adventures
Computer font: CK Script, "The Best of
Creative Lettering " CD Vol. 1, *Creating
Keepsakes*
Leaf punch: Martha by Mail
Embroidery floss: DMC

"Clara Marguerite Hatch"
by Torrey Miller
Lafayette, CO
SUPPLIES
Computer font: Harrington,
package unknown
Ribbon: Offray
Embroidery floss: DMC
Corner punch: Emagination Crafts
Other: Fabric and buttons
Idea to note: Torrey re-created the
look of a French bulletin board on her
page to hold original postcards.

Want to create this fun, quilted look?

❶ Trim a piece of acid-free matting board (available at art supply stores) to just slightly smaller than the page size of your scrapbook.

❷ Cover the matting board with felt until you reach the desired thickness.

❸ Cover the padded matting board with the fabric of your choice.

❹ Crisscross ribbon along the front of the board, creating a diamond pattern. Wrap the ribbon ends around to the back of the board and adhere.

❺ Sew buttons at each ribbon intersection.

❻ Slip photographs underneath the ribbon, adhering lightly if necessary.

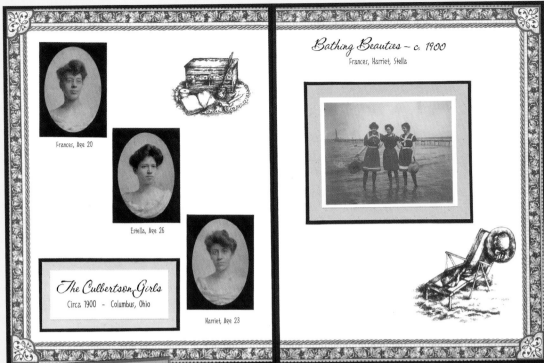

Bathing Beauties ~ c. 1900
Frances, Harriet, Stella

Frances, Age 20

Estella, Age 26

The Culbertson Girls
Circa 1900 - Columbus, Ohio

Harriet, Age 23

BETTY AND BOBBIE

TOP: Betty age 7, Bobbie age 5. Periodically a photographer would show up with props and ask to take pictures for $1.00. This occasion featured a goat pulling a cart.
BOTTOM: Betty age 9 and Bobbie age 7. This photo was taken in Goose Creek which is now Baytown, Texas. The occasion was Easter and they had new dresses. Betty's was pink.

TOP: Betty age 13 or 14, Bobbie age 11 or 12, their Mother Mary age 34 or 35. This photo taken at the open air market on Campostella Road in Norfolk, Va.

MIDDLE: Circa 1955. Betty and Bobbie with their father Thomas Wilson Griffin at Bounds Ranch, Grant County New Mexico
BOTTOM: From left to Right. Aunt Louise, Mary Griffin, Bobbie and Betty. Easter at Aunt Louise & Uncle Rollie's. This photo was taken in the front yard of their big house in Norfolk, Va.

"Bathing Beauties"
by Carolyn Hassall
Bradenton, FL
SUPPLIES
Border stickers: me & my BIG ideas
Computer fonts: CAC Shishoni, package unknown, American Greetings; Scrap Katie, "Lettering Delights" CD Vol. 2, Inspire Graphics
Clip art: Leaves of Time

Page Idea:
Lifespan Pages

❖   ❖   ❖   ❖   ❖

"Through the Years"
by Bonnie Udall
Picture This
Eager, AZ
SUPPLIES
Stickers: me & my BIG ideas
Picket-fence die cut: Memory Lane
Computer font: CK Script, "The Best of Creative Lettering" CD Vol. 1, *Creating Keepsakes*
Chalk: Craf-T Products
Scissors: Deckle edge, Fiskars
Clear photo corners: 3L Corp.

Inheriting hundreds of photographs can be intimidating, especially when you're trying to scrapbook the entire lives of several ancestors at the same time! Instead of trying to create separate pages for each photograph, consider creating a "lifespan" page that highlights major events and photographs from that person's life.

For example, Bonnie Udall of Eager, Arizona, collected several photographs that show two girls, Betty and Bobbie, together at different ages. On her layout "Through the Years," Bonnie created an overview of their lives with photos of the two girls as children, teenagers and adults.

Once you've created a lifespan page for your ancestor or family member, you can rest easy knowing the key events in that person's life have been scrapbooked. This allows you to put the rest of the unscrapbooked photographs aside and work on other projects. If you get inspired to create more detailed pages later, the lifespan page can serve as an introduction or title page to the album you create for that person.

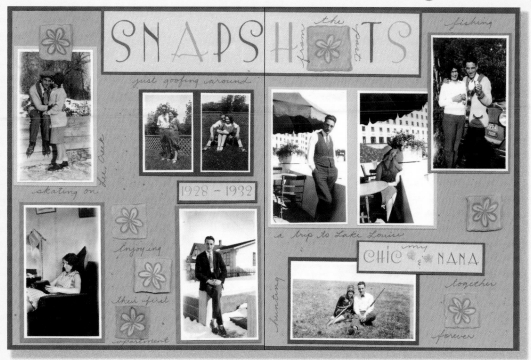

"Snapshots"

by Cheryl McMurray
Cardston, AB, Canada
SUPPLIES
Computer font: Lemon Chicken, downloaded from the Internet
Flower and square rubber stamps: Hero Arts
Pen: VersaMark, Tsukineko
Chalk: Craf-T Products

"John and Miriam"

by Carolyn Hassall
Bradenton, FL
SUPPLIES
Computer fonts: Doodle Do, "PagePrintables" CD Vol. 2, Cock-A-Doodle Design Inc.; Scrap Katie, "Lettering Delights" CD Vol. 2, Inspire Graphics
Leaf punch: The Punch Bunch

Rubber stamps: PSX Design (letters), Just for Fun (sand dollar)
Stamping ink: ColorBox, Clearsnap, Inc.
Color-blocking technique: Carolyn adapted the idea from a layout by Becky Higgins in *Scrapbooking Secrets* (Creating Keepsakes Books).

"Victor and Olga"
by Melissa Caligiuri
Winter Park, FL
SUPPLIES
Dried flowers: Pressed Petals
Computer font: Carpenter, downloaded
from the Internet
Ribbon: Offray

"Joseph and Helen"
by Stefani Meyer
Mustard Moon
San Jose, CA
SUPPLIES
Patterned paper: Mustard Moon
Rubber stamp and stamping ink:
Close To My Heart
Computer font: Mistral,
package unknown
Chalk: Craf-T Products
Embroidery floss: DMC
Pen: Zig Writer, EK Success
Other: Buttons

"Dunn"
by Anne Heyen
Glendale, NY
SUPPLIES
Patterned papers: Anna Griffin
(green), Hot Off The Press (lace)
Vellum: Paper Adventures
Computer font: CK Italic,
"The Art of Creative Lettering"
CD, *Creating Keepsakes*
Lettering template: Chatterbox
Ribbon: Offray
Buttons and bow: Dress It Up,
Jesse James Company
Square punch: Family Treasures

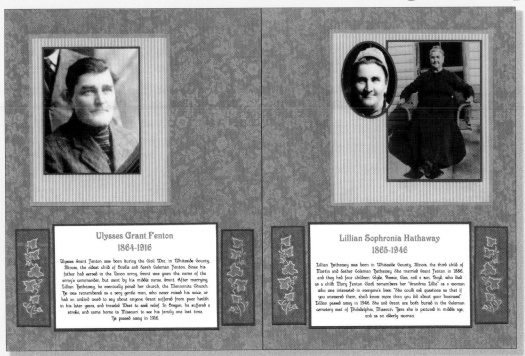

Ulysses Grant Fenton
1864-1916

Ulysses Grant Fenton was born during the Civil War, in Whiteside County, Illinois, the oldest child of Orville and Sarah Coleman Fenton. Since his father had served in the Union army, Grant was given the name of the army's commander, but went by his middle name, Grant. After marrying Lillian Hathaway, he eventually joined her church, the Mennonite Church. He was remembered as a very gentle man, who never raised his voice, or had an unkind word to say about anyone. Grant suffered from poor health in his later years, and traveled West to seek relief. In Oregon, he suffered a stroke, and came home to Missouri to see his family one last time. He passed away in 1916.

Lillian Sophronia Hathaway
1865-1946

Lillian Hathaway was born in Whiteside County, Illinois, the third child of Martin and Esther Coleman Hathaway. She married Grant Fenton in 1886, and they had four children: Glyde, Bessie, Cleo, and a son, Boyd, who died as a child. Mary Fenton Clark remembers her "Grandma Lillie" as a woman who was interested in everyone's lives. "She could ask questions so that if you answered them, she'd know more than you did about your business!" Lillian passed away in 1946. She and Grant are both buried in the Coleman cemetery east of Philadelphia, Missouri. Here she is pictured in middle age, and as an elderly woman.

"Grant and Lillian"

by Janelle Clark
Westerville, OH
SUPPLIES
Patterned paper:
Minigraphics
Vellum: Paper Adventures
(green), source unknown
(striped)

Computer fonts: Victorian
(titles) and Wellsley
(journaling), downloaded
from the Internet
Ivy template: American
Traditional

"Lewis and Velma"

by Janelle Clark
Westerville, OH
SUPPLIES
Patterned paper: Rocky
Mountain Scrapbook Company
*Leaf and background rubber
stamps:* Hero Arts
Stamping inks: Making
Memories, Stewart Superior

Corporation; ColorBox,
Clearsnap, Inc.
Computer fonts: Alison
(titles) and Galant (journaling),
downloaded from the Internet
Photo corner punch: Marvy
Uchida
Ribbon: May Arts

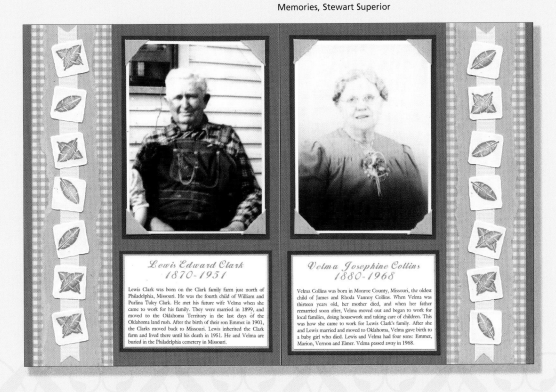

Lewis Edward Clark
1870-1951

Lewis Clark was born on the Clark family farm just north of Philadelphia, Missouri. He was the fourth child of William and Purlina Tuley Clark. He met his future wife Velma when she came to work for his family. They were married in 1899, and moved to the Oklahoma Territory in the last days of the Oklahoma land rush. After the birth of their son Emmet in 1901, the Clarks moved back to Missouri. Lewis inherited the Clark farm and lived there until his death in 1951. He and Velma are buried in the Philadelphia cemetery in Missouri.

Velma Josephine Collins
1880-1968

Velma Collins was born in Monroe County, Missouri, the oldest child of James and Rhoda Vannoy Collins. When Velma was thirteen years old, her mother died, and when her father remarried soon after, Velma moved out and began to work for local families, doing housework and taking care of children. This was how she came to work for Lewis Clark's family. After she and Lewis married and moved to Oklahoma, Velma gave birth to a baby girl who died. Lewis and Velma had four sons: Emmet, Marion, Vernon and Elmer. Velma passed away in 1968.

"A Love Story"
by Anita Matejka
Lincoln, NE
SUPPLIES
Patterned paper: Scrap-Ease
Vellum: The Paper Company
Computer font: Pepita, downloaded from the Internet
Grommets: Impress Rubber Stamps
Thread: On the Surface Fibers
Idea to note: Anita made copies of the original letters her grandfather sent to her grandmother and included them on her layout.

Preservation 101: Including Letters on Layouts

❖ ❖ ❖ ❖ ❖

Handwritten letters, notes, certificates and newspaper clippings add meaning and interest to heritage layouts—but use caution when you're working with the original items. Most papers used in days past contain acid, which will migrate to the other photos and memorabilia in your album, even if the item is enclosed in a sheet protector. The result? Irreparable damage to your keepsakes. To keep your paper items safe, try one of these options:

♦ **Make a color copy.** Make sure you're using a copier with powder toner (the store attendant should be able to tell you what type of toner their copiers use) and copying onto acid- and lignin-free paper. This will provide a copy of the item that will last for hundreds of years.

♦ **Wash newspaper articles.** As a general rule, this should be done on clippings smaller than 10" x 12" and older than 10 years. First, pour distilled water into a flat glass baking dish. Immerse the article in the water and let it soak for 20 minutes. Carefully lift out the paper and lay it on a flat surface (you may want to slip a piece of paper under the article to provide stability while removing it from the water). Let the paper dry in a place with an even temperature. This process seems intimidating, but it's actually very easy—and good for the paper! In addition to removing acid, the wet fibers expand and bind together, making the paper stronger.

♦ **Use a deacidification spray.** Any uncoated paper item can be deacidified using a deacidification spray, such as Archival Mist by Preservation Technologies. The solvents in Archival Mist will not dissolve or affect inks, colors or adhesives. (To be extra cautious with your heritage items, test a small area to make sure the inks will not be affected.) Follow the directions on the specific deacidification spray you choose for the best results. Once you've deacidified your item, attach the original using photo corners instead of adhesive in case you need to remove it from your album in the future.

a new look at letters

Write a letter—to yourself or someone you love—to be opened at a future date. *Page by Rebecca Sower.* **Supplies** *Acrylic paints:* Golden Paints; *Rhinestones:* Darice; *Pen:* Zig Writer, EK Success; *Vellum envelope:* European Papers; *Other:* Angel wings, netting and embroidery floss.

*A tisket, a tasket,
a green and yellow basket
I wrote a letter to my love,
and on the way I lost it.*

REMEMBER SINGING this little ditty as a child? I do. Hmmm, a lost letter. Wouldn't it be fun to know just how many letters have been addressed to you in your lifetime?

Which lost letters would I most like to find? My husband and I lived in separate states for one year before we were married. You'd better believe I saved every one of those letters (all 200 or so of them). But what about the letters from those guys I didn't marry? Or the notes from my grade-school friends? What about the letters from my parents while I was at summer camp? *All* of them would add interesting little twists to my personal history.

Last year, a boy in my daughter's sixth-grade class wrote what I thought was an impressive letter. (I found out later that his mom helped him.) My daughter didn't feel as affectionately

ARTICLE BY REBECCA SOWER

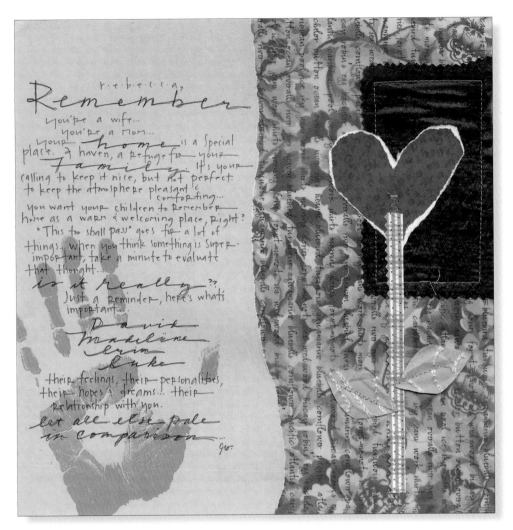

Figure 1. Write a letter to remind you about what's really important. *Page by Rebecca Sower.* **Supplies** *Patterned papers:* Laura Ashley, EK Success; *Specialty paper:* Provo Craft; *Double-coated cardstock:* Making Memories; *Acrylic paint:* Golden Paints; *Pinking shears:* Fiskars; *Pen:* Zig Writer, EK Success; *Other:* Fabric and thread.

toward the boy as he did toward her, so she wanted to destroy the letter and pretend it never happened. Oh no, not my daughter! First, she had to thank him for writing the letter. Then she had to, as sweet as sugar, tell him she would rather just be friends. (C'mon, girls, we all had to do this several times throughout our school years, remember?) And

then, she really had to be his friend. Well, that part worked—they're great friends today.

Back to the letter. I didn't let her trash it because the letter's part of her history. I think it will come into play at some point in her future. When she falls madly in love with Mr. Wonderful and he lacks letter-writing pizazz, she can show him—in a light-hearted

way, of course—how a letter to a girl should be written. You get my point: keep those letters!

Beyond Baby

Many of us write letters to our children. Whether it's on their birthdays or more or less often, we've gotten good at pouring our hearts into letters for our children's scrapbooks.

Do you have a certain letter that holds a special place in your heart? If you haven't scrapbooked that letter, now's the time.

Figure 2. Write a letter to a recipient who's long gone—it's therapeutic. *Pages by Rebecca Sower.* **Supplies** *Watercolor paper:* Molly Hawkins; *Walnut ink:* Anima Designs; *Photo corners:* Canson; *Letter stamps:* PSX Design; *Stamping ink:* Nick Bantock, Ranger Industries; *Pen:* Zig Writer, EK Success; *Other:* Old photo mat.

So, should we write any other letters? Most certainly! I'd propose the following recipients:

• Ourselves—that's right, ourselves
• A significant other
• Our parents
• Our nation's leaders
• Our friends (forget the e-mail—dust off the old pen and paper and use them)
• People we've never met (yep, like an unborn child, or even a future spouse)
• Someone who's passed away

Dear Me

Well, that sounds a little weird. Why in the world would you write a letter to yourself? It has all the makings of wasted time. I beg to differ. It's cleansing, therapeutic and motivating.

I chose to write a letter reminding me of what's truly most important in my life (Figure 1). I posted a copy in my studio so I see the letter every day. It helps me prioritize in a very real way.

Another fun project? Write a letter to yourself to be opened at a future date, then seal the envelope. No peeking! I did this when my daughter turned 12 (see page 71). It's a milestone year—she's no longer a little kid and is fast becoming an adolescent.

I thought about when my daughter will go out on her own. That day is going to kill me emotionally. So I wrote a letter to myself to be opened on that day. Although the contents of this private "pep talk" are too personal to share here, the premise of the letter is encouragement, consolation and a reminder that this is what moms do—we give our children wings. Go ahead. Write yourself a "Dear Me" letter.

If Only

Rarely do many of us verbalize our feelings for special people in our lives. After a loved one dies, we often regret that we didn't take time to write a letter, make a call and share our feelings. After a person is gone, it's too late, right? Maybe for them, but not for you.

My step-grandpa passed away

during my senior year of high school. Did I ever actually *tell* him how much he meant to me? I was in high school, remember? Of course I didn't. And yes, it's too late for him to hear it now. So I decided to write a long-overdue letter (Figure 2). I needed to do it for me, and I needed to do it for my children so they know about a wonderful man they never met.

Don't let more time pass before you sit down and write a letter telling someone who's passed away all the things you wished you'd said.

Sincerely Yours

Remember the letters from my husband-to-be that I mentioned earlier? Do you have a certain letter that holds a special place in your heart? If you haven't scrapbooked that letter, now's the time. Instead of just putting it on the page and jotting down a subtitle, journal about how the letter came into your life. Or, if you're still waiting to find your Prince Charming, write a letter to him (Figure 3).

What kinds of letters have you been writing? Keep it up! Now, what kinds of letters *should* you be writing? Aren't there at least a few that might be "lost"? Make it a goal to write at least three or four letters a year to these non-traditional recipients. No more "lost" letters! ♥

Figure 3. Is marriage still in your future? Write a letter to your future spouse. *Page by Lanna Carter.* **Supplies** *Patterned paper:* Karen Foster Design; *Vellum:* Provo Craft; *Computer fonts:* CK Sketch (journaling), "The Art of Creative Lettering" CD, CK Elegant ("I Love You") and CK Carbon Copy ("but who are you"), "Fresh Fonts" CD, *Creating Keepsakes; Fibers:* All My Memories; *Printed ribbon:* Lavish Lines; *Chalk ink:* ColorBox, Clearsnap; *Brads:* Lasting Impressions for Paper. *Idea to note:* Lanna tinted the ribbon with four chalk ink colors.

JOURNALING SPOTLIGHT

"You mean the world to me! If only I knew who you were. You wander into my thoughts a thousand times a day, yet I don't even know your name. You sneak into my nocturnal musings, but I wouldn't recognize you if we passed on the street. Sometimes I can close my eyes and almost imagine you behind me, whispering melodious nothings into my ear, yet I don't know anything about you.

"On quiet nights, I wonder if you are thinking of me. I catch myself glancing at the door hoping to see you waltz in with a smile on your face as if you've been a part of my life since before time began. But for now, the door doesn't open and I am left to my daydreams and hopes for some future time.

"I may not know your name, where you live or your hair color (if you even have hair), but I do know that regardless of how I imagine you to be, I will love you."

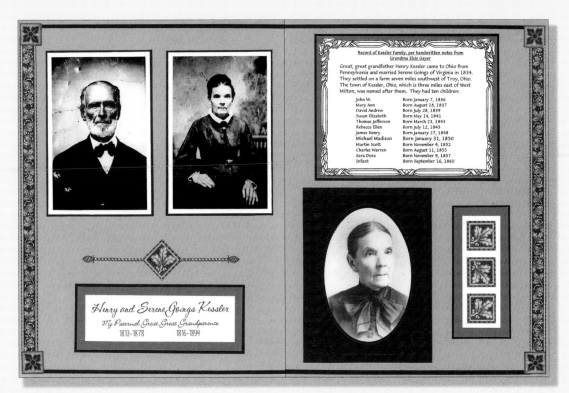

"Henry and Serene"

by Carolyn Hassall
Bradenton, FL
SUPPLIES
Computer fonts: CAC
Shishoni, package unknown,
American Greetings; Scrap
Calligraphy, "Lettering
Delights" CD Vol. 2, Inspire
Graphics
Border stickers: me & my BIG
ideas
Frame: Keeping Memories
Alive

"Joel and Mary"

by Janelle Clark
Westerville, OH
SUPPLIES
Patterned paper: K &
Company
Computer fonts: Jugend and
Bookman Old Style, down-
loaded from the Internet
Leaf stamp: Hero Arts
Stamping ink: VersaColor,
Tsukineko
Wave template: Christmas
Tracer, Pebbles in my Pocket

"My Heritage"

by Lynnette Carruthers
Belvidere, IL
SUPPLIES
Patterned paper: Paper Pizazz,
Hot Off The Press
Rose die cuts: The Family Archives
Corner punch: Southwest, Marvy
Uchida

Flower stickers: The Gifted Line,
Michel & Company
Idea to note: To preserve the
grainy look of old newspaper and
antique photos, Lynnette scanned
and enlarged her photos, then
printed them out on Velveteen
paper by Paper Adventures.

"Iola McIver"

by Darlynn Kaso
All About Scrapbooks
Virginia Beach, VA
SUPPLIES
Patterned paper: Close To My Heart
Butterfly stamp: Close To My Heart
Ink pad: Close To My Heart
Computer font: Edwardian Script, Microsoft Word
Photo corners: Canson

Paper edge: Corkscrew by Fiskars

"Katie Claude Johnson"
by Debra A. Stulik
El Cajon, CA

SUPPLIES

Patterned paper: Autumn Leaves
Punches: Family Treasures (double scallop corner slot punch), Marvy Uchida (crown border punch)
Pressed flower accent: Nu Century
Computer font: Crusader Gothic Extended, Microsoft Word
Idea to note: Debra created her own photo corner decorations by combining the border and corner slot punches.

"F. R. C. Ellis"
by Debra A. Stulik
El Cajon, CA

SUPPLIES

Clock stationery: The Paper Company
Pen: Zig Writer, EK Success
Idea to note: Debra cut the clocks from an 8½" x 11" piece of stationery and used them to create her own patterned paper for a 12" x 12" layout.

3 WAYS TO ADD MEANING TO HERITAGE PAGES

Heritage pages are often the hardest to create, because it is so hard to backtrack to find information about the people pictured. Adding meaning to heritage pages now will help future generations appreciate their past.

1. Ask older family members for information about the people pictured. You may stumble upon a "time machine"— a family member who knows story after story but never realized the importance of telling them!

2. Connect generations by showing photographs of family members together. Including information about how young family members are similar to their older relatives will help form bonds despite the age difference.

3. Recognize opportunities to create pages that will become heritage pages in the future. Scrapbooking changes in government, monetary systems, location and culture will help your future generations understand their roots.

Byron
Moore
Adams

Born May 5, 1907
Parowan, Utah

About 6 months old

Adams Children

Byron Adams was one of the fastest runners in elementary school and enjoyed sports all of his life. When he was about eight years old he was going up the mountain to get wood with his dad and brother Louis. The team was "spooked" and Byron was thrown under the wagon wheel. The heavy iron wheel ran over his upper back and neck paralyzing his legs and arms. He was in a coma for 3 months. After his recovery he spent the summers herding sheep on Cedar Breaks Mountain.

Byron loved and cherished his mother who was a school teacher and relief society president for sixteen years. He went on many assignments with her. Byron loved to read and was taught the importance of education. He finished high school in Tempe, Arizona where he earned money by working at a dairy. He graduated from Tempe High School and then went on to Lambson's Business College. He raised chickens to pay for his education.

Byron returned to Parowan, Utah to work as bookkeeper for the local cheese factory and other businesses. After 10 years he moved back to Arizona settling in Mesa. He sold Watkins Household Products for a time and later became bookkeeper for Farmers Independent Oil Company. He eventually bought the oil company and later built his own service station. He was a very successful businessman full of integrity, honesty and hard work.

He met Prudence Millet Allred in the Mesa 2nd Ward. They were married March 9, 1945 in the Mesa Arizona Temple.

Lola, Byron (back center), Louis and Harvey

Byron

James Leach Adams

Melinda's Parents

Vina Patten Moore and John Harvey Moore jr.

Melinda Moore Adams

"Byron Moore Adams"
by Laury Moulton
Pullman, WA
SUPPLIES
Photo corners: Close To My Heart
Computer font: Footlight MT Light, Source unknown

"Paula Seltsam"
by Darlynn Kaso
All About Scrapbooks
Virginia Beach, VA
SUPPLIES
Patterned paper: Minigraphics
Punches: Family Treasures (suns, daisy, small circle, large flowers, heart and birch leaf), Emagination Crafts (maple leaf)
Computer font: Edwardian Script, Microsoft Word
Pen: Zig Millennium, EK Success

Paula Seltsam
Southgate High School, Class of 1962

Osteopathic Hospital

Philadelphia 1937

"Philadelphia, 1937"

by Beth Turchi
Glassboro, NJ
SUPPLIES
Specialty paper: Paper
Adventures (Velveteen),
Source unknown (patterned
vellum)
Rose and corner stickers:
Class-A-Peels, Mark Enterprises
Alphabet stickers:
Mrs. Grossman's

Gold studs: Style Studs,
Gemcraft, Inc.
Rubber stamp: Uptown
Rubber Stamps
Idea to note: Beth used a
hot iron to impress the rubber
stamped images onto the
velvet paper.

"I Wish You Could Have Known Him"

by Julie Lowry
Montgomery, AL
SUPPLIES
Stickers: Design Lines,
Mrs. Grossman's
Lettering idea: "Classic,"
The Art of Creative Lettering,
Creating Keepsakes Books
Pens: Zig Writer and Zig Millennium,
EK Success

Idea to note: Julie used cardstock
and stickers to recreate the ribbons
worn on her dad's and husband's
uniforms.
Journaling idea: Julie's dad died
before she was married, so she
recorded some of the special things
about her dad and her husband that
they would have loved about each
other.

"My Grandfather"

by Marilyn Healey
West Jordan, UT
SUPPLIES

Patterned paper: Provo Craft (lavender thatch and splatter dot), Paper Adventures (pastel border and title background)

Handmade paper (blue): Solum World Paper

Ivy stationery: NRN Designs (large ivy around corners), Keeping Memories Alive (small ivy on title block)

Computer fonts: CK Script, "The Best of Creative Lettering" CD Vol. 1 (journaling) and CK Wedding,

"The Best of Creative Lettering" CD Vol. 2 (title), *Creating Keepsakes*

Punches: Family Treasures (circles), All Night Media (swirl border)

Other: Marilyn got the idea for the paper wisps from the article "Playful Paper Wisps" by Desirée Tanner in the May/June 1999 issue of *Creating Keepsakes* magazine.

Idea to note: Instead of cutting patterned paper and mounting it on the letters in the title, Marilyn cut the center out of the letters and backed the title block with the thatched patterned paper.

"George and Anna Seltsam"

by Darlynn Kaso
All About Scrapbooks
Virginia Beach, VA
SUPPLIES

Patterned paper: Frances Meyer

Circle and oval punches: Family Treasures

Hole punch: Punchline, McGill

Computer font: Edwardian Script, Microsoft Word

Pen: Zig Writer, EK Success

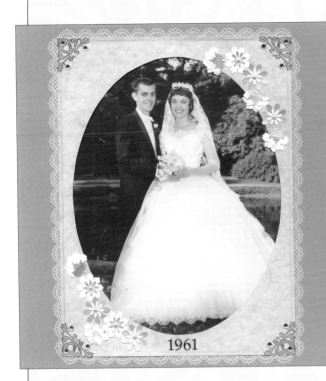

1961

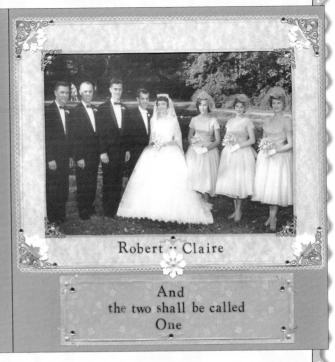

Robert · Claire

And
the two shall be called
One

"And the Two Shall Be Called One"

by Beth Turchi
Glassboro, NJ
SUPPLIES
Marbled cardstock: Westrim
Floral vellum: Source unknown
Stickers: Paper Whispers (lace borders) and
Classic Alphabet (letter stickers), Mrs. Grossman's;
Class-A-Peels, Mark Enterprises (silver corner stickers)
Punches: Family Treasures (silhouette punch flower and
small daisy), CARL Mfg. (large daisy), McGill
(small sun, maple leaf and crown border)
Jewel accents: Magic Pearls and Magic Gems,
Gemcraft, Inc.
Pen: Creative Memories

The Hand's of a Loving
Mother.
Jim, Kathy, Sue, and mother.
In our yard in Placerville.
Mother always had a beautiful
garden of pansies.
Spring 1955

"The Hands of a Loving Mother"

by Kathy Stott
Mom and Me Scrapbooking
Salt Lake City, UT
SUPPLIES
Flower stickers: The Gifted Line, Michel & Company
Computer font: Lucinda Handwriting, Microsoft Word

What turns an ordinary page into an extraordinary page? A single accent is often all it takes to give your work a signature look. Adapt the following accents to pages that celebrate the milestones of your life. The only limit is your imagination!

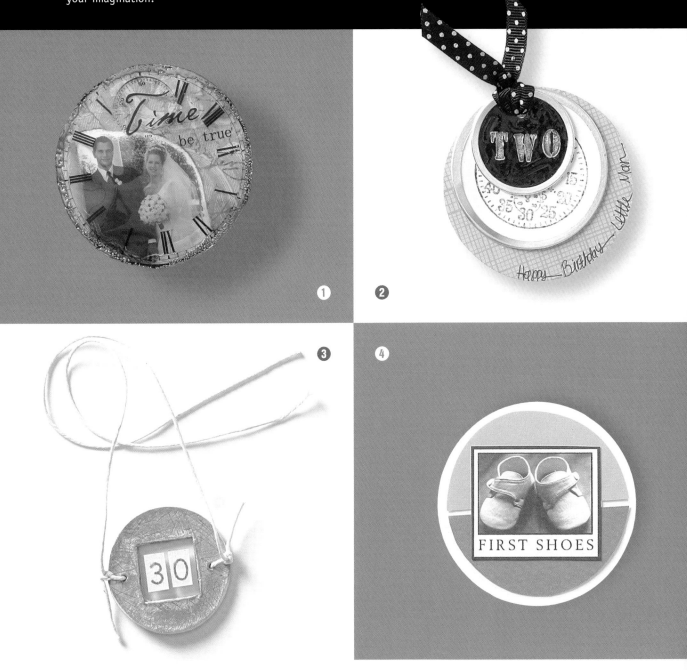

❶ **"TIME BE TRUE" by Karen Russell, Grants Pass, OR. Supplies** *Patterned paper:* 7 Gypsies; *Decoupage tissue:* DMD, Inc.; *Embossing powder:* Suze Weinberg; *Transparency:* Karen's own design. ❷ **"TWO" by Jenni Bowlin, Mount Juliet, TN. Supplies** *Patterned paper:* Chatterbox; *Letter stamps:* Turtle Press; *Metal-rimmed tags:* Avery; *Stamping ink:* Stampendous!; *Rubber stamp:* Postmodern Design; *Ribbon:* Hobby Lobby. ❸ **"30" by Julie Turner, Gilbert, AZ. Supplies** *Paper clay:* Creative Paperclay Company; *Silver-leafing pen:* Krylon; *Rub-ons:* Craf-T Products; *Other:* Glass, string and numbers cut from an old magazine. *Ideas to note:* This embellishment is a variation of the popular trend of tying a ribbon around a photo. The tag, marked with the birthday year, could be tied across a photo or journaling block. ❹ **"FIRST SHOES" by Marissa Perez, Issaquah, WA. Supplies** *Computer font:* Times New Roman, Microsoft Word.

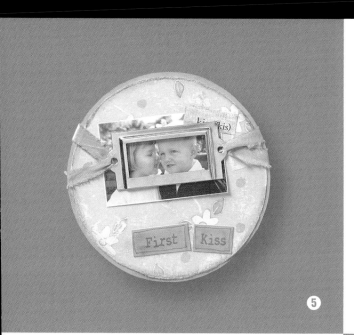

❺　　**❻**

❼　　**❽**

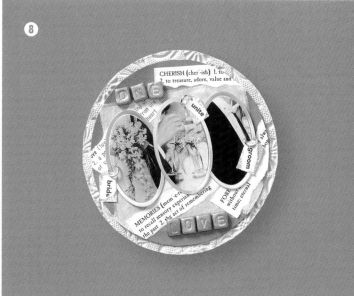

❾

❺ **"FIRST KISS" by Shannon Jones, Mesa, AZ. Supplies** *Patterned paper:* Kangaroo & Joey; *Silver frame:* Magic Scraps; *Ribbon:* Memory Lane; *Chalk:* Craf-T Products; *Computer font:* CK Corral, "Fresh Fonts" CD, *Creating Keepsakes*; *Definition:* Making Memories. **❻** **"YOUR FIRST SMILE" by Renee Camacho, Nashville, TN. Supplies** *Patterned paper:* KI Memories; *Circle tag:* Making Memories; *Letter stamps:* PSX Design; *Embossing powder:* Ranger Industries; *Snaps:* Making Memories; *Pen:* Zig Millennium, EK Success. **❼** **"SWEET SIXTEEN" by Gail Robinson, Herriman, UT. Supplies** *Charms:* Pebbles; *Ribbon:* C.M. Offray & Son; *Number stamp:* Making Memories; *Letter stickers:* me & my BIG ideas; *Rocks:* JudiKins; *Other:* Stamping ink, watch crystal and flower accent. **❽** **"ONE LOVE" by Denise Pauley, La Palma, CA. Supplies** *Embossed paper:* Books by Hand; *Definitions:* Making Memories; *Clay:* Makin' Clay, Provo Craft; *Tags:* Making Memories; *Jump rings:* GoneScrappin.com; *Other:* Metal stamps and fabric. *Idea to note:* Denise layered definition stickers over a swatch of fabric and decoupaged them to the background. **❾** **"LOVE" by Lynne Montgomery, Gilbert, AZ. Supplies** *Patterned paper:* Daisy D's; *Eyelet word:* Making Memories; *Coin holder:* Memory Lane; *Dimensional adhesive:* Diamond Glaze, JudiKins; *Other:* Ribbon.

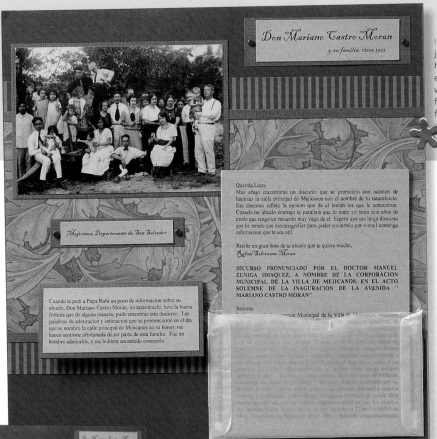

IDEA TO NOTE: Lizzy presented her journaling in Spanish to celebrate her family's heritage. She also included the English translation of her words so her non-Spanish speaking family members can enjoy the page for years to come.

"Don Mariano Castro Moran"

by Lizzy Mayorga
Seattle, WA
Supplies *Patterned paper:* K & Company; *Textured paper:* Bazzill Basics; *Computer fonts:* Times New Roman, Microsoft Word; Blackadder ITC, package unknown; *Glassine envelope:* Twopeasinabucket.com; *Other:* Mini-brads.

"Princess"

by Jennifer Bourgeault
Macomb Township, MI
Supplies *Printed vellum, frame and flower accents:* Leeco Industries; *Textured papers:* K & Company (cream), Bazzill Basics (peach); *Flower stickers:* Jolee's Boutique, Sticko; *Computer fonts:* 2Peas Katherine Ann, downloaded from www.twopeasinabucket.com; Brock Script, downloaded from the Internet.

"Love at Home"
by Jennifer Gallacher
Savannah, GA
Supplies *Patterned paper:* Anna Griffin; *Vellum:* Making Memories; *Corrugated cardstock:* DMD, Inc.; *Textured paper:* Source unknown; *Ribbon:* C.M. Offray & Son; *Computer font:* Times New Roman, Microsoft Word; *Hanger accent:* Westrim Crafts; *Stamping ink:* Memories; *Chalk:* Craf-T Products; *Pop dots:* All Night Media; *Other:* Buttons.

"Auckland to Sydney"
by Helen McCain
Sun Prairie, WI
Supplies *Patterned and embossed papers:* K & Company; *Floral and photo-corner stickers:* K & Company; *Computer font:* CK Bella, "The Best of Creative Lettering" CD Vol. 3, *Creating Keepsakes; Eyelets:* Making Memories; *Watercolor pencils:* Rexel-Derwent; *Green tags:* Helen's own designs; *White and manila tags:* The Paper Cut; *Pen:* Zig Writer, EK Success; *Pop dots:* All Night Media; *Other:* Mini-brads.

"U.S. Navy"
by Erin Lincoln
Frederick, MD
Supplies *Patterned paper:* Mustard Moon;
Vellum: The Paper Company; *Borders:*
Chatterbox; *Computer font:* CK Journaling,
"The Best of Creative Lettering" CD Vol. 2
and CK Template, "Fresh Fonts" CD, *Creating
Keepsakes; Eyelets, tags and letters:* Making
Memories; *Pen:* Slick Writer, American Crafts;
Anchor punch: Emagination Crafts; *Other:*
Bead chain and vintage magazine cartoon.

"Kenneth Ward Lerner, 1964"
by Julie Lowry
Montgomery, AL
Supplies *Embossed foil paper and vellum:*
Club Scrap; *Computer font:* Baskerville Old
Face, Microsoft Word; *Metal letter:* Making
Memories; *Quote:* Downloaded from
www.twopeasinabucket.com.

"Father and Daughter"

by Shannon Freeman
Bellingham, WA

Supplies *Specialty paper and circle accents:* CG-Creations; *Computer font:* Cezanne, package unknown; *Poem:* Shannon's own work.

"Cub Scouts"

by Leah Yourstone
Issaquah, WA

Supplies *Patterned papers:* Club Scrap (brown), Autumn Leaves (music); *Computer font:* Adler, downloaded from the Internet; *Letter stamps:* Hero Arts (small), Club Scrap (large); *Stamping ink:* ColorBox (topaz), Clearsnap; *Color It* (white); *Cub Scout clip art and song lyrics:* Downloaded from the Internet; *Pumice gel medium:* Golden; *Ribbon:* Loose Ends; *Eyelet letters:* Making Memories; *Other:* Photo corners, jewelry tags, mini-brads and cardboard tiles.

12·27·45

First
Christian
Church

Wilkinsburg
PA

A time
for new
beginnings

"John and Virgina's Wedding"

by Joanne Ellis, Petite Motifs
Bellevue, WA
SUPPLIES
Specialty paper: Petite Motifs
Background paper: Autumn Weave
Frames: Autumn Check, Autumn Weave
Stickers: Mrs. Grossman's
Page accents: ScrapArts

"A Perfect Day"

by Karen Burniston
Littleton, CO
SUPPLIES
Handmade paper: Artistic Scrapper
Mesh paper: Scrap-Ease
Leaf vellum: Source unknown
Lettering template: Brush Letters, Wordsworth
Computer font: GabbyGauguinSH,
package unknown
Clip art: Microsoft Design Gallery
Shrink plastic: CoMotion
Beads: JewelCraft
Colored pencils: Prismacolor, Sanford
Craft wire and mini-eyelets: Making Memories

shrink charms accent

Have you noticed all the great wedding clip art available on the Internet? Combine clip art with shrink plastic to make charms for your heritage pages.

◆ Select clip-art images and size them to be 2½" tall. Print them out in grayscale or black and white.

◆ Using a fine-tip permanent black pen, trace the images onto clear shrink plastic. Take detail out of the images as desired— remember, they will be very small when finished.

◆ Turn the shrink plastic over and sand the back until it has enough grain to hold colored pencil. (Or you can purchase pre-sanded shrink plastic.)

◆ Color the images with colored pencils (colors will intensify upon shrinking).

◆ Trim around the images and punch a ⅛" hole near the top of the charm.

◆ Shrink with a heat gun or on a cookie sheet in a 350° oven.

◆ Once cool, hang your charms from thread, ribbon or wire.

—by Karen Burniston

a blessed union

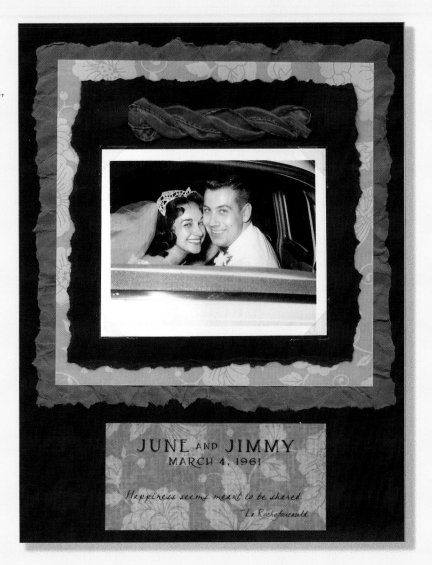

"June and Jimmy"
by Jamie Carney
Germantown, TN
SUPPLIES
Patterned vellum: Frances Meyer
Computer fonts: Caldera,
downloaded from the Internet;
CK Bella, "The Best of
Creative Lettering" CD Vol. 3,
Creating Keepsakes
Ribbon: Horizon Fabrics, Inc.

JUNE AND JIMMY
MARCH 4, 1961

Happiness seems meant to be shared.
~La Rochefoucauld

QUOTABLE QUOTE:

"Some memories are realities, and
are better than anything that can
ever happen to one again."

—WILLA CATHER

"Great-grandparents Rau"

by Jennifer Ditz
Cincinnati, OH
SUPPLIES
Punches: NanKong (mega
blossom and leaf)

Computer fonts: Pompeii
Capitals, Harrington and
English 157BT, downloaded
from the Internet
Pen: VersaMark, Tsukineko

"Our Parents"

by Barbara Gardner
Scottsdale, AZ
SUPPLIES
Computer fonts: CAC
Shishone Brush and
Monotype Corsiva,
Microsoft Word
Corner rounder:
Creative Memories
Corner punch: CARL Mfg.
Corner-slot punch:
Family Treasures
Idea to note: Barbara used
a brad by HyGlo to mark
which person in the main
photograph is her father.

Problem Solving:
Creating a Page Map

❖ ❖ ❖

Q. I'm overwhelmed by how much information I'd like to include on my heritage pages. With photos, stories and personal
details, I don't have room for everything. How
can I include more information?

A. Barbara Gardner, of Scottsdale, Arizona,
came up with an excellent solution,
shown on her layout "Our Parents." Barbara
wanted to include certain photographs and
facts on her layout, but also wanted to identify the people in the photos in a detailed way.
The answer? She created a miniature "page
map" to include on the back of her layout.

First, Barbara scrapbooked her photographs. Then, using her computer, she created
basic shapes to represent each photograph on
her layout. Inside each shape, she listed the
names, events, dates and other information
she wanted available but not visible on the
layout. This is an ingenious way to make sure
information stays with the photographs but
doesn't clutter a layout!

Consider using a page map to record secondary information, too. If the page focuses on
memories, use a page map to record events
and dates for historical purposes. If the page
focuses on an event, use a page map to record
thoughts and feelings about the photographs
that may not be related to the events pictured.
The extra few minutes it takes to create a page
map will be worth it when complete information is preserved for generations to come.

"Wedding Portrait"
by Alannah Jurgensmeyer
Rogers, AR
SUPPLIES
Patterned paper, embossed paper and
photo corners: K & Company
Computer font: Lucia BT, Corel Draw
Chalks: Stampin' Up!

NORTH DAKOTA

At the age of 23, William Walter Marvel left his father's small homestead for a job as a ranch-hand in Sterling in 1910. He worked there for a year before he met his future wife, Martha Ellen Slater. During the summer of 1911, when Martha was 17 years old and tending to the general store, she met William. Her father ran the general store in town and supplied many of the outlying farms and ranches.

They fell in love and married. The photograph to the right shows them in their wedding attire. They married on January 28, 1913.

William and Martha moved to a small farm in Bismarck. While living there, they had three children, Isabel, Dwight (1918) & Eleanor.

Our family history continues to unfold because two people met and fell in love... one summer's day during 1911.

1913

"Love at the General Store"
by Laura Hudson
Boise, ID
SUPPLIES
Patterned paper: The Paper Stuff
Computer fonts: Algerian (title) and Garamond
Bold, Microsoft Publisher
Eyelets: Stamp Studio, Inc.
Photo corners: Canson
Pop dots: All Night Media

Joined in Matrimony

Noah Weaver and Fannie Martin were married in Chambersburg, Pennsylvania, on November 26, 1908. This was their wedding portrait: They spent a few months visiting relatives before settling at the Weaver family farm outside Columbiana, Ohio.

"Joined in Matrimony"
by Janelle Clark
Westerville, OH
SUPPLIES
Patterned paper: Paper
Adventures
Silver paper: Canson
Suede paper: Paper Adventures
Computer fonts: Brandywine

(title) and Papyrus (journaling),
downloaded from the Internet
Leaf punch: Paper Adventures
Photo corners: Canson
Pen: Gelly Roll, Sakura
Idea to note: Janelle colored
white photo corners with a silver
pen to match her layout.

"The Bride"
by Mary Larson
Chandler, AZ
SUPPLIES
Patterned paper: Making Memories
Border and accents: Shotz! by Danelle Johnson, Creative Imaginations
Photo corner punch: All Night Media

Journaling Starter:
Interview Questions

❖   ❖   ❖   ❖   ❖   ❖

At your next family gathering, take a moment to record the unique perspectives and life experiences of your older family members. Be sure to have a tape recorder ready to catch all of the informa- tion—more often than not, once people start talking about their personal reflections, they can't stop! This information will be valuable on your heritage layouts.

Having some questions prepared will ease the pressure of trying to decide what to talk about first. Once the question has been asked, let the person you're interviewing talk about whatever comes to his or her mind. If one story leads to another, that's just more information to be captured! Here are some sample questions you may want to consider:

- ◆ What is your favorite childhood memory?
- ◆ What do you consider to be your greatest accomplishment in life, and why?
- ◆ What advice would you give to future generations?
- ◆ If you had to summarize your life philosophy, what would it be?
- ◆ What is the hardest thing you've had to deal with in your life?
- ◆ What is the happiest moment in your life?
- ◆ What do you want people to remember about you?
- ◆ What people have been most important in your life, and why?

"Lyle and Louree"
by Lori Allred
Bountiful, UT
SUPPLIES
Embossed patterned paper: K & Company
Vellum: The Paper Company
Computer fonts: Edwardian Script (title)
and unknown (journaling),
downloaded from the Internet
Chalk: Stampin' Up!
Eyelets: rememberwhenonline.com
Pop dots: All Night Media
Idea to note: Lori scanned the original
photo and printed it onto vellum, then
she tore the edges and chalked them.
She also placed vellum over the journaling
to soften the look of her layout.

"Shhh … We Eloped"
by Cheryl McMurray
Cardston, AB, Canada
SUPPLIES
Computer font: Civilian, downloaded
from the Internet
Border stickers: K & Company
Punches: Creative Memories (corner
rounder), Marvy Uchida (medium circle),
Family Treasures (small circle)
Scissors: Colonial edge, Fiskars
Chalk: Craf-T Products

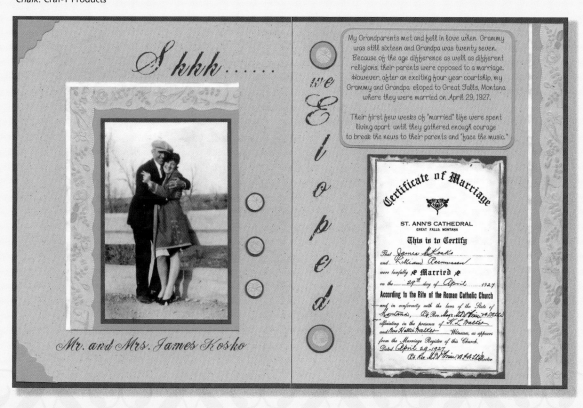

"Souter and Mills Wedding"
by Heather Lancaster
Calgary, AB, Canada
SUPPLIES
Patterned papers: The Robin's Nest Press (plaid),
Scrap in a Snap (swirls)
Vellum: Paper Adventures
Computer font: Source unknown
Other: foil

Donald Willis
Souter
&
Alice Irene
Mills

December 24th
1957

"Family/Sisters"
by Anne Heyen
Glendale, NY
SUPPLIES
Patterned paper: Colors By Design
Vellum: Keeping Memories Alive
Computer fonts: CK Italic and CK Gala,
"The Art of Creative Lettering" CD,
Creating Keepsakes
Buttons: Dress It Up, Jesse James Company
Pen: Gelly Roll, Sakura

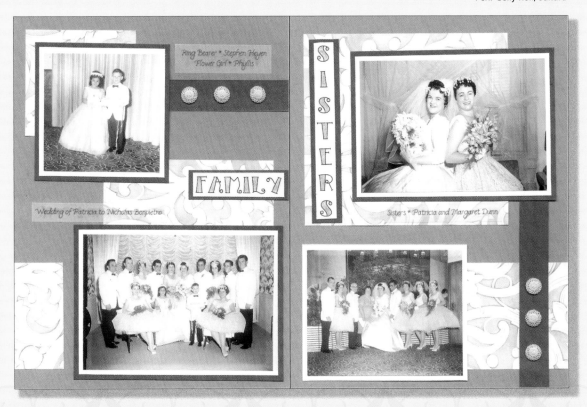

Ring Bearer * Stephen Heyen
Flower Girl * Phyllis

SISTERS

FAMILY

Wedding of Patricia to Nicholas Bonpietro

Sisters * Patricia and Margaret Dunn

My Grandparent's Wedding

My grandparents were married in 1940 at a time when a lot of westernized customs were reaching Japan but the old country traditions were still prominent. As you can see, most people in the wedding party were wearing traditional Japanese kimonos, but some younger men and my grandfather, the groom, wore western tuxedoes. This western style of clothing exhibits the groom's modern, powerful image. In contrast, the traditional Japanese kimono that the bride is wearing displays a quiet, virgin like graciousness. The kimono's many white layers represent purity and allow the bride to hide herself while presenting her gorgeously as a heroin of that day.

My grandparent's wedding pictures are evidence that a dramatic mixing of cultural concepts was occurring at that time. It was a time when East met West. History tells us that it was not easy, but through their determination and sacrifice a better world emerged.

It means a lot to me to know that my grandparents lived in this time of great change in Japanese history; they carried with them the new and the old parts of Japan to the generations that have followed. I am glad they kept the old traditions and adopted new ones. Our lives will be forever blessed.

"My Grandparents' Wedding"
by Satomi Thornock
Layton, UT
SUPPLIES
Patterned paper: Japanese origami paper, source unknown
Speckled vellum: The Paper Company
Gold metallic paper: Making Memories
Computer font: Times New Roman, Microsoft Word
Japanese writing: Satomi's own design
Embroidery floss: DMC
Circle punch: EK Success

Getting Organized:
Sorting Supplies

As you prepare to begin your heritage scrapbooking projects, take a moment to evaluate your supplies. Consider storing cardstock, patterned paper and page accents you might use with heritage photographs in one place. Make sure you have an appropriate adhesive, and plenty of it. Check your chalks, embossing templates and other materials to get a good feel for the supplies you already have at home.

Keeping your heritage-appropriate supplies in one place will prevent you from buying duplicate items, and help you know when you're running low on supplies. And, if you know what products you have on hand, you can easily select supplies that will coordinate with the items you already have. While scrapbooking, keep a running list of items you need. Keeping your supplies stocked and organized is one of the biggest money- and time-savers there is!

Heritage Albums

Even if you've already scrapbooked your wedding photos—or if you don't have wedding photos to scrap—you can still enjoy the wonderful wedding products available. Lisa Bluhm created this beautiful heritage album to celebrate her in-laws' 50th wedding anniversary. Using wedding-themed supplies and photos and newspaper announcements she found in a long-neglected box, Lisa created a heartfelt gift that truly is a keepsake.

"Bride, Groom"

by Lisa Bluhm
Tumwater, WA
S U P P L I E S
Embossed paper: K & Company
Ribbon: C.M. Offray & Son
Letter stickers: Déjà Views,
The C-Thru Ruler Co.
Stamping ink: ColorBox,
Clearsnap, Inc.

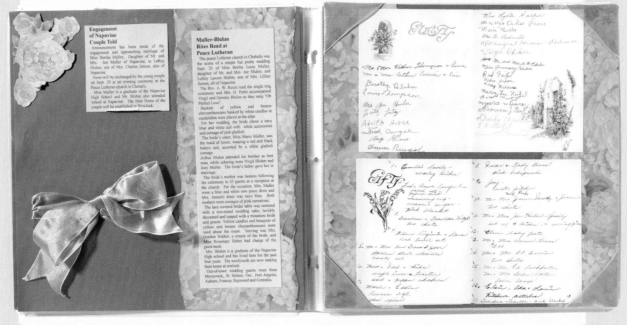

"Our Marriage"

by Lisa Bluhm
Tumwater, WA
S U P P L I E S
Embossed paper and page accent: K & Company

Ribbon: C.M. Offray & Son
Computer font: Times New Roman, Microsoft Word
Stamping ink: ColorBox, Clearsnap, Inc.

Idea to note: Lisa re-typed the newspaper announcement on cardstock and included it on the layout.

"LeRoy and Bertha Bluhm"

by Lisa Bluhm
Tumwater, WA
SUPPLIES
Embossed paper, photo corners,
frame and tag: K & Company
Ribbon: C.M. Offray & Son
Sticker letters: Déjà Views,
The C-Thru Ruler Co.
Stamping ink: ColorBox, Clearsnap, Inc.
Other: Charm

"Happy Ever After"

by Lisa Bluhm
Tumwater, WA
SUPPLIES
Embossed paper: K & Company
Ribbon: C.M. Offray & Son
Photo corners and page accents: K & Company
Letter stickers: Déjà Views,
The C-Thru Ruler Co.
Stamping ink: ColorBox, Clearsnap, Inc.

"Today"

by Jennifer Bester
Reading, MA
S U P P L I E S
Vellum: Paper Source
Computer font: Garamouche,
Impress Rubber Stamps
Eyelet letters: Making Memories
Eyelets: Doodlebug Design
Flower ribbon: Hirschberg
Schutz & Company
Other: Tulle and sheer ribbon
Idea to note: Jennifer included
the wedding invitation on
her layout.

"Joe Ragnor and Francis Durbin"

by Margaret Goehring
Boise, ID
S U P P L I E S
Patterned paper: Anna Griffin
Mulberry paper: PSX Design
Ribbon: C.M. Offray & Son
Buttons: Favorite Findings
Paper yarn: Twistel, Making Memories

preserving
your album

I NEVER THOUGHT an album would destroy my wedding photos, but that's exactly what happened. My wedding album was a fancy, coated-paper binder with fill-in-the-blank pages. I thought it was a treasure. Now it's discolored and cracked, and has totally fallen apart. The pages I lovingly assembled as a tribute to my special day are an unsalvageable mess.

Luckily, today's knowledgeable scrapbooker doesn't have to have the problems of yesteryear. From the album and its contents to the methods you use to assemble it, you'll find an array of supplies that will ensure the archival soundness of your album. Read on to find out what you need to know before your put your wedding album together.

Albums

Preserving your wedding memories starts with a safe album—one made from an acid- and lignin-free binder board, safe glue and an archival covering. Stay away from vinyl albums, commonly known as "naugahyde." They contain harmful chemicals that emit chlorine gases that will bleach your photos and special documents. And don't rely on sheet protectors to save the contents of your album—the destructive gases will penetrate them.

For ideal storage, consider choosing an album with a slipcase, which will put the album in dark storage, protecting it from dust and providing a safe housing.

Paper

You can't have a scrapbook without paper—that's why it's so important to choose papers that won't adversely affect your photos and memorabilia. Acid and lignin—two chemicals found in some papers—are a scrapbook's worst enemies.

They cause papers and photos to become yellow and brittle over time. When choosing paper for your album, follow these tips:
◆ Don't use colored paper with one-of-a-kind photos—the color in most papers isn't permanent. Use duplicate photos, or consider adding color to your pages with colored pencils, permanent watercolors, chalks or safe markers.
◆ Don't be fooled by handmade papers. Even pure cotton paper can be acidic. And keep in mind that foliage, glitter and jute all have lignin in them.
◆ Use vellum and metallic papers with care. Some brands are safe and some are not, so look for the CK OK seal when using vellum or metallic papers.
◆ You can make your own patterned paper by scanning the lace from your wedding dress and printing it out (remember to use a permanent-ink printer).

Binder with slipcase,
Preservation Source

ARTICLE BY JEANNE ENGLISH

Page Protectors

Page protectors guard photos and memorabilia, keeping them safe from fingerprints and harmful contaminants. When choosing them, be sure to select safe plastics, such as Polypropylene and Polyester, and avoid harmful plastics, known as "vinyl" PVC and acetate.

Another option that works well if you're using a non-standard album size is interleaving—tucking blank sheets of paper between album pages. Interleaving sheets should be unbuffered, and acid and lignin free.

Mounting Photos and Memorabilia

When it comes to mounting photos and memorabilia on your album pages, make sure the method you use isn't permanent. You may want to remove snapshots and documents from your album in the future, so avoid any adhesive that won't give you that option. Only use as much adhesive as you absolutely need.

Labeling and Journaling

You don't want important dates, names and facts to disappear in the future because you've used unsafe ink in your album. Here are some tips to remember:

◆ **Photos.** In addition to your journaling, label the backs of your photos with names, places and dates. Use a soft graphite pencil, such as General's Sketch and Wash, which writes on slick surfaces. A fine-tipped marker is also a good choice for labeling colored photos.

◆ **Pens.** For ink to last on a scrapbook page, is has to be permanent. When recording names, dates and other important information, use permanent, pigment-based ink.

◆ **Computer printers and copy machines.** If you use your computer to print journaling, titles and clip-art images, make sure the printer uses a permanent, powder-based toner. Pages printed with liquid toners will change color and fade away with time.

Adding Embellishments

Use common sense when adding embellishments to your scrapbook pages. What will they look like 20 or 50 years from now? Will they stand the test of time, or will they look dated? Never allow the embellishment to express more than the memento itself. More importantly, make sure each accent you use is safe for your album. Keep these guidelines in mind:

◆ The more layers of paper you add (die cuts, laser cuts, pre-cut frames), the more bulk you add to your album.

◆ Stickers are an easy way to add interest to a scrapbook page, but make sure they're safe. Never put stickers on the front of a photograph.

◆ Natural embellishments (dried flowers, raffia, twine, wood, leather) have a high lignin content. In time, they'll discolor and age the contents around them. If you choose to include these items, tuck them into poly bags before attaching them to your pages.

◆ To eliminate harmful dyes and sizing in fabric embellishments (cloth, ribbon, tulle), wash the items before adding them to your pages (keep in mind that most craft ribbons can't be washed because they will lose their shape).

Don't risk losing your special wedding memories to unsafe practices. Armed with the right knowledge and supplies, you're ready to create a sentimental treasure that will last for generations. ❤

From the album and its contents to the methods you use to assemble it, you'll find an array of supplies that will ensure the archival soundness of your album.

Our photographer wanted to take most of the portraits pre-ceremony, which meant that Brad and I got to see each other before the actual wedding. We marveled at each other's transformations while we were standing outside, but I don't think the true magnitude of what we were about to do hit us until we were standing on the altar together, preparing for portraits. I looked out at the empty church, soon to be filled with our family and friends, and then looked back at Brad, not quite believing that our day was finally here. Brad seemed just as awestruck as I did, for we both realized at the same moment that we were truly on the edge of eternity. August 14, 1993

"On the Edge of Eternity"

by Jennifer Wohlenberg
Stevenson Ranch, CA
SUPPLIES
Computer fonts: Daly Hand and Daly Text, downloaded from the Internet
Mulberry paper: Pulsar Paper Products
Frame: Memory Lane
Nailheads: JewelCraft
Metallic rub-ons: Craf-T Products
Stamping ink: Source unknown

Ralph & Cloteal Gierisch
Reception Photo
Married: September 29, 1936

When Ralph and Cloteal were married in the Logan Temple, they had no family with them. After they were married, Ralph and Cloteal went to Burley, Idaho for their reception, which is where this photo is taken.

"Ralph & Cloteal"

by Kerri Bradford
Orem, UT
SUPPLIES
Patterned paper and ribbon: Anna Griffin
Vellum: Paper Adventures
Computer font: Unknown

Anthony and Rose Curto
June 10, 1939

"Anthony and Rose Curto"

by Christine Daly
Lake Wales, FL
SUPPLIES
Patterned papers: Carolee's Creations
Vellum: Stampin' Up!
Computer font: Gradl, WordPerfect
Rhinestones: The Beadery
Craft wire: Star Gazer
Twine: The Beadery
Photo corners: Canson

our family ties

remembering my

ROOTS

When I look at this photo of my relatives, I don't see a group of Oklahoma sharecroppers struggling to make ends meet in the face of oppression. I don't see their torn clothes or unkempt hair. I see a group of people who are a family. I see men, women and children who are strong and determined. I see individuals who are committed to overcoming obstacles and knocking down barriers. I see people who are empowered and resilient in the face of all the challenges life has brought their way. I see me. I see my heritage, but most of all I see my family.

The McClarty Family

Pictured from left to right are Grandpa Green, Grandma Green, Georgia, Willie (my great-grandfather), Lula Mae, Ludi, Archie & Jimie Lou

"Remembering My Roots"
by Taunya Dismond
Lee's Summit, MO
SUPPLIES
Textured paper: Solum World Paper
Lettering template: Block, ABC Tracers, Pebbles for EK Success
Computer fonts: CK Cursive, "The Best of Creative Lettering" CD Vol. 2, *Creating Keepsakes*; BernhardMod BT, Microsoft Word
Square punch: Marvy Uchida
String: On the Surface Fibers
Other: Buttons

QUOTABLE QUOTE:

"He who has done his best for his own time has lived for all times."

—JOHANN VON SCHILLER

"Camp Blanding, Florida"
by Lori Houk
Lawrence, KS
SUPPLIES
Vellum: Paper Adventures
Computer font: CK Bella, "The Best of Creative Lettering" CD Vol. 3, *Creating Keepsakes*
Brads: American Pin & Fastener

"This Day of Sadness"
by Mary Larson
Chandler, AZ
SUPPLIES
Patterned paper: The Family Archives
Computer fonts: Lambo HMK and Lambo HMK Bold, "Hallmark Card Studio" CD, Hallmark
Photo corners: me & my BIG ideas

Idea to note: The journaling box under the photo was scanned from the back of the picture. Mary also included her father's recollections, written in his handwriting. It explains why this picture was taken and what happened to him and his siblings after it was taken.

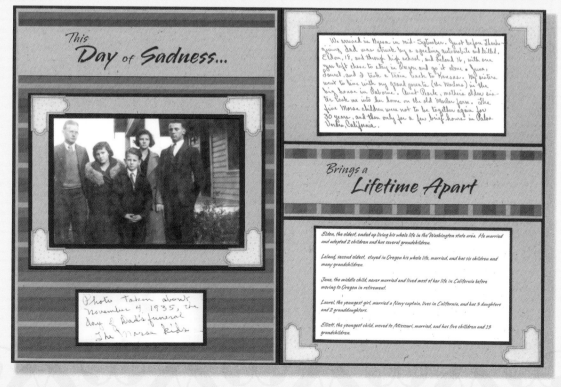

"The Steenblock Famiy"

by Amy Brenton
Tucson, AZ

SUPPLIES

Patterned papers: Making Memories (blue), Sonburn (paper frame)

Computer font: Unknown
Stickers: Mrs. Grossman's
Brads: HyGlo
Fiber: On the Surface Fibers
Rubber stamp: Art Impressions
Stamping ink: Close To My Heart

Problem Solving:
Enlarging Photographs

❖ ❖ ❖ ❖ ❖

Q: I want to create a scrapbook page about a certain person, but I can't seem to find any photographs of her alone. Any suggestions?

A: Janelle Clark, of Westerville, Ohio, came up with a great solution to this problem, shown on her layout "The Shank Family" (see right page). Janelle had a family photograph that showed her great-grandmother, Emma, as a child and needed a close-up shot of her to use on a layout. Janelle simply made a copy of the family photograph, enlarging it until the image of her great-grandmother was the correct size for her layout. Then, to eliminate the back-

ground, she cropped her great-grandmother out of the family picture using an oval cutter. At first-glance, you'd never guess there is a person standing behind her!

This technique is easy to do with a computer scanner, color-copy machine or photo-imaging machine (like the Kodak Picture Maker or Fuji Aladdin). Some of the picture quality may be lost if you enlarge the photo too much, so keep a close eye on how clear your enlargement looks. If you have negatives for the photograph you want to enlarge, you can get a good-quality enlargement at a photo lab.

Clyde,
Lewis,
and
Emma
Fenton

1912

"1912"

by Janelle Clark
Westerville, OH
SUPPLIES
Patterned paper and vellum: Paper Adventures
Computer fonts: Brandywine and Niederwald (date),
downloaded from the Internet
Photo corners: Hero Arts

The Fenton Family

Clyde and Emma Fenton with their children (left to right):
Helen, Florence, Mary, Lewis, Esther and Walter. This
picture was taken in Kansas in the mid-1930s.

"The Fenton Family"

by Janelle Clark
Westerville, OH
SUPPLIES
Patterned paper: Lasting Impressions for Paper
Computer fonts: CAC Pinafore and Bookman
Old Style, downloaded from the Internet
Stickers: Susan Wheeler

The Shank Family

This is our great-grandmother, Emma Anne Shank, as a child, with
her parents, Lewis and Mary Wenger Shank, and some of her brothers and sisters. From left to right: Josephus, Mollie, Charles,
Lewis, Sarah, Emma, Mary holding Fannie, and John Shank.
Emma's older brother, Jacob, is not pictured, and her brother Benjamin died as an infant. This picture was taken about 1890, probably
in Kansas. Shortly afterward, the family moved to Florida in the hopes
that the climate change would help Mary Shank's tuberculosis. The family's
tenth child, Florida Rose, was born there. Emma told her children that when the family
lived in Florida, she and her brothers and sisters would play with baby alligators in the
river. The move to Florida did not help Mary's health, and she died there in 1894;
Emma was ten years old. Emma spent the rest of her growing up years helping to raise
her younger siblings, and also caring for her uncle's children after their mother died.

"The Shank Family"

by Janelle Clark
Westerville, OH
SUPPLIES
Patterned paper: Lasting
Impressions for Paper
Computer fonts: Texas Hero (title)
and Galant (journaling), down-
loaded from the Internet

Thread: On the Surface Fibers
Photo corner punch: Marvy Uchida
Stamping ink: VersaMark,
Tsukineko
Idea to note: To create a textured
look on the green photo mat,
Janelle used a crumpled ball of
plastic wrap to dab ink on it.

"Reames Family Photo"
by Peggy Adair
Fort Smith, AR
SUPPLIES
Patterned paper: Hot Off The Press
Computer fonts: Valiant, Print Shop,
Broderbund; Freehand 575, Microsoft Word
Idea to note: Peggy used a craft knife to cut
out part of the flowers from the patterned
paper, then she slid her photo underneath
the flowers.

REAMES FAMILY PHOTO
Taken About 1909

Front Row Seated: Jeff Johnson, Buford Johnson, Elisha Reames, Virgie Reames
& Voyrie Reames.
2nd Row: Marion Bonnie Reames (standing) behind John Johnson (seated), Mollie
Johnson holding Hazel Johnson, Benjamin Franklin Reames holding Cecil Johnson,
Rebecca Henson Reames, Betty Ann Gideon, Verna Reames (child) and Mary Reames
holding Gustava.
3rd Row: Virgil Cotton holding Grace Cotton, Bertha Reames Cotton, Bessie Reames,
Julia Reames, Iwa Harris, Willie Gideon, Ora Johnson, Nora Gideon, Doshia Reames
Lelah Reames, Will Gideon.
Back Row: Robert Gideon, Sherman Reames, Elbert Reames, Ed Reames, Frank
Reames, Tom Johnson.

"Adene"
by Carol A. Thomson
Oyama, BC, Canada
SUPPLIES
Laser-cut page: Scherenschnitte Design
Computer font: CK Calligraphy, "The Best of
Creative Lettering" CD Vol. 1, *Creating
Keepsakes*
Sticker: Creative Memories

"Sadie"
by Lori Houk
Lawrence, KS
SUPPLIES
Patterned paper: Anna Griffin
Metallic paper: Family Archives
Corrugated paper: Art Cornerstone
Leaves: Black Ink
Brads: Office Max
Computer font: CK Bella, "The Best of Creative Lettering" CD Vol. 3, *Creating Keepsakes*
Stick: Fru Fru
Craft wire: Wig Jig

"Family Portrait"
by Carolyn Hassall
Bradenton, FL
SUPPLIES
Flower frame: Carolyn created the frame from an invitation.
Computer font: Shishoni Brush, package unknown, American Greetings; Scrap Katie, "Lettering Delights" CD Vol. 2, Inspire Graphics
Border stickers: me & my BIG ideas
Rubber stamp: PSX Design

"Shirk"
by Lori Houk
Lawrence, KS
SUPPLIES
Patterned paper: Scrap-Ease
Computer font: Adinekirnberg,
downloaded from the Internet
Chalk: Craf-T Products
Tags: Office Max
Other: Buttons

"My Family Line"
by Teresa Snyder
Pebbles in my Pocket
Orem, UT
SUPPLIES
Patterned paper: Debbie Mumm,
Creative Imaginations
Computer font: CK Sketch,
"The Art of Creative Lettering" CD,
Creating Keepsakes
Chalk: Craf-T Products

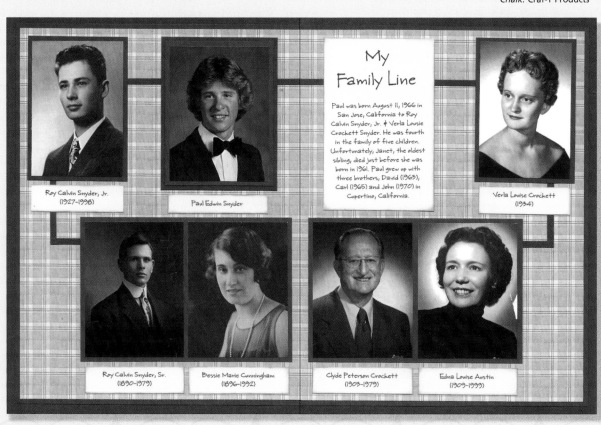

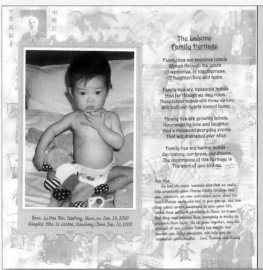
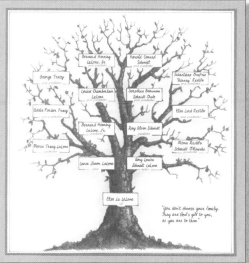

"The LaLone Family Heritage"
by Joyce Schweitzer
Greensboro, NC
SUPPLIES
Patterned paper: Keeping Memories Alive
Family tree stationery: Creative Memories
Border punch: All Night Media
Rubber stamps: Stampington
Ink pad: ColorBox
Pens: Pigma Micron, Sakura; Tombow
Computer fonts: Harrington, Microsoft Word; Doodle Cursive, "PagePrintables" CD Vol. 1, Cock-A-Doodle Design, Inc.
Chalks: Craf-T Products
Idea to note: Joyce made a color copy of the family tree stationery in sepia tones, then colored in the tree with chalks and markers.

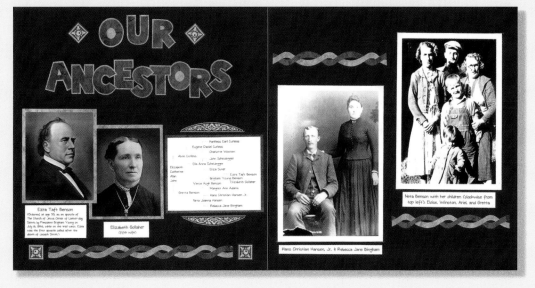

"Our Ancestors"
by Catherine Schulthies
College Station, TX
SUPPLIES
Patterned paper: Creative Press
Lettering template: Block, ABC Tracers, Pebbles for EK Success
Computer font: CK Journaling, "The Best of Creative Lettering" CD Vol. 2, *Creating Keepsakes*
Stickers: me & my BIG ideas
Template: Creative Memories

Page Idea: Family Tree Pages

As you're creating pages about your family roots, don't forget to include a family tree page to show exactly how you're related to the people in your album. Showing the links between ancestors is a great way to begin or finish a heritage album—and it's a helpful way to display technical information that may be hard to explain in text.

Check your local scrapbook store for pre-printed family tree papers, like the beautiful family tree illustration used above by Joyce Schweitzer of Greensboro, North Carolina. You can also use your home computer to create a family tree, as Catherine Schulthies of College Station, Texas, did. If you're already using a computer program to keep track of your genealogy, simply print the information and dress it up before including it on your layout.

Four Generations of Strength and Beauty

Mary Jane McIver Smith Circa 1909

Circa 1906

Flowers of the Past
These are some of the women in Grandpa John Horace Smith's life. His wife (at left) and niece, Hazel Bennett; sister, Jennie Smith Bennett; mother, Mary Alameda Schull Smith & grandmother, Grandma Schull Lyons (above).

"Silhouettes Past"

by Sharon Whitehead
Vernon, BC, Canada

SUPPLIES

Title and wire flowers: Sharon's own designs
Computer fonts: Gradl and Pristina, Microsoft Word
Flowers: Velvet Treasures, NagPosh
Chalk: Craf-T Products
Covered craft wire: Darice
Pen: Zig Writer, EK Success
Other: Cord

"Smith Family Roots"

by Sharon Whitehead
Vernon, BC, Canada

SUPPLIES

Vellum: Paper Adventures
Computer fonts: Amazon BT and Brushscript, Microsoft Word
Chalk: Craf-T Products
Colored pencils: Memory

Pencils, EK Success
Jute: Darice
Ribbon: Offray
Sewing thread: DMC
Other: Buttons
Idea to note: Sharon adapted the idea for her picture frames from a frame she refinished for her mother.

Smith **F**amily **R**oots

Seen here at the age of 18 in 1944. She was born Virginia Grace Smith on April 26, 1926 the seventh of ten children, at Bestville P.O. Saskatchewan. Her father sent for her birth certificate from the Bestville P.O. using that as his return address so that's what is listed as her place of birth. She was born at home with Grandma Smith attending as midwife.
See how much she looks like her father, John Smith. She has his eyes, chin and nose, as well as his feisty disposition and heart of gold. She spent her early years in Saskatchewan, at Bestville until 1928 when they moved to Hazlet, because there was a brand new high school there. They then moved to Creston B.C. Sept./36. where she attended high school. She was on the basketball team and good at gymnastics.

John and Mary were married on July 20, 1914 in Cabri Saskatchewan. They had ten children in total; the first was stillborn and the last died of an unfortunate accident when he was 1 ½. Of the remaining eight, there were six girls and two boys.

John Smith - circa 1899 Age 20

Mary Jane McIver circa 1909 – age 18

"Four Generations"
by Blyss Capell
Brigham City, UT
SUPPLIES
Patterned paper: Amscan
Computer font: Christie,
downloaded from the Internet
Stickers: Class-A-Peels, Mark Enterprises

"Another Smith Generation"
by Sharon Whitehead
Vernon, BC, Canada
SUPPLIES
Vellum: Paper Adventures
Computer font: American Text BT, Microsoft Word
Punches: Martha by Mail (fern),
Marvy Uchida (flower)
Stickers: me & my BIG ideas
Chalk: Craf-T Products
Vase: Sharon's own design
Idea to note: Sharon scanned and enlarged
the picture on the left and used it as part
of the background paper. She also re-created
the flower arrangement in the photo to
draw attention to the picture.

Four Generations
Tabitha Hendricks Ricks, Joseph Ricks,
Margaret Ricks Pearson, John Theo Pearson

Another
Smith
Generation

John Downie Smith,
b. July 4, 1852
d. July 1, 1931
marriage
in October 1878 to
Mary Alemeda Schull,
b January 20, 1861
d. 1957

Circa 1878

Circa 1889

Gibson   PEORIA ILL.

John Downie Smith and Mary Alemeda Smith
were married in October 1878 and lived in
Peoria, Illinois raising two sons and three
Daughters: John H., Jennie, Fred, Edna, and
Marguerite.
John H. became a cabinet maker, taking his
apprenticeship starting at age 16. Then he
opened a boat building shop. John was in the
merchant marines when he was 21.
Fred died at age 21 from pneumonia. Jennie
married Willis Bennett and had one daughter
Hazel. Edna married Elmer Hiersphiel. They
had two daughters — Evelyn and Edna-Ruth.
Marguerite married and had two daughters
And two sons. In 1911 John H. sold his
business and immigrated to Canada. He and his
father took out adjoining homesteads at
Bestville, Saskatchewan.
John H. married Mary Jane McIver in 1914 at
Cabri, Saskatchewan. John D. built a small
house and a sod barn in Bestville and his
family moved up from Illinois.
They raised pigs, sheep, turkeys, and chickens
besides wheat farming. They lived there until he
retired in 1928. They celebrated their 50th
anniversary in Bestville and were presented with
gold watches. John D. was a kind and jolly
man with a long white beard and he always
played Santa at all the Christmas parties.
Mary R. hand sewed a quilt for each one of her
grandchildren. She also crocheted and tatted.
They moved back to Detroit around 1929.

John Horace Smith, b. July 21, 1879
Edna Smith, b. January 4, 1890; Jennie Smith, b. August 1, 1882
Fred Smith, b. June 16, 1884

1800'S

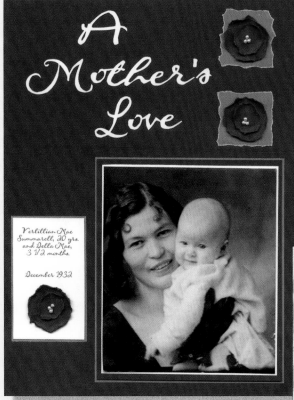

"A Mother's Love"
by Amy Grendell
Silverdale, WA
SUPPLIES
Vellum: Keeping Memories Alive
Computer font: Scrap Cursive, "Lettering Delights" CD
Vol. 3, Inspire Graphics
Flowers: Amy's own designs
Other: Pearl beads

Verlillian Mae
Summarell, 20 yrs.
and Della Mae,
3 1/2 months.

December 1932

"The Grogan Girls"
by Torrey Miller
Lafayette, CO
SUPPLIES
Patterned paper: K & Company
Vellum: Paper Adventures
Computer font: Desdemona, package unknown
Basket: Torrey's own design
Punches: All Night Media (corner), Emagination Crafts
(corner pocket), The Punch Bunch (leaf)
Poem: Downloaded from the Internet

~ Sisters ~

For many years
We've shared our lives
One roof
we once lived under...
Sometimes we laughed
Sometimes we cried
Through winter storms
And thunder.
As summer brings
The happy times.
The autumn winds
Will whisper...
A closer friend
I'll never find
Than the one I call
My sister

~Vernon

The Grogan Girls

Accent Idea: Popular Arts and Crafts

❖   ❖   ❖   ❖   ❖

Before televisions and the Internet, people relied on arts and crafts to fill their time. If you're struggling to find an accent for a page, consider some of the popular arts and crafts of the time you're scrapbooking and adapt them to your pages. Here are a few suggestions:

◆ **Cross-stitch or embroidery.** Cross-stitch and embroidery can be as simple or intensive as the patterns and designs you choose. Either way, they're a terrific addition to a scrapbook page.

◆ **Paper quilling.** A visit to a craft or book store will reveal hundreds of patterns and ideas for quilling

designs. Include the designs on your pages for a sophisticated yet homemade look.

◆ **Paper pricking.** Paper pricking involves using a stylus and pattern to make tiny holes in paper to reveal a design. Try raising your pricked accent on pop dots to let some light shine through the back.

◆ **Quilting.** The concept of piecing together scraps of fabric works in scrapbooking, too. Create mini-quilts of fabric to include on your layout, or re-create the look with paper to use as a background for your page.

"The Fenton Sisters"

by Janelle Clark
Westerville, OH
SUPPLIES

Patterned paper: Sweetwater Linens
Computer fonts: A Yummy Apology (title) and
Bookman Old Style, downloaded from the Internet
Punches: EK Success (leaf); 2Grrrls, Colorbök (flower)
Scissors: Scallop edge, Fiskars

"Two Sisters Bound"

by Mary Larson
Chandler, AZ
SUPPLIES

Patterned paper: Source unknown
Computer font: Isabella, downloaded from
the Internet
Punches: Family Treasures (heart and circle)
Embroidery floss: DMC

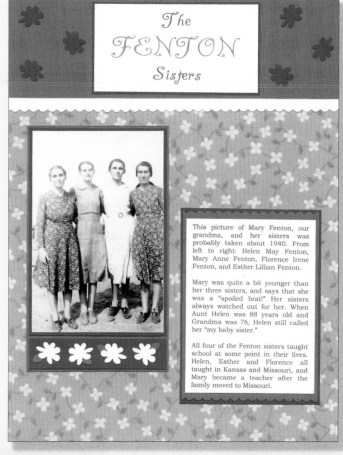

The
FENTON
Sisters

This picture of Mary Fenton, our grandma, and her sisters was probably taken about 1940. From left to right: Helen May Fenton, Mary Anne Fenton, Florence Irene Fenton, and Esther Lillian Fenton.

Mary was quite a bit younger than her three sisters, and says that she was a "spoiled brat!" Her sisters always watched out for her. When Aunt Helen was 88 years old and Grandma was 76, Helen still called her "my baby sister."

All four of the Fenton sisters taught school at some point in their lives. Helen, Esther and Florence all taught in Kansas and Missouri, and Mary became a teacher after the family moved to Missouri.

Two Sisters Bound
Forever by a child

Pearl and Bertha Marlar

Mike and Pearl Tollis

Laurence and Bertha Morse

"Pieces of Yesterday"

by Taunya Dismond
Lee's Summit, MO
SUPPLIES
Lettering template: Whimsy,
ScrapPagerz.com
Computer fonts: Invitation,
Microsoft Word; Girls Are Weird,
downloaded from the Internet
Flowers: Taunya's own designs
Other: Brads

"Erna Caroline Augusta (Rau) Fehnder"

by Jennifer Ditz
Cincinnati, OH
SUPPLIES
Patterned paper: Anna Griffin
Mulberry paper: PrintWorks
Flower accents: Cut from
Anna Griffin paper
Computer fonts: Scrap Rhapsody and
Scrap Oval, "Lettering Delights" CD
Vol. 2, Inspire Graphics
Eyelets: Impress Rubber Stamps
Fiber thread: On the Surface Fibers

Journaling Starter:
Interpreting Facts

❖ ❖ ❖ ❖ ❖

In heritage scrapbooking, we often feel lucky if we have even minimal information about the photographs of our ancestors. Adding the facts you do have to your layouts is important, but you can add so much more! Let those facts teach you lessons about the ancestors you're scrapbooking. If you know, for instance, that your great-grandfather started working as an apprentice at the age of 12, you know he had a great amount of determination and knew the value of hard work. Why not include those personal thoughts on your layout?

Jennifer Ditz, of Cincinnati, Ohio, created a layout about why her grandmother is an amazing woman, but instead of just listing her grandmother's accomplishments, she also included what she's learned from those accomplishments. Your personal insights will add meaning—and make the journaling process more fun!

The Drama of Hands

PHOTO TIPS BY ANITA MATEJKA

PHOTOS BY ANITA MATEJKA

When I think of family, I think of togetherness and a deep connection between individuals. One way I like to symbolize this connection in my snapshots is by photographing hands. Try these ideas:

◆ Take a picture of your family holding hands during the prayer at mealtime. Focus on a specific set of hands.
◆ Photograph the special bond between a grandparent and his or her grandchild. Snap a shot of them holding hands while taking a walk, caressing each other's hands while sitting in the rocking chair, or playing a game of patty-cake.
◆ Are there any arm wrestlers in the family? Snap a close-up shot of the action.
◆ Take a picture of a husband's and wife's hands, then take another photo 25 or 30 years later. The difference in age will show dramatically in their hands.

And, don't forget to capture:
◆ A child's hand while painting or drawing
◆ Hands working on carving a pumpkin, wrapping a present, or dying Easter eggs
◆ Hands gripping a golf club, basketball or baseball bat
◆ Hands working in the garden

Once you've taken all the hand shots you can muster … what about feet? Your child's bare feet in the grass, your husband's dirty work boots, your and your best friend's fresh pedicures—the list goes on and on!

scrapbooking "trendy" photos

Capture the '60s, '70s and '80s in your album

BELL-BOTTOMS. Mood rings. Shag carpet. Platform shoes. Blue eye shadow. Jordache jeans. Do these trends from the '60s, '70s and '80s sound familiar? Chances are you have a stash of photographs from these decades you haven't dared to touch yet. After all, how exactly do you scrapbook photographs of someone in a polyester shirt with orange, red and brown geometric designs on it?

Trends come and go, and when they're gone, you're left with dated photographs of great memories—in hard-to-scrapbook disguises. Instead of storing these photos under the bed, give them the place they deserve in your scrapbooks. Easier said than done, right? Wrong. The seven tips listed below will make scrapbooking those "trendy" photos a cinch!

1 Sort through your photographs. When was the last time you pulled that box of photographs out and looked through them, anyway? Now's the time to simplify, simplify, simplify by looking at each and every photo and deciding whether to scrapbook it, store it or toss it. Don't hesitate to throw away photographs you feel no emotional connection with, or poor-quality photographs you know you'll never scrapbook.

When you come across a photo you just can't bear to part with, despite the hippy hairdo and peace-sign necklace, reserve a place for it in your scrapbook. Consider for a moment what you love so much about the shot—is it the freedom you felt when the photograph was taken? The event pictured? The fact that your dad actually *bought* you the peace-sign necklace? When you sit down to scrapbook it, flash back to what made you hold on to it.

Figure 1. Making a personal connection with '60s, '70s and '80s photographs can help you see past the trends and focus on the meaning. *Page by Nicole Gartland.* **Supplies** *Patterned paper:* The Robin's Nest Press; *Computer fonts:* Fontdiner.com and Sketched Out, downloaded from the Internet; CK Journaling, "The Best of Creative Lettering" CD Vol. 2, *Creating Keepsakes; Watch clip art:* Arttoday.com; *Metallic paper:* Canson; *Pen:* Zig Writer, EK Success.

ARTICLE BY CATHERINE SCOTT

Focus on that memory, event or idea as you scrapbook, and you'll be happy with the results no matter what trends are pictured in the photographs.

While looking through a box of old photos, Nicole Gartland of Portland, Oregon, found a photograph of her partner, Neil, taken in the early 1970s. Even though the photograph showed Neil in plaid pants and his dad in the typical polyester shirt, Nicole was struck by the sentimental moment captured between a father and son. She was even more charmed by Neil's notes in a nine-year-old's handwriting on the back of the photograph. The personal connection Nicole made with the photograph helped her find meaning and made the process of scrapbooking the photo easier. The resulting page (Figure 1) is a perfect tribute to the memory.

❷ Pay attention to warm and cool colors. Remember when all make-up colors were classified as either warm (with yellow undertones) or cool (with blue undertones)? This color principle is actually quite handy when you're dealing with photographs from the '60s, '70s and '80s. Many photos from these decades have distinctly warm or cool undertones.

Be sure to decide which category your photos fit in before you select the supplies you'll use on your pages. For example, a photograph from the '80s showing a girl in a hot-pink shirt would look best with cool colors, while a photograph from the '70s showing a girl in an orange-red shirt will probably look best with warm colors. (A good tip to remember is that off-white is warm, and pure white is cool.) Once you've mas-

Figure 2. Before making color selections for your layout, evaluate whether your photograph has warm or cool undertones. *Page by Traci Rancier.* **Supplies** *Vellum:* Close To My Heart; *Computer font:* LD Notebook, downloaded from *www.letteringdelights.com*.

tered this color principle, you'll be less intimidated by the photographs you're working with.

Traci Rancier of Euless, Texas, followed the warm/cool color principle when she created her layout "The 1970s" (Figure 2). The photograph shows orange drapes and yellow carpet—typical color choices for that time period. By choosing warm shades for her

scrapbook page, such as yellow, rust, brown and off-white, Traci created a layout that truly represents the decade.

❸ Do your research. Don't worry—this is fun research! If you know you'll be scrapbooking photos from the '60s, '70s, '80s or any other decade, why not have some fun while you're doing it? Head to

Now's the time to simplify, simplify, simplify by looking at each and every photo and deciding whether to scrapbook it, store it or toss it.

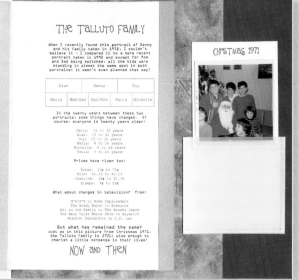

Figure 3. Use movies, television shows, music and other resources from decades past to spark your creativity. *Pages by Pam Talluto.* **Supplies** *Patterned paper:* Scrap-Ease; *Computer fonts:* Abadi, Courier New, French Script and Flowerchild, downloaded from the Internet; *Vellum:* Paper Adventures; *Ribbon:* Stampendous.

watching shows or flipping through magazines appropriate to the decade you're scrapbooking will get you in the groove in no time. If you don't believe me, put in your ABBA CD (or record, or eight track) and see what happens!

❹ Don't try to hide it. Trying to scrapbook photographs with obvious "dated" trends the same way you would scrapbook photographs from today could end in disaster! Instead of trying to ignore the trends, be proud that you have a little piece of history in your photos, and treat them appropriately. Look for retro scrapbooking products that will help highlight the trend, or at least complement it.

Make sure you mention the trend in your journaling if appropriate. On her layout "Tu-tu

your local library or video store and stock up on movies, CDs, magazines and books to inspire you. Think of all the ideas you could glean just by watching reruns of *The Monkees, The Brady Bunch, Three's Company*, and *Miami Vice*!

As you're watching movies and television reruns, pay attention to popular color combinations, trendy hairstyles and clothing,

and slang words and phrases—they'll be helpful as you scrapbook photographs from these decades.

Pam Talluto of Rochester Hills, Michigan, for example, used a quote from the movie *Willy Wonka and the Chocolate Factory*, created in 1971, on a layout showing photographs of her husband's family in 1971, 1972 and 1992 (Figure 3).

You'll find that playing music,

Figure 4. Don't try to hide or ignore trends that are obvious in your photographs—acknowledge or even accent them when it's appropriate for your layout's theme. *Pages by Sharon Whitehead.* **Supplies** *Computer fonts:* CK Concave, "The Art of Creative Lettering" CD, *Creating Keepsakes;* Monotype Corsiva and Brushscript BT, Microsoft Word; *Ballet clip art:* Print Master Gold; *Chalks:* Craf-T Products; *Pen:* Zig Millennium, EK Success; *Other:* Brads and ribbon.

Figure 5. If your photograph doesn't show obvious signs of the decade in which it was taken, don't force a trendy theme on the layout you create. Focus on the theme instead. *Page by Nicole Gartland.* **Supplies** *Patterned paper:* Paper Adventures; *Computer fonts:* Whisper Write, downloaded from the Internet; CK Journaling, "The Best of Creative Lettering" CD Vol. 2, *Creating Keepsakes;* *Pen:* Milky Gel Roller, Pentel; *Craft wire:* Hillman Fastener; *Rattle:* Nicole's own design; *Other:* Beads.

Cute" in Figure 4, Sharon Whitehead of Vernon, British Columbia, Canada, scrapbooked several photographs of her younger sister in her ballet classes, wearing the then very fashionable cat's eye glasses. Sharon made sure to mention the glasses in her journaling along with the rest of her memories. As a result, her layout captures personal experiences *and* popular culture, adding perspective and historic documentation to her album.

5 Remember your theme. While you don't want to hide trends that are obvious in your photographs, you do want to focus on the general theme of your page, especially if your '60s and '70s photos don't show the typical "signs" of the decade. Instead of forcing a '60s or '70s feel on your layout, look at the photographs and decide

On the scrapbook page:

"Cooling Off"

This is a picture of me at age 6 months. No flash baby pools in those days. A 70's baby was given a baby bath under a tree to keep the summer heat off. Doesn't look like I had need to complain though—such fun!

Ellington Street 1972

Figure 6. Focus on the theme of your photograph, no matter when it was taken, to create an appropriate look and feel on your layout. *Page by Debra Fuller.* **Supplies** *Vellum:* Paper Adventures; *Rubber stamps:* Stamp-It; *Watercolor crayons:* Pentel; *Other:* Safety pin and ribbon.

and accent focus on the true theme of the layout—her baby picture.

Debra Fuller of Mordialloc, Victoria, Australia, followed the same principle in her "Cooling Off" layout (Figure 6). Her choice of page accents—a classic rubber stamp showing children playing and a pastel-colored ribbon—keep the focus on the youthful theme of her layout.

6 Keep it simple. In your "trendy" scrapbooking endeavors, you may come across photographs that seem impossible to scrapbook at first glance. Many trends of days gone by included loud colors and patterns, and some of your photographs will show two or three at the same time (think plaid pants and geometric-print shirts). Don't give up so soon. Put on your problem-solving hat and think about ways you can keep the look simple. If the photograph has several patterns, consider using a solid-colored background and few accents on your layout. If the photograph has conflicting color schemes, change it to black and white. If too many different elements overwhelm the photo, crop in on your subject and make a new print.

When, Juilien Jiang of San Jose, California, created her "Dear Brother" layout in Figure 7, she

what the theme of the layout is, such as a particular holiday or milestone, like the first day of school. Choose supplies and techniques that support that theme instead of trying to incorporate accents that highlight the decade.

For example, you'll probably find that baby photographs from the '60s and '70s look a lot like today's baby photographs—a baby is a baby no matter when he or she was born! When Nicole Gartland came across a baby photo of herself taken in 1971, she created a layout that focused on the memories her mom shared with her about the photograph (Figure 5). While Nicole mentioned in her journaling when the photograph was taken, she didn't dwell on the decade she was born in since the photograph looks timeless. Instead, her papers, title

Scrapbooking photos from decades past doesn't have to be intimidating. Enjoy the fact that you're capturing valuable memories that have gone unscrapbooked for too long.

changed a color photo of her brother on his first birthday to black and white. This eliminated any conflicting color schemes and allowed her to add color to her page with a pleasing background mosaic. The graphic pattern is representative of the style in the 1960s, but it doesn't overwhelm the adorable photo of her brother with his cake. Her journaling focuses on the event and her purpose in scrapbooking the photograph.

❽ Have a ball! Retro is all the rage, so take advantage of its popularity and have a retro scrapbooking night. Invite your friends to bring photographs from the '60s, '70s and '80s, dress up and have a blast scrapbooking the night away. You'll have fun reminiscing, and you'll get tons of great ideas from the photographs, scrapbooking styles and supplies others are using.

Scrapbooking photos from decades past doesn't have to be intimidating. Enjoy the fact that you're capturing valuable memories that have gone unscrapbooked for too long. Celebrate relationships, as Lori Allred of Bountiful, Utah, did in her layout "My Little Brother" (Figure 8). Appreciate the times you've lived through and the lessons they've taught you. Most of all, recognize your own creativity and determination and how these traits have developed over the years. That's what scrapbooking is all about! And who knows—when the trends go full circle and come back in style, you may be the first on the block with a completed album full of hip pages! ♥

Figure 7. Simplify a busy photograph or layout by changing your color photos to black and white before including them on your page. *Page by Juilien Jiang.* **Supplies** *Vellum:* IFR; *Computer fonts:* CK Primary, "The Art of Creative Lettering" CD and CK Handprint, "The Best of Creative Lettering" CD Combo, *Creating Keepsakes; Square template:* Coluzzle, Provo Craft; *Pop dots:* All Night Media; *Embroidery floss:* DMC; *Other:* Charms.

Figure 8. Have fun while you're scrapbooking important relationships and aspects of your life—that's what scrapbooking is all about! *Page by Lori Allred.* **Supplies** *Patterned paper:* Making Memories; *Computer font:* CK Penman, "The Best of Creative Lettering" CD Vol. 3, *Creating Keepsakes; Chalks:* Stampin' Up!; *Eyelets:* Impress Rubber Stamps; *Charms:* magicscraps.com; *Poem idea:* twopeasinabucket.com.

Ephemera
of My World

Preserve tomorrow's mementos today

I love to scrapbook with vintage ephemera—you know, items such as old greeting cards, labels, antique buttons, currency and more. They add authenticity and interest to my artwork.

But what about today's ephemera, mementos from today's pop culture? They're the everyday items we typically throw away. I can create a glimpse of my life in the early 21st century by incorporating items such as receipts, ticket stubs and product labels into my scrapbook pages. You can, too. Following are five ideas to get you started.

by Kelly Anderson

Remembrances of an Era

I always imagined that once people became "grown-ups" they stopped growing. Having reached adulthood, I now realize that we never stop changing. Life is dynamic (thank goodness) and we continually progress. I created this layout to remind me of this point in my life's journey.

"In My Life"
by Kelly Anderson

Supplies *Patterned paper:* Ink It; *Transparencies:* Li'l Davis Designs; *Definition sticker:* Making Memories; *Rubber stamps and stamping ink:* Creative Block; *Pen:* Zig Millennium, EK Success; *Ruler:* Nostalgiques, EK Success; *Gold number:* Walnut Hollow; *Magnetic typewriter keys and metal sheet:* Barnes & Noble; *Clips:* OfficeMax; *Chalk:* Craf-T Products; *Logo:* P22 Type Foundry; *Preservation spray:* Archival Mist, EK Success; *Other:* Foam core, antique house number, gold letter, negative strip, staples, receipt, brown bag, parking citation, dry cleaning tag, lip gloss label, magazine clippings and notepad image.

Idea to note: Kelly used a golf scorecard booklet to create a mini altered book, which includes journaling, magazine subscription cards, baggage claim tickets, a newsletter and product labels.

Clip a mini altered book to your page as a creative twist.

Note how each spread includes everyday items, displayed in a fun, fresh way.

Life's Ephemera

Not only can ephemera document pop culture, it can also reflect *your* life. This layout documents my life's comings and goings. To express my passion for photo and paper arts, I included a *Creating Keepsakes* subscription card and a label from a favorite scrapbooking product.

"Ephemera of My World"

by Kelly Anderson

Supplies *Album:* DMD, Inc.; *Ribbon loop:* 7 Gypsies; *Envelopes:* Ink It; *Tape measure:* JoAnn Crafts; *Pen:* Zig Millennium, EK Success; *Chalk:* Craf-T Products; *Other:* CK subscription card, postage stamp, merchandise tags, negative strip, magazine card, silk flower, photo corners, ribbon, metal rings and charm.

Examples of Ephemera

Ephemera includes anything that documents everyday life. The items are produced for an immediate, practical purpose, with no thought of preservation. Following are examples of ephemera that future generations could treasure:

CD covers	Receipts	Currency	Political buttons	Invitations
Gift tags	Ticket stubs	Sheet music	Postcards	Programs
Price tags	Pamphlets	Candy wrappers	Labels	Playing cards
E-mail headings	Certificates	Awards of merit	Maps	
Negative strips	Greeting cards	Advertisements	Stamps	

College Collectibles

College graduation involves much more than just photos in a cap and gown. Why not display information about all the work involved in reaching that coveted commencement?

For this layout about my master's program, I included small color copies of textbooks and a list of course requirements. The alumni key chain represents the transition to my new status.

"Arizona Sun Devils"
by Kelly Anderson

Supplies *Leather paper:* Ink It; *Computer font:* CK Newsprint, "Fresh Fonts" CD, *Creating Keepsakes; Bookplate and brads:* Making Memories; *Acrylic paint:* Golden; *Stamping ink:* Fresco, Stampa Rosa; *Envelopes:* Ink It; *Gold numbers:* Walnut Hollow; *Preservation spray:* Archival Mist, EK Success; *Other:* Photo corners, textbook images, key chain, university seal and stickers, newspaper clippings, ribbon and thread.

Shadow Box Souvenirs

Consider displaying bulky mementos in a shadow box. For this layout, I included make-up and costume props used for my role in "Steel Magnolias." I created an interactive flap, then tucked newspaper clippings, script pages and the program into a clear envelope on the back of the flap. This also allowed more room for journaling and extra mementos.

"Steel Magnolias"

by Kelly Anderson

Supplies *Textured paper:* Ink It; *Computer font:* Broadway and Times New Roman, Microsoft Word; *Pen:* Zig Millennium, EK Success; *Metal squares and letter:* Making Memories; *Ribbon:* Midori (narrow) and JoAnn Crafts (wide); *Slides and bookplate:* Scrapworks; *Wood letters:* Walnut Hollow; *Stamping ink:* Brilliance, Tsukineko; *File tab:* Avery; *Hinges:* Michaels; *Other:* Slide holder sheet, thread, bobby pins, paint chips, pearl strand, flower, transparency, make-up, script, newspaper clippings and program.

Ideas to note: Kelly sewed the slide-holder sheet to her cardstock. She colored the wood letters with stamping ink.

Ephemera without the Bulk

Love the look of ephemera but want to avoid the bulk? Try some of these real and faux products:

"Experience"

by Loni Stevens • Pleasant Grove, UT

Supplies *Tag, currency and label:* Limited Edition Rubber Stamps; *Computer font:* 1942 Report, downloaded from the Internet; *Bookplate, definition and jump ring:* Making Memories; *Pearl snap:* Prym-Dritz; *Flower:* The Robin's Nest; *Other:* Embossed paper, twine, eyelet, thread and ribbon.

Idea to note: To make the cut-out tag more sturdy, Loni backed it with cardstock.

Foreign Bank Currency and Ephemera Sheets, Limited Edition Rubber Stamps

EpHemerA

"Missing You"

by Katherine Brooks
for Two Busy Moms by Deluxe Designs

Supplies *Patterned paper and stamp accents:* Chronicles, Two Busy Moms, Deluxe Designs; *Letter stamps:* PSX Design; *Square brad:* Creative Impressions; *Metal tag:* Magic Scraps; *Other:* Ribbon and stamping ink.

During the 1940's my grandmother would receive many wonderful letters and photos from her boyfriend (my now grandfather). She kept them all wrapped with a bow and tucked safely inside a shoebox, which she placed next to her bed. This was one of her favorite photos; my grandfather (Sam Harker Sr.) is third from left in the photo.

Chronicles, Two Busy Moms by Deluxe Designs

"Vegetable Guy"

by Mary Larson • Chandler, AZ

Supplies *Seed packet images:* Click-n-Craft, The Vintage Workshop; *Textured paper:* Magic Scraps; *Patterned paper:* The Paper Garden; *Metal word:* Li'l Davis Designs; *Computer fonts:* TagXtreme (title) and Grunge Caltek Bold (journaling), downloaded from the Internet; *Brads:* Lasting Impressions for Paper; *Charm:* QVC.

Click-n-Craft CD-ROM, The Vintage Workshop

"Megan and Mikaela"

by Joy Uzarraga • Clarendon Hills, IL

Supplies *Ephemera tag and letter stickers:* me & my BIG ideas;
Stamp letter stickers: Sonnets, Creative Imaginations; *Definition:*
Elements; *Chalk:* Craf-T Products; *Stamping ink:* Ranger Industries.

Scrappy Chic, me & my BIG ideas

"Play by the Rules"

by Carol Wingert • Gilbert, AZ

Supplies *Bingo and playing cards:* The Ephemera Book,
Design Originals; *Metal corners and twill tape:* 7 Gypsies;
Rubber stamps: Stamp Camp and A Stamp in the Hand;
Letter charms: Making Memories; *Stamping ink:* Clearsnap
and Ranger Industries.

Idea to note: To keep her layout flat, Carol scanned bingo
markers and stamped the Scrabble letters and dice.

The Ephemera Book, Design Originals

Tradition Trinkets

What traditions are prominent in your life? On a layout, incorporate mementos associated with those traditions.

To introduce freshmen to collegiate traditions as part of my job, I asked student leaders to list 101 things every student must experience. For this layout, I used clips from the newspaper article that featured the list as well as photos that reflect the advice from upperclassmen. I also incorporated collegiate trinkets to show my school spirit.

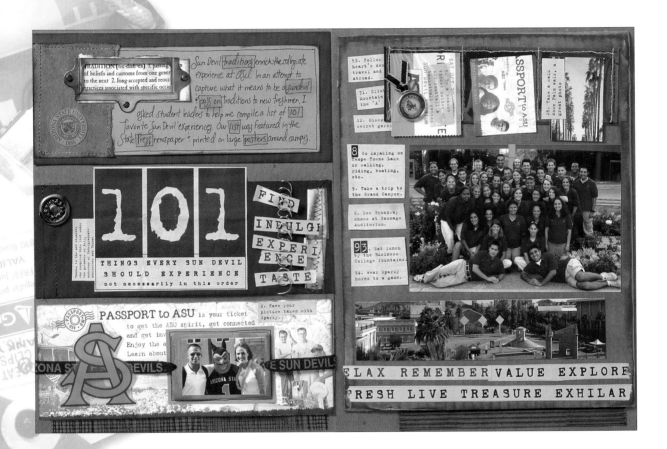

"101 Sun Devil Traditions"
by Kelly Anderson

Supplies *Corrugated paper:* DMD, Inc.; *Definition:* Making Memories; *Bookplate and brads:* Ink It; *Metal plaque and wire:* 7 Gypsies; *Stamping ink:* Fresco, Stampa Rosa; *Pen:* Zig Millennium, EK Success; *Chalk:* Craf-T Products; *Other:* Slide holder sheet, cardboard, chipboard, wax seal, college stickers, shoelace, ribbon, thread, newspaper clippings, brochures and football tickets.

places from our past

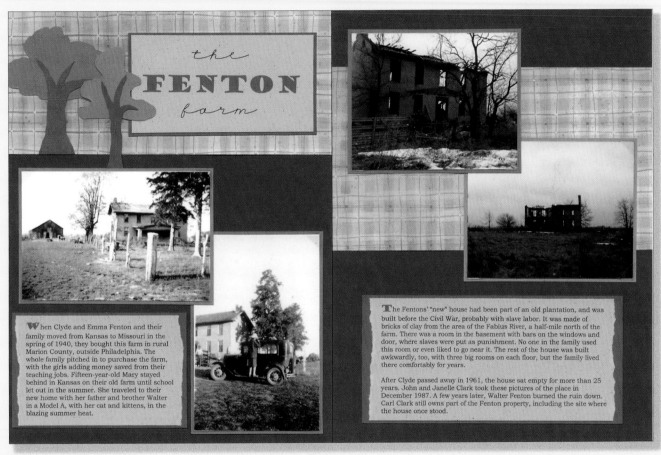

the
FENTON
farm

When Clyde and Emma Fenton and their family moved from Kansas to Missouri in the spring of 1940, they bought this farm in rural Marion County, outside Philadelphia. The whole family pitched in to purchase the farm, with the girls adding money saved from their teaching jobs. Fifteen-year-old Mary stayed behind in Kansas on their old farm until school let out in the summer. She traveled to their new home with her father and brother Walter in a Model A, with her cat and kittens, in the blazing summer heat.

The Fentons' "new" house had been part of an old plantation, and was built before the Civil War, probably with slave labor. It was made of bricks of clay from the area of the Fabius River, a half-mile north of the farm. There was a room in the basement with bars on the windows and door, where slaves were put as punishment. No one in the family used this room or even liked to go near it. The rest of the house was built awkwardly, too, with three big rooms on each floor, but the family lived there comfortably for years.

After Clyde passed away in 1961, the house sat empty for more than 25 years. John and Janelle Clark took these pictures of the place in December 1987. A few years later, Walter Fenton burned the ruin down. Carl Clark still owns part of the Fenton property, including the site where the house once stood.

"The Fenton Farm"
by Janelle Clark
Westerville, OH
SUPPLIES
Patterned paper: Carolee's Creations
Computer fonts: CK Cursive (title),
"The Best of Creative Lettering" CD
Vol. 2, *Creating Keepsakes*; Goudy
Stout (title) and Bookman Old Style
(journaling), downloaded from
the Internet
Trees: Janelle's own designs

QUOTABLE QUOTE:

"We live in a moment of
history where change is so
speeded up that we begin to
see the present only when it
is already disappearing."

—R.D. LAING

"The Old Home"

by Eva Flake
Mesa, AZ
SUPPLIES
Computer font: PC Type,
"For Font Sakes" HugWare
CD, Provo Craft

Leaf punch: Family Treasures
Fence: Eva's own design
Chalk: Craf-T Products
Pen: Zig Writer, EK Success
Photo corners: Canson
Other: Twine

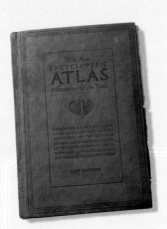

Accent Idea: Vintage Magazines and Books

❖ ❖ ❖ ❖ ❖

If you're at a loss for ideas for accenting your heritage layouts, gather your photographs and head to the library. It's a treasure trove of valuable time-specific designs and illustrations. Take an afternoon to browse through back issues of magazines from the 1940s, or ask your librarian where you can find dated copies of social etiquette books or other publications with illustrations from the time period you're scrapbooking. You can color-copy the designs onto acid-free paper to include in your album.

Paging through vintage magazines and books will also give you a feel for color schemes that were popular in the past, the "in" fashions and hairstyles, and interesting tidbits of information you can include on your layouts. Let your creativity roam as you wander through the library—you may find yourself making color copies of old maps, stamps or documents. This blast from the past may be just what you need to jump-start your creativity!

"A Home for the Ages"
by Alannah Jurgensmeyer
Rogers, AR
SUPPLIES
Patterned paper: Scrap-Ease
Computer font: Bangle, Corel Draw
String: On the Surface Fibers
Chalks: Stampin' Up!

A HOME for the AGES

1903 to Present
In 1903, Conrad Jurgensmeyer and his wife Mary built their house on the top of the hill at the farm in St. Elizabeth, MO. where it still stands today.
This picture was taken in 1915 and shows Conrad's family and some of his grandchildren. Conrad and Mary lived in this home until 1928 when they leased it to their son, Joseph. Joseph and his wife Clara raised their 9 children in the home and then sold it to their 8 sons in 1968. His sons are still the current owners.

"Seasons of Farmlife"
by Pam Talluto
Rochester Hills, MI
SUPPLIES
Vellum: Paper Adventures
Computer fonts: Aeolus, 39 Smooth and Ballads, downloaded from the Internet
Stamps: Hero Arts
Stamping ink: Stampa Rosa

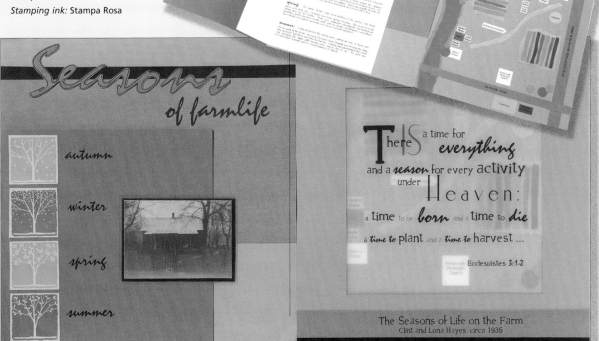

Seasons of farmlife
autumn
winter
spring
summer

There IS a time for *everything* and a *season* for every activity under **Heaven:** a time to be ***born*** and a time to *die* a *time to* plant and a *time to* harvest ...
Ecclesiastes 3:1-2

The Seasons of Life on the Farm
Clint and Lona Hayes · circa 1935

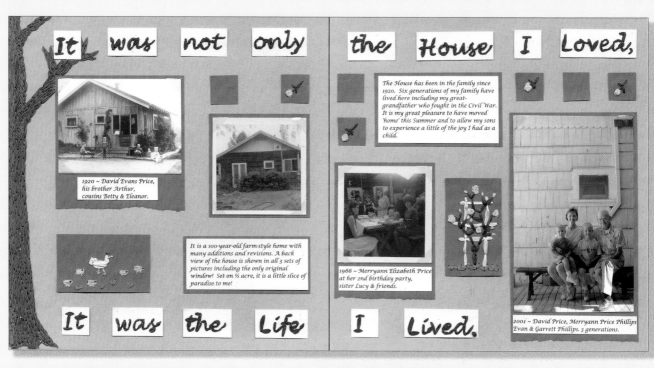

"The House I Loved"

by Merryann Phillips
San Diego, CA

SUPPLIES

Computer font: Lucida Calligraphy, Microsoft Word
Tree and rose trellis: Merryann's own designs
Idea for chickens: From *An Encyclopedia of Ribbon*
Embroidery by Deanna Hall West
Embroidery floss: DMC
Embroidery ribbon: Pure Silk

"This Old House"

by Lynette Jensen
Jennings, LA

SUPPLIES

Patterned paper: Stamping Station
Vellum: The Write Stock
Computer fonts: CK Journaling (journaling), "The Best of Creative Lettering" CD Vol. 2 and CK Leafy Capitals (title), "The Art of Creative Lettering" CD, *Creating Keepsakes*

Embossed frames: Keeping Memories Alive
Stickers: Frances Meyer
Memorabilia pocket: 3L Corp.
Clear embossing powder: Mark Enterprises
Other: Brads
Idea to note: Lynette picked a magnolia from the house and included it on her layout.

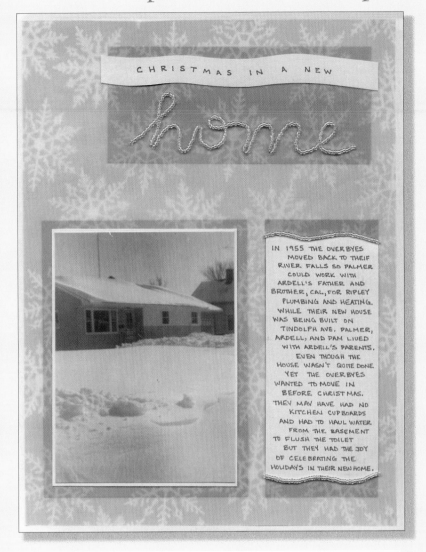

"Christmas in a New Home"
by **Lisa Brown**
Berkeley, CA
SUPPLIES
Vellum: Paper Adventures
Snowflake vellum: Whispers,
Autumn Leaves
Pen: Zig Writer, EK Success
Crystal beads: Darice

CHRISTMAS IN A NEW *home*

IN 1955 THE OVERBYES MOVED BACK TO THEIR RIVER FALLS SO PALMER COULD WORK WITH ARDELL'S FATHER AND BROTHER, CAL, FOR RIPLEY PLUMBING AND HEATING. WHILE THEIR NEW HOUSE WAS BEING BUILT ON TINDOLPH AVE. PALMER, ARDELL, AND PAM LIVED WITH ARDELL'S PARENTS. EVEN THOUGH THE HOUSE WASN'T QUITE DONE YET THE OVERBYES WANTED TO MOVE IN BEFORE CHRISTMAS. THEY MAY HAVE HAD NO KITCHEN CUPBOARDS AND HAD TO HAUL WATER FROM THE BASEMENT TO FLUSH THE TOILET BUT THEY HAD THE JOY OF CELEBRATING THE HOLIDAYS IN THEIR NEW HOME.

Preservation 101: Choosing and Storing Paper

❖ ❖ ❖ ❖ ❖

Ensuring your heritage album is made with archival-quality paper products is essential, particularly if you're scrapbooking original photographs and documents. Follow these tips for choosing and storing paper items:

- Choose acid- and lignin-free paper.
- Store acidic items away from acid-free items—acid will migrate.
- Never glue paper documents onto your scrapbook pages. Use acid-free or safe plastic mounting corners or corner slots.
- Store paper in moderate temperatures and moderate humidity.
- Keep your storage area free of pests that could eat your paper or adhesives.
- Keep paper away from light, especially direct sunlight.
- Unfold letters and store them in safe boxes, plastic sleeves or envelopes.
- Newspaper articles and paper documents should be acid free before storing them—test and deacidify them if necessary.

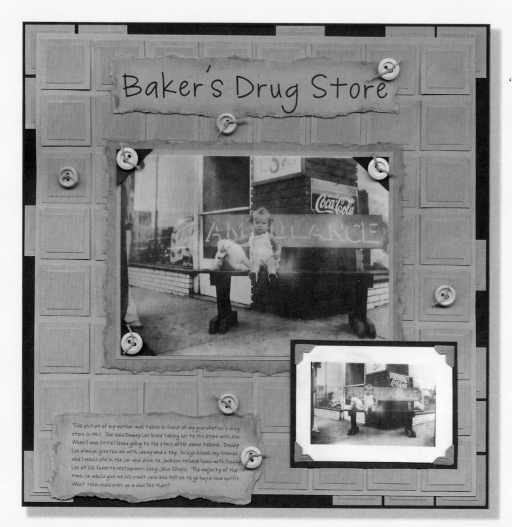

This picture of my mother was taken in front of my grandfather's drug store in 1937. She said Daddy Lee loved taking her to the store with him. When I was little I loved going to the store after dance lessons. Daddy Lee always greeted me with candy and a toy. In high school, my friends and I would pile in the car and drive to Jackson to have lunch with Daddy Lee at his favorite restaurant, Long John Silvers. The majority of the time he would give me his credit card and tell me to go buy a new outfit. What teen could pass up a deal like that?

"Baker's Drug Store"
by Lee Anne Russell
Brownsville, TN
SUPPLIES
Computer font: CK Jot,
"The Art of Creative Lettering"
CD, *Creating Keepsakes*
Buttons: Lara's Crafts
Chalk: Craf-T Products
Photo corners: Canson
String: On the Surface Fibers

Getting Organized: Grouping

❖ ❖ ❖ ❖ ❖

Scrapbooking heritage photographs can be difficult—it may seem that every time you finish a page, another photograph or item pops up that would have been perfect for your layout! To help, consider taking a block of time to focus on one ancestor, rather than scrapbooking photos in random order.

For example, start by choosing an ancestor you've got a few materials for already. In the next week or two, ask family members for any informa-tion, photographs or heirlooms they may have that relate to that ancestor. Gather as much informa-tion as you can before you sit down to scrapbook.

While this process may take more time, it'll pre-vent the frustration of feeling the need to create a new layout in order to include information or photos you discover at a later time. It'll also help you incorporate interesting and important items onto one layout, making it more meaningful and complete.

The Barnesville Methodist Church was built in 1900, when my grandfather, Clint Hayes, was five years old. His father, Allen Hayes, donated part of his farmland for the church and helped to build it. Typically, in those days and in that area, the women and girls organized societies to raise money for building of the church. Ice cream suppers, pie suppers, friendship quilts - all went toward the collection of funds for the new building. Landowners donated trees to be sawed into lumber for construction.

When Clint was ten years old, a new little girl moved to the area. She was only five years old and her name was Lona. Lona and her family also attended the Barnesville Methodist Church. Eleven years later, Clint and Lona were married. They built their home within sight of the church and began to raise their family. My mom, Dell, was the sixth of their nine children.

My mom, along with her parents, grandparents, brothers and sister, attended this church throughout her childhood. So many of their social activities centered around the church. They attended services, morning and evening, every Sunday; but besides that there were also prayer meetings, Vacation Bible Schools, Christmas Programs, and Ice Cream Suppers. Sometimes there would be Dinners where everyone would bring something to share. After dinner, everyone would clean all the grounds of the church and cemetery.

The Barnesville Methodist Church still stands today. Its little cemetery is right across the road; my grandparents, Clint and Lona Hayes, are buried there. I don't get to visit Tennessee very often; but when I do, I always have to make my way to Barnesville to visit this church and this land; to feel the peace that is there.

"Barnesville Methodist Church"

by Pam Talluto
Rochester Hills, MI
SUPPLIES
Patterned paper: Making Memories
Patterned vellum: Papers by Catherine
Computer fonts: Tahoma, Courier New and American, Microsoft Word; PC Ratatat, package unknown, Provo Craft
Snowflake punches: Family Treasures
Other: Beads
Idea to note: Pam scanned four photographs and used Adobe PhotoDeluxe to size them together into a panoramic photo.

"Middleton"

by Allison Strine
Atlanta, GA
SUPPLIES
Patterned paper: Carolee's Creations (blue plaid), Rocky Mountain Scrapbook Company (brown), Colors By Design (clocks)
Computer font: Brush Art, downloaded from the Internet
Rubber stamps: Above the Mark (ribbon, clock), Stampendous (texture cube)
Stamping inks: Adirondack, Ranger Industries
Lettering template: Calligraphy, ScrapPagerz.com
Scissors: Deckle edge, Fiskars
Square punch: All Night Media
Chalks: Craf-T Products
String: On the Surface Fibers

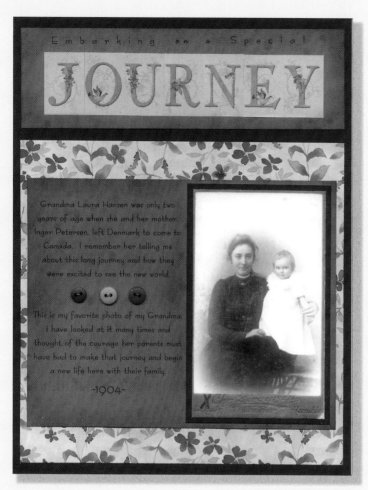

"Journey"
by Cindy Schow
Cardston, AB, Canada
SUPPLIES
Patterned paper: Colors By Design
Computer fonts: Bernhard Fashion HMK and
Cluff HMK, "Hallmark Card Studio 2" CD,
Hallmark
Letter stickers: K & Company
Chalk: Craf-T Products
Other: Buttons and wire

"Moving West"
by Janelle Clark
Westerville, OH
SUPPLIES
Patterned paper: Rocky Mountain
Scrapbook Company
Computer fonts: Fancy Pants (title) and
Bookman Old Style (journaling),
downloaded from the Internet
Clip art: "Remember When"
HugWare CD, Provo Craft
Chalk: Craf-T Products
Stamping ink: Ancient Page,
Clearsnap, Inc.

A story from this time has become part of family folklore. When the family was living in Wyoming, they lived in a log cabin on the Bighorn River. Clyde worked on the ranch across the river. On March 2, 1915, Helen's second birthday, she and Lewis were playing church, sitting on a chair next to the red-hot pot-bellied stove. Helen fell off the chair into the coal bucket, which tipped her toward the stove, burning her face and her right eye. Lewis grabbed Helen's skirt and pulled her back from the stove, which saved her from a terrible injury.

Emma put egg whites and Vaseline on Helen's burns, and bundled her and Lewis up, because it was very cold outside. Emma was pregnant (she would give birth to Esther just a few weeks later) so she could not carry Helen. She and four-year-old Lewis took Helen's hands and led her across the frozen river to find Clyde.

The boss of the ranch got two horses that had not been broken yet, and hitched them to a buckboard. Helen remembers being wrapped up in a comforter in her father's arms, then the boss slapped the horses and they took off across the prairie to the nearest town, which was 15 or 20 miles away, to go to the doctor.

Emma was greatly relieved when the doctor found that Helen's eye was not damaged. The doctor told her that her quick action and treatment had been just the right things to do.

After Clyde and Emma's first child, Lewis, was born in 1911, the Fenton family decided to move west. Grant, Clyde's father, had respiratory problems, and it was thought that the dry air of the western states would help his health. Clyde, Emma and Lewis, along with Clyde's parents, Grant and Lillian, and Clyde's brother Elsie, left Missouri. Clyde worked at many jobs along the way, as they searched for a place to settle.

This picture was taken in Nebraska, where their daughter Helen was born. The year was 1913. Helen remembers that her mother covered the dirt floor of their tent with feed sacks. Helen would dig in the dirt with her spoon! Clyde worked for the railroad in Nebraska, and also on a ranch.

The family moved on to Wyoming, where their second daughter, Esther, was born in 1915. In Wyoming, Clyde worked on the ranch that Buffalo Bill Cody owned, outside Thermopolis. Here he broke horses and delivered goods.

The Fentons ended up moving all the way to Oregon, but the western climate did nothing to help Grant Fenton's health. Clyde and his parents took the train home to Missouri, and Emma followed with their belongings and the three children. Their fourth child, Florence, was born outside Philadelphia, Missouri, in late 1917.

"Homeland"
by Pamela Kopka
New Galilee, PA
SUPPLIES
Patterned paper: Scrap-Ease
Vellum: Paper Pizazz, Hot Off The Press
Velveteen paper: Paper Adventures
Computer font: Amazone BT, downloaded from the Internet
Pens: Pigma Micron, Sakura; Wet Looks, Marvy Uchida
Chalk: Craf-T Products
Embossing powder: Rubber Stampede
Idea to note: Pamela created her own vintage map using chalk and gold embossing powder.

Journaling Starter: Places from Your Childhood

❖ ❖ ❖ ❖ ❖

Take a moment to think about the memories associated with certain places from your childhood. Whether you spent afternoons in a tree house in your backyard or visited the same drive-in for a dipped ice cream cone every Monday night, you likely have poignant memories from the places where you spent time as a child. As you work on your album, consider capturing this aspect of your heritage on your pages. Here are a few questions to get you started:

◆ How many homes did you live in while you were growing up? Where did you play? What was your room like? Did you share a room or have your own? What was your favorite room to spend time in? Were there things about the home you loved, or didn't like? Thinking of each room you remember, are there specific memories that should be recorded about that room or the things that happened there?

◆ What places were included in your daily routines? Did you stop at the same corner store for a drink on the way home from school, or visit a friend or relative on a regular basis? Did you head to the pond after school for a refreshing swim, or head to the barn to do afternoon chores?

◆ What type of city or town did you grow up in? Did it have a charming drug store with a soda fountain, a gazebo where the town met for special occasions, or a candy store that sold penny candy of every kind? Did the man at the grocery store always remember your name, or did neighbors spend the evening on their front porches, greeting other neighbors out for a walk?

Memories about places in your childhood can be triggered by a question, a smell, a photograph or a sound—just make sure that as the memories start flowing, you're ready with a pen and pencil to jot them down. This way, they'll be available when you're ready to create pages about the places you loved (or hated!) the most.

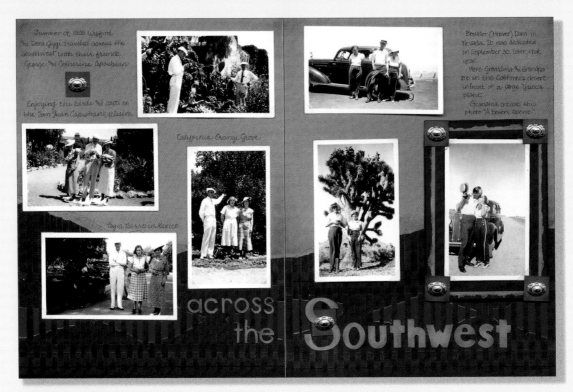

"Across the Southwest"

by Noralee Peterson
Orem, UT

SUPPLIES

Vellum: Paper Adventures
Title: Noralee's own design (small letters and large "s")
Punches: EK Success (ABC letters), Family Treasures (circle), CARL Mfg. (oval)
Metal accents: The Leather Factory
Chalk: Craf-T Products
Pen: Pigma Micron, Sakura

"Moscow 1947"

by Allison Strine
Atlanta, GA

SUPPLIES

Patterned paper: Scrap-Ease (pocket paper and title letters), Mustard Moon (red and orange)
Vellum: Paper Adventures
Computer font: Lucida Handwriting, Silfvens and Robot Teacher, downloaded from the Internet

Nails: Anchor Wire Corp.
Stamping ink: Ranger Industries
Scissors: Deckle edge, Fiskars
Ideas to note: Allison color-copied original baggage claim checks, menus and postcards and included them on her lay-out. She also used stamping ink to distress the title mat, title and cardstock.

HOMETOWN, USA,

CAPTURE the SPIRIT of a SPECIAL PLACE

by Allison Strine

The mere mention of my hometown—Magnolia, Massachusetts—gives me an evocative blast of memories. I haven't been there in 10 years, but I can close my eyes and remember how it felt to walk to Doc Viera's pharmacy for a root-beer Popsicle. I think of the salty sea air, and I picture myself shopping for penny candy with my precious dime. My sense of who I am evolved while searching for sea glass on Magnolia Beach.

That's what hometowns do. Without our even knowing it, hometowns weave their way into the fabric of our very being. We may move away, but we never leave. We grow up, and suddenly what was hokey becomes historical. What seemed silly is now significant. Hometowns are at the heart and soul of our being. There's something powerful and patriotic about having our own hometowns, and it's important to us as scrapbookers to capture these emotions and memories on paper.

When I say "hometown" to you, what images and feelings spring to mind? Challenge yourself to scrapbook a layout or even an album about your hometown. Capture what you find most meaningful. You'll find inspiring ideas on the pages that follow!

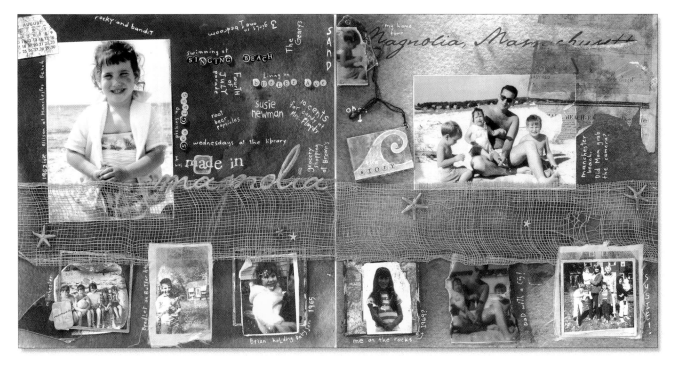

Supplies *Patterned paper:* Wordsworth; *Pen:* Milky Gel Roller, Pentel; *Stickers, poemstone, metal frames and mini book:* Sonnets, Creative Imaginations; *Letter rub-ons:* Bradwear, Creative Imaginations; *Calendar page:* Anima Designs; *Image transfer paper:* Lazertran; *Polymer clay:* Sculpey, *Metallic rub-ons:* Craf-T Products; *Netting:* Magic Scraps.

MAGNOLIA

by Allison Strine   ★   Atlanta, GA

Since my Magnolia memories are a collage in my mind, I tried to recreate that impression in my layout. Close your eyes and think about your hometown. Let the memories wander through your head. Jot down as many random thoughts as you can think of. Now, how can you transfer those thoughts to paper?

- To evoke a feeling of the old days, add a small calendar. Crumple it, chalk it, tear it, ink it!

- If you're feeling brave, rough up the corners of a color photo with sandpaper for "character."

- Experiment with transferring images to clay and silk.

- Tuck design elements in front of and behind netting.

Supplies *Photo-editing software:* PictureIt!, Microsoft; *Photo paper:* Premium Matte, Hewlett-Packard; *Vellum:* Paper Adventures; *Pens:* Ultimate Gel Pen, American Crafts; Zig Calligraphy, EK Success; *Computer font:* Love Letters, downloaded from the Internet; *Glaze:* Diamond Glaze, Judikins; *Chalk:* Stampin' Up!.

VALLEY GIRL

by Colette Stucki ✦ Glen Allen, VA

While growing up, Colette didn't realize how big her hometown was. "The San Fernando Valley, which is located in the suburbs of L.A. and has millions of residents, is actually larger than some U.S. states!" says Colette. While creating her layout, Colette included a filmstrip section of photos on the left-hand side to commemorate the show-business connections of people living in the valley.

- Add a glint of shine to certain page elements by applying a thin coat of glaze.
- Tear, fold and spindle corners and edges of design elements. Have fun!
- Enlarge an aerial photo to use as background on your page.

THE BRIDGES OF MORGAN CITY

by Leslie Davis ✦ Baton Rouge, LA

Sometimes home is defined by a chunk of metal. For Leslie, the skyline of the two bridges is an icon of her city. "Even now, people in town still call them the 'old bridge' and the 'new bridge,' even though the latter is 23 years old," says Leslie. "My husband and I met there, so it's very important to our family history."

- Make a super design element by creating a mosaic out of punched rectangles.
- Include your children in photographs of your hometown. What does it mean to you to mix the past and the present?
- Use white cardstock as a background for a clean, graphic look.

Supplies *Computer font:* Scrap Sweetness, downloaded from *www.letteringdelights.com*, Inspire Graphics; *Rectangle punch:* Paper Shaper, EK Success.

Supplies *Patterned paper:* Debbie Mumm; *Paper-piecing pattern:* Bumper Crops, EK Success; *Chalk:* Craf-T Products; *Ribbon:* C.M. Offray & Son; *Hat pins:* Westrim Crafts; *Photo corners:* Dress-It-Up; *Sticker:* Mrs. Grossman's; *Flowers:* Card Connection; *Computer font:* CK Elegant, "Fresh Fonts" CD, *Creating Keepsakes*; *Letter stamps:* PSX Design; *Date stamp:* OfficeMax; *Stamping ink:* Tsukineko; *Embossing powder:* Stamp'n Stuff; *Scissors:* Jumbo Scallop edge, Provo Craft; *Adhesive:* Glue Dots International; *Photo:* Tintype Photo Parlour.

ST. CHARLES

by Jeniece Higgins ★ Northbrook, IL

As a child, Jeniece treasured her special visits to St. Charles with her mother. "It was always quality time because we were never in a hurry," says Jeniece. Once, they even commemorated their day out by getting photos of themselves dressed up in costumes.

Jeniece continues this precious tradition with her own daughter, even revisiting the same photographer for pictures. Consider taking a family trip to *your* hometown, so you can share the memories.

- Rub chalk around the edges of paper for an antiqued look.

- Construct a shop window by rolling paper under itself. Tie with a pretty ribbon.

- Make a valance by cutting paper with decorative scissors. Mount it with foam tape for depth.

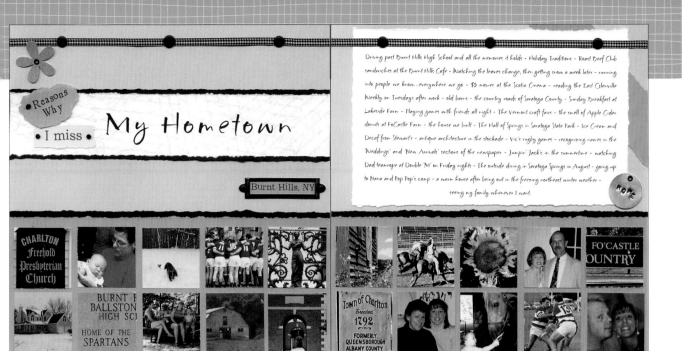

Supplies *Buttons, eyelet charms and eyelets:* Making Memories; *Computer fonts:* McBooHmk, Hallmark Scrapbook Studio; CK Newsprint, "Fresh Fonts" CD, Creating Keepsakes; *Square punch:* Marvy Uchida; *Ribbon:* C.M. Offray & Son; *Rubber stamps:* Hero Arts (title background) and PSX Design (title); *Metal stamps:* C.M. Hanson & Co.; *Stamping ink:* Clearsnap and Memories; *Other:* Brads and bookplate.

REASONS

by Lisa Russo ⭐ Chicago, IL

What do you miss about your hometown? Growing up, what were the little things that made it important to you? Reminisce in the form of a list and jot down memories as they pop into your head.

Lisa's photo collage matches the list theme in her journaling. "By itself, each of the photos might not mean as much," says Lisa, "but as a montage they get me all weepy."

- Stamp into a metal tag with metal stamps. Highlight the letters with a marker.

- Journal specific things you want to remember. A few of Lisa's?

"Jumpin' Jacks in the summertime, old barns, Vic's rugby games, and roast beef sandwiches at the Burnt Hills Café."

- To create a sense of unity in a two-page layout, place ribbon in a strip across both pages.

- To emphasize a subtitle, place it inside a metal bookplate.

FAVORITE HANGOUTS in your HOMETOWN

Think about the places that make up your hometown. Consider including some of the following in a layout:

- The drive-in theater. What movies did you see there? Is it still around?

- How often did you go to the library? What was the librarian like?

- What's unique about stores such as the pharmacy, grocery store or ice-cream parlor?

- If a friend came to town, where did you take her for fun? Did you go to the golf course? The video store?

- What special landmarks does your town have? Is there a train station? A duck pond?

- What about the government buildings? Was there something special about the fire station or the post office?

- What school did you go to? What was great (and not so great) about that particular school?

- How many playgrounds were there?

- Who were your favorite neighbors?

- Did you have a secret hangout?

- Think nature. Were there interesting parks to hike in? Walking trails?

Supplies *Patterned paper:* All About Me, Pebbles in my Pocket; *Die cuts:* Mini Fresh Cuts, EK Success; *Stickers:* Mary Engelbreit, Creative Imaginations; *Craft wire and snaps:* Making Memories; *Computer fonts:* 2Peas Evergreen, downloaded from *www.twopeasinabucket.com*; CK Journaling, "The Best of Creative Lettering" CD Combo, *Creating Keepsakes*; *Pen:* Pigma Micron, Sakura; *Glue dots:* Glue Dots International; *Plastic:* Paint Blank, Deco Arts; *Other:* Non-glass. *Ideas to note:* Erin cut the plastic easily after scoring it several times with a craft knife placed alongside a ruler. She hammered the snaps flat, then attached them with glue dots.

HOMETOWN USA

by Erin Lincoln ⭐ Frederick, MD

For Erin, growing up in four states and five houses wasn't the ideal way to plant roots. "But now, a little older and wiser," says Erin, "I can see the benefits of experiencing life throughout the USA."

- Stack and stagger. If you have a lot of photos to fit in a small space, mount them on cardstock, then create a photo stack that flips up to reveal each photo beneath.

- Use a "non-glass" product to adhere journaling blocks in a visual manner.

- Repetition can be a good way to carry a design element throughout the layout. Erin used brads to hang the flag accent, to anchor the photo stack, and to attach the non-glass to her layout.

SMALL TOWN GIRL

by Michelle Tardie ⭐ Richmond, VA

When Michelle was a child, she wanted nothing more than to explore life outside her tiny hometown of Fairfield, Vermont. "I sometimes longed to live in a town where the cows didn't outnumber the people," admits Michelle.

"Now that I live outside a large city, I sometimes catch myself wishing I could go back to the quiet and safety of my little hometown." Reflect on the changes adulthood has brought to your views of your hometown.

- Add texture and an "aged" appearance by applying metallic rub-ons.

- To enhance the look of old photos, choose a muted color scheme for your layout.

- Place ribbon on mesh to add texture and create a darker look.

- Use a rubber stamp to apply dates on vellum tags.

Supplies *Patterned paper*: Karen Foster Design; *Title letters*: Farmer Alphabet, Forget Me Not Designs; *Rubber stamps*: Antique Alphabet, PSX Design; *Stamping inks*: Page Craft, Clearsnap; *Computer font*: 2Peas Chestnuts, downloaded from www.twopeasinabucket.com; *Mesh*: Magic Mesh, Avant Card; *Vellum tags*: Making Memories; *Brads*: Boxer Scrapbook Productions; *Metallic rub-ons*: Craf-T Products; *Fiber*: Strands; *Embroidery floss*: DMC.

IDEAS to GET YOU STARTED

Your hometown deserves to be commemorated. Start your creative juices flowing with these ideas:

- How has the town changed over time?

- What is explicitly unique about your town?

- Do a page about the history of your town. Use the Internet to help with facts.

- Create a layout explaining how your family ended up living in the house they did.

- What would you want your great-grandchild to know about how you feel about your town?

- What was one of the most emotional experiences you ever had in your town? Scrapbook it!

- What does your town do to celebrate the Fourth of July? Any other special celebrations?

- Spend an afternoon recording the cost of living in your town. Include a photograph of the family and list the day's financial expenditures.

- Does your town have a famous resident? Consider interviewing him or her!

Supplies *Patterned paper:* Frances Meyer; *Computer fonts:* Typewriter (journaling) and RS Font (title), both downloaded from the Internet; *Beads:* Westrim Crafts; *Tag:* Julie's own design; *Markers:* Fibracolor; *Other:* String and reinforcement.

GROWING UP IN TORONTO

by Julie Hillier ★ Toronto, ON, Canada

OK, Toronto isn't in the United States, but it's close! Scrapbooking about your "hometown" works whether you live in Australia, Italy or any other country.

For Julie, the time spent creating this layout was especially significant. Notes Julie, "I did some reminiscing about a lot of great things from my childhood."
Julie chose to highlight her hometown with a photo of a famous Toronto landmark.

- To give photos an "older" look, convert them to black and white with image-editing software.

- Highlight a computer-generated title with pen to lend a hand-made touch.

- Be patriotic! Find a way to include your country's flag in your hometown layout.

Supplies *Patterned paper, die cuts and eyelets:* Leaving Prints; *Letter stickers:* Creative Memories; *Pen:* Zig Writer, EK Success; *Stamping inks:* Archival Ink (sepia) and Memories (black); *Computer font:* Mom's Typewriter, downloaded from the Internet; *Mesh:* Magic Mesh, Avant Card.

LAWRENCE, KANSAS

by Sarah Ackerman-Hale ⭐ Spring Hill, KS

Do you know what it's like to grow up in the middle of an important landmark and take it for granted? Sarah didn't appreciate the remarkable history of her hometown until she married a Civil War buff. "I've learned so much about my hometown's rich and exciting past," says Sarah. "It's the perfect framework for an album about my childhood."

- Tuck personal journaling notes behind lift-up cards and photos.

- Want to create a smoky, burned look? Apply sepia-toned ink with a make-up sponge to photos printed on cardstock.

- To add a personal touch to computer-generated journaling, leave space to highlight some words by hand. ♥

Protect your memories in a theme album that's attractive and easy to fill. *Album and protecting sheets:* Kolo.

BY BECKY HIGGINS

Memories of Home

The leaves crunched with every step as I walked around the

garden. The sky was the purest shade of blue, and a gust of

autumn wind nearly took my breath away as I reminisced over

this beautiful place I

called home for 17 years.

Create an album about a special place in your life

In that very moment, I

received my inspiration for a project I was eager to create—a

scrapbook about my childhood home. I began brainstorming

and snapping pictures almost immediately. →

It's been a while since I've lived in that home in Brunswick, a rural town in the rolling hills of central Maryland. My parents bought this home nearly 30 years ago, and they still live there. I currently live in Cleveland, Ohio, where my husband and I recently moved for his medical residency. For now, this is home. In several years, "home" may be somewhere else. But, no matter where I live—and I've lived in several different places in my life—I will always have a place in Maryland that I call home.

The happy feelings I get whenever I think about the home where I grew up gave me the motivation to get this project

Show the entrance to your property on your title page. Provide the address as well.

Include your parents' memories of how they found and purchased your childhood home. Explain why you wanted to revisit and record the home you lived in as a child.

Editor's note: The scrapbook pages pictured contain these supplies: *Patterned paper and stickers:* Magenta; *Photo corners:* Pioneer; *Computer fonts:* Beatty (journaling) and Garrison (title page), Microsoft; CK Sketch and CK Jot (foreword), "The Art of Creative Lettering" CD, *Creating Keepsakes.*

Nature Trees

This is one of the magnificent trees around the yard, and specifically, where we had our ultimate tree house on the west side of the house. We built the tree house many, many years ago and I can't even remember how many levels it had. I do remember always coming out of the house with plenty of [sap] on my skin and clothes!

This is the wheel barrel, next to Dad's windmill, in the Fall (the flowers were blown over by the wind. Elinn picked out this fence in Amish Country and they (Steven & Elinn) plan to include it in their yard since they currently live just down the road from Mom & Dad (moved into their new home Fall 2000).

Autumn time in Brunswick

rolling. In my mind, this was more than just a fun idea for a future date. This was an album I knew I would complete without hesitation. I'll walk you through the thought process of creating this simple album.

PURPOSE

As with any page layout or album, I first established a goal. I asked myself, "What is my purpose? What message do I want to leave with others who see what I've created?"

For this album, I wanted to include beautiful photographs of my parents' home and surrounding property. To preserve those

memories, I decided to include written stories that reminded me of each picture. One day, I plan to share this album with my children and even my grandchildren so they will know how special my childhood home is to me.

FORMAT

This scrapbook didn't need divided sections, so I began with a title page (see example at left). I designed an introduction layout for the next page, which included two forewords. My parents, the homeowners, wrote the first one. As the album's creator, I penned the other introduction. The rest of the album is page

after page of 26 individually featured photographs.

SETTING THE TONE

In a theme album, mood is important. I traditionally set the tone by choosing an appropriate album as well as papers and other accents to best convey that mood. Ideally, all the pieces come together for an attractive, unified look. With that in mind, the focus is drawn to the "meat" of the album (the photos and journaling) instead of the accents.

I love the classy products by Kolo, so I chose their Newbury photo album to house this project. A simple ribbon in the spine

This flower box has always been here, but it wasn't until a couple of years ago that Jonathan & Bob, our neighbor, did the brick layer to finish it off. of course Dad and Tyler were there to help, too. Mom has always planted beautiful flowers in this flower bed. In the background, those steps (a little overgrown with ivy right now) lead you to the garden area

By the Front Door

This is Dad's favorite statue. When Mom & Dad were visiting Grandma Johnson in North Carolina one time, they went to a local pottery place looking for flower pots and found this charming statue of a child engrossed in his book. They proudly display this on the flowerbed along the driveway, just outside the front door where the cars are parked

Record what others see when standing by the front door. Spotlight a favorite yard decoration.

When including single pages in a theme album, keep them visually harmonious with facing pages as well.

holds everything together and adds a pretty touch. The acid-free pages were included with the album.

I added protecting sheets (also from Kolo) separately to protect the photographs from little fingerprints. Patterned papers and stickers from Magenta, another company that offers elegant products, conveyed the beauty and homey theme of my album.

PROJECT PREPARATION
Last fall, I visited my parents and took time to capture scenes during my favorite season. Adorned with my trusty camera, I walked around the yard and surrounding property, taking pic-tures of anything that had special meaning to me. I took more photos this past summer, for a glimpse of different seasons.

When I took the film to a photo lab, I specifically asked for white borders around my pictures. (Many photo developers will do this if you ask.) Not only does it add a clean finish to each photograph, it also saves time and cardstock since I don't have to mat the photos!

Photos in hand, I began brain-storming and taking notes about each picture. I jotted down signif-icant memories I wanted to share. I asked for my parents' help with missing information and addition-al stories. This was a huge help. Because they've lived in the house longer than I have, they know more about the history and have different perspectives.

PUTTING IT ALL TOGETHER
My goal was to complete the album in a weekend. With my album, photos and supplies in front of me, I went to work. To keep the look consistent through-out the album, I chose four pat-terned papers that complemented the photos and each other. I selected a fifth paper in a lighter shade (golden yellow) for the journaling.

You'll notice that a similar for-mat is used in the design of each layout. I use a block of patterned paper on every outside edge (which, by the way, is exactly half an 8½" x 11" sheet of paper). The photo on each page is attached with gold photo corners by Pioneer. A small title is placed in a larger block, which is then added to the page, coming off the edge. The journaling is printed and torn around the edges to help soften the look. Little stickers from Magenta are the finishing touches.

Everything came together quickly, and I'm pleased with the unified look. With very little time and effort, I was able to combine my favorite home photos with reflections, memories and even a little history. There's nothing like the feeling of a completed project!

My childhood home will always be a piece of me, a part of my life. Reflect on the places you've lived or love to visit. Perhaps you're in a home now that you want to preserve. Maybe it's the family farm, the apartment you live in, or even your grandparents' home that you cherish. Ready for the challenge?

Grab your camera and a roll of film and snap those pictures while the memories are fresh. Involve other family members if you need help with details or want added perspectives. When you complete this simple theme album, you're sure to have a treasure that will be enjoyed today, tomorrow and for generations to come.

Show your childhood home from the front and the back.

6 heritage theme-album ideas

Explore the connections that mean the most

Scrapbooking hundreds of heritage photographs can be a daunting task—but there are ways to spice it up a bit! If you're looking for a shorter, focused project that captures important aspects of your heritage without an overwhelming time commitment, try one of the following theme-album ideas. Most can be completed in a few days, and they'll re-inspire you to get to work on that hefty pile of photographs!

When you're ready to get started, branch out a bit. Try a new album size; repeat themes, accents or techniques throughout the album for continuity and convenience; and be creative with your subject matter. The sense of accomplishment you'll feel when you realize you've finished an album that's ready to be shared with loved ones will be all you need to get you hooked on creating theme albums once and for all! Read on for six great heritage theme-album ideas to get you started.

"Things We've Handed Down" Album

A "Things We've Handed Down" theme album is a fantastic way to show the connections between generations past and present. It's fascinating to see how physical characteristics, talents, abilities and interests can be traced back through the years—and this information will add meaning to yours and family members' lives as they realize they are a part of a much larger picture.

Figure 1. Show how physical characteristics and abilities or personality traits have been passed through the generations of your family in a "Things We've Handed Down" theme album. **Supplies** *Vellum:* Paper Cuts; *Computer fonts:* Calligrapher and Caslon Old Face BT, Print Shop, Broderbund; *Clip art:* Print Shop, Broderbund; *Pen:* Milky Gel Roller, Pentel.

ARTICLE BY CATHERINE SCOTT

Be creative in the topics you include in your album. In my Things We've Handed Down album in Figure 1, I included such physical characteristics as the "Weber nose," height (my mom is 5' 8" and my dad is 6' 0", but my younger brother shot up to 6' 5" at an early age), and curly hair.

Think about talents you have, such as gardening, musical ability or writing. These are all fun topics to trace in your album. Be sure to include photographs or sound clips of family members sharing their talents for future generations to enjoy!

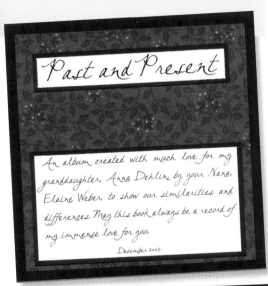

"Past and Present" Album

At first glance, you might look at the faces in your heritage photos and think you have absolutely nothing in common with the people pictured. That may or may not be true, but you can connect your life with theirs in a Past and Present album that shows the similarities and differences between their lives and yours. Some subjects you may want to explore include:

◆ Details about your family (how many brothers and sisters you have, where you fall in the age order, what growing up in your family was like)

◆ Particulars about yourself (what you look like; how you dress; what your favorite things, hobbies or talents are)

◆ Information about your education (when you started school, how much schooling you completed, what you studied, what your grades were like, what your classes were like)

◆ Historic information about your life (where you grew up, when you were born, what was happening in the world at key

moments in your life)

Start by gathering as much information, photographs and memorabilia from the life of the ancestor you'd like to scrapbook, then collect information, photographs and memorabilia from your own life. In your album, create two-page spreads on each subject, with the page on the left highlighting your ancestor and the page on the right highlighting the same subject in your own life. The pages can be as detailed or as general as you'd like, depending on how much information is available to you.

A Past and Present album makes a great gift, as well. Consider creating an album paralleling your life with that of your grandson or granddaughter (Figure 2), or create an album comparing the life of your child with that of the person he or she is named after. Remember to include a dedication or explanation in the album so the recipient will understand its importance and sentimentality.

Figure 2. A "Past and Present" album that parallels the life of a granddaughter or grandson with your own life is sure to make a treasured gift. **Supplies** Patterned paper: Déjà Views; Computer font: CK Bella, "The Best of Creative Lettering" CD Vol. 3, Creating Keepsakes.

Figure 3. A "Random Heritage Photos" album is a great solution if you have several unrelated heritage photographs and not a lot of information to go with them. **Supplies** *Patterned paper:* Mara-Mi; *Metallic paper:* Paper Adventures; *Pen:* Milky Gel Roller, Pentel; *Photo corners:* Canson.

"Random Heritage Photos" Album

This great heritage theme-album idea, taken from Stacy Julian, editor-in-chief of *Simple Scrapbooks* magazine, is the perfect solution if you have several unrelated heritage photographs and not a lot of information to go with them. Simply decide on a format for your pages (the format can be as basic or as ornate as you'd like) and mount each photograph in the album without worrying about name or date order. Underneath each photo, write a title or name (Figure 3).

Create an index that shows each title or name in alphabetical order. As you meet with family members who have information or memories about a particular photograph, add it to your index. You can update and print a new version of your index for your album as you gather new information.

Helpful hints: Consider using a larger format for your Random Heritage Photos album to leave enough space for all of your photographs. If you plan to crop photographs so you can fit more on a page, use color copies or duplicates. Also, consider adding a title page with an explanation of the album's format and concept, along with a dedication or an explanation of why

you created it. And don't forget to include your name and the date you're starting the album so future viewers understand the perspective the photographs were scrapbooked from. They're sure to appreciate the historic information, as well as any memories or stories you've managed to capture in your index.

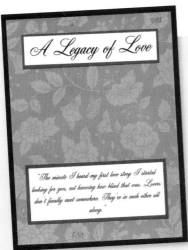

"Legacy of Love" Album

Love is a timeless subject, making it the perfect theme for a heritage album. Look through your photographs and memorabilia, and talk to family members about love stories in your family line. Perhaps you have love letters or poems shared between a husband and wife (Figure 4), a piece of lace from your great-grandmother's wedding dress, or a dried flower from a wedding bouquet. Include stories about how ancestors met and courted if you have access to this information.

Don't forget to include the present in your Legacy of Love album, as well. Include a page for your grandparents, your parents, and you and your spouse. If you haven't found your "one and only" yet, consider making a page about what you're looking for in a companion, or what you've learned from the relationships of your ancestors.

Capturing the romantic aspects of your heritage will add meaning to the relationships you share by showing the legacy of love in your own family.

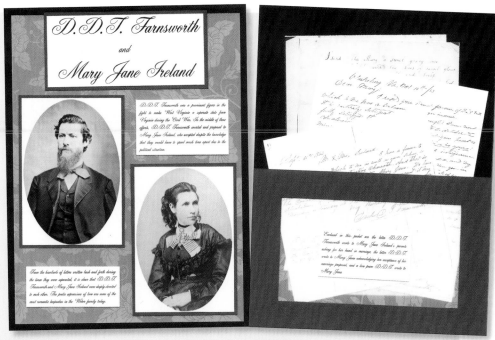

Figure 4. Capture the romantic photographs, memorabilia and stories from your ancestral line in a "Legacy of Love" album. **Supplies** *Patterned vellum:* Frances Meyer; *Computer font:* Quill, Print Shop, Broderbund.

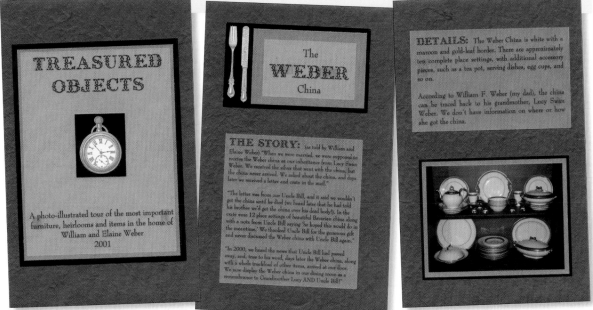

"Treasured Objects" Album

How many times have you walked through your parents' home and wondered why they've kept certain items all these years? Have you ever wondered what the story is behind a particular piece of furniture or art, or how your parents ended up with the family china? A Treasured Objects album is fun from beginning to end, and the finished result will be a valuable record of the most important physical objects your family possesses (Figure 5).

The first step to creating the album is arranging a tour of your parents' (or relative's) home. If you have a video camera or tape recorder, you'll want to bring it along. Ask them to walk you through each room of their house and talk about their decorations, furniture and trinkets—where did they get them, when, and why are the objects meaningful to them? Take pictures of the most meaningful

Figure 5. Create a "Treasured Objects" album about the most important furniture, heirlooms and items in your home, your parents' home, or the home of a close relative. **Supplies** *Handmade paper:* Marco's Paper; *Metallic paper:* NRN Designs; *Vellum:* Paper Cuts; *Computer fonts:* Antique and BernhardMod BT, Print Shop, Broderbund; *Stickers:* The Gifted Line.

objects or the ones that have amusing, touching or particularly historic stories that go along with them. These are the objects you'll want to include in your album.

Once your film is developed, play back your video or audio tape and decide what information to include in your album. Focus on information that makes the objects more emotionally valuable to you or other family members.

You'll be surprised at how many stories, memories and feelings are associated with physical objects in your home. Be sure to capture them for future generations so they can fully appreciate the meaning of the heirlooms they receive.

My Favorite Memories of Growing Up with Elizabeth

Referring to pictures clockwise, starting in the top left corner

1. *Elizabeth was my constant companion.* This is a picture of my first day of kindergarten, and Elizabeth is standing right beside me, holding my hand as I wait for the bus. For some reason, this picture reminded me of the night time ritual we had while living in Ohio. We shared a room, and I used to call out from the top bunk, "Elizabeth?" as we were falling asleep. "Yeah?" she'd always answer. "Nevermind," I'd say, because all I wanted to know was that she was awake with me. For some reason, this was so comforting to me, and I'll never forget the sense of security I felt when I knew she was with me. (Photo was taken in Hudson, Ohio, in 1982)

2. *Elizabeth and I liked to pretend we were twins.* We were felt close enough to be twins! People were always asking us if we were twins, especially in high school, and a few times we said yes just for fun. It wasn't uncommon for me to be raising my hand in a class and have the teacher call out, "Elizabeth?" instead of my name, and the same thing was always happening to her. A lot of our friends would just call us both "Weber" to avoid the difficulty of telling which one we were. This was strange to us, because to us we look pretty different, but we still enjoyed the little game. (Photo was taken in Clearwater, Florida, in 1989)

3. *Elizabeth reminded me to have fun.* I tend to be very reserved and controlled, especially in public, and Elizabeth is exactly my opposite. She is such a free-spirited, energetic person, and I think that's why we got along so well. She was constantly getting me to do crazy, silly things, and I never laughed more than when we were together. (Photo was taken at Clearwater Beach in 1985)

4. *Elizabeth taught me to celebrate other people's victories.* Being only two years apart in age made us a bit competitive with each other. We participated in many of the same activities and usually went to the same school, so growing up with Elizabeth taught me that I can't be the best at everything. In track and cross-country we ran in the same races, and she beat me in every race but one. Seeing her victories reminded me that winning isn't as important as loving, and I learned to be happy for her successes, even when it meant she had "beat" me at something. (Photo was taken in Clearwater, Florida, in 1987)

5. *Elizabeth was quick to forgive.* Being playmates, classmates and teammates gave us plenty of chances to fight with each other. Yet, no matter how nasty I got when Elizabeth and I were fighting, five minutes later she'd be knocking on my door, asking if I wanted to go do something fun. She had no place in her life for holding grudges, and I try to model her forgiving spirit in all I do. (Photo was taken in Hudson, Ohio, in 1983)

6. *Elizabeth kept an eye on me.* Elizabeth is one of the most honest people I know, and if I was doing something she didn't approve of, she never hesitated to let me know. Her straight-to-the-point attitude and watchful eye made me aware that I was setting an example for someone and helped me make good decisions. (Photo was taken in Clearwater, Florida, in 1994)

7. *Elizabeth was my best friend.* And no matter how far apart we are, she always will be. (Photo taken in 1981 at an unknown location)

Figure 6. Your heritage doesn't always come from ancestors and heritage photographs—be sure to capture key aspects of your personal history by using lists and photo collages in a "Favorite Memories" album. **Supplies** *Vellum:* Paper Cuts; *Computer font:* Monotype Corsiva, Microsoft Word.

The best thing about having a sister was that I always had a friend. *Cali Rae Turner*

"Favorite Memories" Album

Your heritage doesn't always come from the ancestors before you; much of your heritage is the life experiences you've had, where you've lived, and what you've accomplished. Capture a portion of your heritage by creating a Favorite Memories album that breaks aspects of your life down into lists and photographs on the topics you choose to include.

For example, one section in your Favorite Memories album could be about the relationships within your family (Figure 6). Choose a favorite photograph to include on the main title page for each relationship, then make a list of your favorite memories with that person. Include a collage of photographs that illustrates your favorite memories (the photographs don't have to show exactly what you're talking about—they can be favorite shots of you with that person), and you've captured important aspects of a relationship that would have otherwise gone unscrapbooked.

Your Favorite Memories album can include endless topics, such as relationships, places, moments, holidays, school days or accomplishments. Remember to stick to a brief list format to keep things simple. It'll be easier to scrapbook your memories if you list your top-ten memories on each topic, then select your favorite photographs that illustrate them.

Are you ready to dig into those piles of heritage photographs? Remember, a guaranteed way to find inspiration in scrapbooking is to look for meaningful connections between yourself and the subjects you're scrapbooking. Those connections will help you capture your heritage in a way you'll enjoy and appreciate in years to come! ♥

"School Marm"
by Mary Larson
Chandler, AZ
SUPPLIES
Patterned paper: Rocky Mountain
Scrapbook Company
Letter and block stickers:
K & Company
Computer font: Americana,
downloaded from the Internet
Photo corners: Canson
Idea to note: Mary included a
color copy of the ledger from the
class of 1914–1915 on her layout.

QUOTABLE QUOTE:

"To find out what one is
fitted to do, and to secure
an opportunity to do it, is
the key to happiness."

—JOHN DEWEY

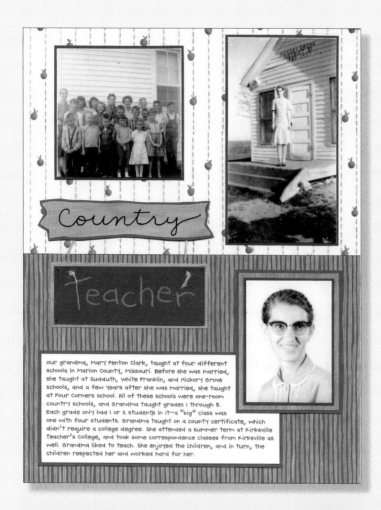

"Country Teacher"
by Janelle Clark
Westerville, OH
SUPPLIES
Patterned papers: Debbie Mumm,
Creative Imaginations (apple);
Keeping Memories Alive (striped)
Wood veneer: Paper Adventures
Computer font: CK Handprint,
"The Best of Creative Lettering" CD
Combo, *Creating Keepsakes*
Colored pencils: Prismacolor, Sanford
Pen: Pigment Liner Calligraphy,
Staedtler, Inc.
Jute: Darice

Our grandma, Mary Fenton Clark, taught at four different schools in Marion County, Missouri. Before she was married, she taught at Sudduth, White Franklin, and Hickory Grove schools, and a few years after she was married, she taught at Four Corners school. All of these schools were one-room country schools, and Grandma taught grades 1 through 8. Each grade only had 1 or 2 students in it—a "big" class was one with four students. Grandma taught on a county certificate, which didn't require a college degree. She attended a summer term at Kirksville Teacher's College, and took some correspondence classes from Kirksville as well. Grandma liked to teach. She enjoyed the children, and in turn, the children respected her and worked hard for her.

"Miss Walker's Class"
by Cheryl McMurray
Cardston, AB, Canada
SUPPLIES
Computer font: Doodle Basic,
"PagePrintables" CD Vol. 1,
Cock-A-Doodle Design, Inc.
Punches: Marvy Uchida (apple),
Darice (heart)
Chalk: Craf-T Products
Pens: Zig Millennium, EK Success;
Milky Gel Roller, Pentel

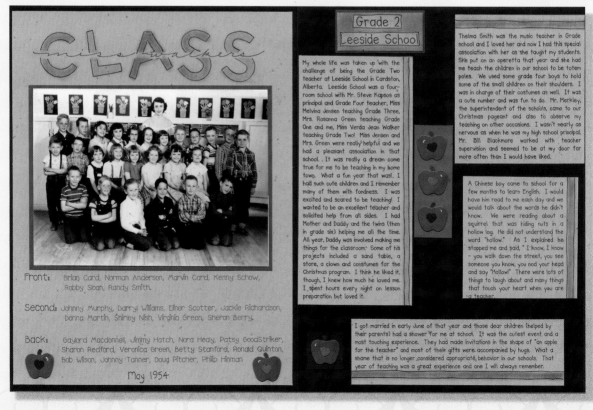

CLASS *Miss Walkers*

Grade 2
Leeside School

Front: Brian Card, Norman Anderson, Marvin Card, Kenny Schow, Robby Sloan, Randy Smith.

Second: Johnny Murphy, Darryl Williams, Elinor Scotter, Jackie Richardson, Donna Martin, Shirley Nish, Virginia Green, Sheron Berry.

Back: Gaylord Macdonnell, Jimmy Hatch, Nora Healy, Patsy GoodStriker, Sharon Redford, Veronica Green, Betty Stanford, Ronald Quinton, Bob Wilson, Johnny Tanner, Doug Pitcher, Philip Hinman

May 1954

My whole life was taken up with the challenge of being the Grade Two teacher at Leeside School in Cardston, Alberta. Leeside School was a four-room school with Mr. Steve Kapsos as principal and Grade Four teacher, Miss Melvina Jensen teaching Grade Three, Mrs. Rosana Green teaching Grade One and me, Miss Verda Jean Walker teaching Grade Two. Miss Jensen and Mrs. Green were really helpful and we had a pleasant association in that school. It was really a dream come true for me to be teaching in my home town. What a fun year that was!. I had such cute children and I remember many of them with fondness. I was excited and scared to be teaching! I wanted to be an excellent teacher and solicited help from all sides. I had Mother and Daddy and the twins (then in grade six) helping me all the time. All year, Daddy was involved making me things for the classroom. Some of his projects included a sand table, a store, a clown and costumes for the Christmas program. I think he liked it, though, I knew how much he loved me. I spent hours every night on lesson preparation but loved it.

Thelma Smith was the music teacher in Grade school and I loved her and now I had this special association with her as she taught my students. She put on an operetta that year and she had me teach the children in our school to be totem poles. We used some grade four boys to hold some of the small children on their shoulders. I was in charge of their costumes as well. It was a cute number and was fun to do. Mr. Merkley, the superintendent of the schools, came to our Christmas pageant and also to observe my teaching on other occasions. I wasn't nearly as nervous as when he was my high school principal. Mr. Bill Blackmore worked with teacher supervision and seemed to be at my door far more often than I would have liked.

A Chinese boy came to school for a few months to learn English. I would have him read to me each day and we would talk about the words he didn't know. We were reading about a squirrel that was hiding nuts in a hollow log. He did not understand the word "hollow." As I explained he stopped me and said, " I know, I know - you walk down the street, you see someone you know, you nod your head and say "Hollow!" There were lots of things to laugh about and many things that touch your heart when you are a teacher.

I got married in early June of that year and those dear children (helped by their parents) had a shower for me at school. It was the cutest event and a most touching experience. They had made invitations in the shape of "an apple for the teacher" and most of their gifts were accompanied by hugs. What a shame that is no longer considered appropriate behavior in our schools. That year of teaching was a great experience and one I will always remember.

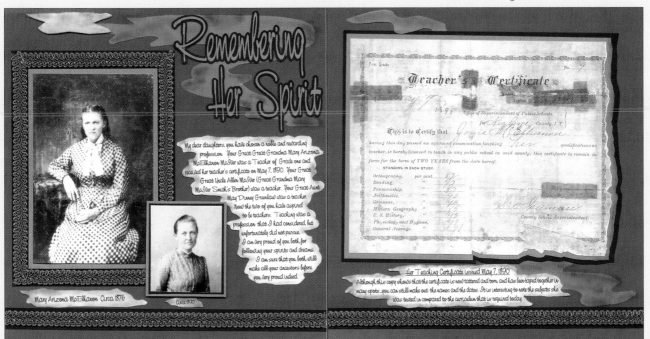

"Remembering Her Spirit"

by Sharon Whitehead
Vernon, BC, Canada
SUPPLIES
Vellum: Paper Adventures
Computer font: NevisonCaseD, Microsoft Word
Chalk: Craf-T Products
Pop dots: All Night Media
Other: Ribbon

"A Teacher and Her Students"

by Anita Matejka
Lincoln, NE
SUPPLIES
Vellum: Paper Adventures
Side borders: Shotz! by Danelle Johnson, Creative Imaginations
Computer fonts: Brush Script and CurcacBlack, packages unknown
Pen: Zig Writer, EK Success

Chalk: Craf-T Products
Pop dots: All Night Media
Ideas to note: Anita used actual pages from her grandmother's school planner to create the background paper. She designed the title using Ulead PhotoImpact, then printed it on vellum.

"Stewart Park Maxwell"
by Nancy Maxwell-Crumb
Whitmore Lake, MI
SUPPLIES
Border stickers: me & my BIG ideas
Computer font: Black Chancery, package
unknown
Army sticker: Creative Memories
Photo corners: Canson

"Brothers Serving the USA"
by Nancy Maxwell-Crumb
Whitmore Lake, MI
SUPPLIES
Computer fonts: Lucida Hand and Verdana,
downloaded from the Internet
USA title: Idea from *Heritage Scrapbooks*
by *Creating Keepsakes*
Map and metals: Downloaded
from the Internet
Photo corners: Canson
Idea to note: Nancy included maps
showing where her father and his
brothers served during World War II.

"U.S. Navy"

by Dayna Gilbert
McMinnville, OR
SUPPLIES
Computer fonts: Gill Sans MT and
Ext Condensed Bold, downloaded
from the Internet
Title: Dayna's own design

Hemp: Darice
Slot punch: Family Treasures
Ideas to note: Dayna braided the
hemp to re-create the patterns
that are shown in the postcard.
She also adapted the idea for her
title from the postcard.

Problem Solving: Memorabilia Collections

❖ ❖ ❖ ❖ ❖

Q: I have a collection of war medals from a family member's service in the U.S. Army. I want to include the medals in my album, but they take up too much space. What should I do with them if I don't put them in my scrapbook?

A: Collections of memorabilia, such as military medals, are valuable heirlooms you'll want to preserve for future generations. The medals may be too big to keep in your album, but you can include reduced color copies (or photographs) of the medals, along with a description of how each was earned. To save space in your scrapbook, slip the color copy behind a layout about his or her military service so the information stays together.

Another option is to create a shadowbox to display the medals, then include a photo of the shadowbox in your scrapbook. This way, the medals will be stored safely, and the information about them will be available in your scrapbook. Not only will the color copies or photographs be an interesting addition to your heritage layouts, they'll also serve as a record of how many medals you inherited in case you need the information for insurance or historical purposes.

"Sawyer's Heroes"

by Janice Clifton
Wilmington, DE

SUPPLIES
Patterned paper: NRN Designs
Mulberry paper: PrintWorks
Computer fonts: CK Single Serif, "The Best of Creative Lettering" CD Combo, *Creating Keepsakes*; Franklin Gothic No. 2, Adobe

Corner punch: Family Treasures
Stickers: Mrs. Grossman's
Photo corners: Canson (gold), Pioneer (clear)
Idea to note: To avoid cropping her original photos, Janice created photo mats to hide the white borders. She also used photo corners so the original prints can be removed.

"A Soldier and Gentleman"

by Kathleen Paneitz
Loveland, CO

SUPPLIES
Patterned paper: The Family Archives
Embossed paper: K & Company
Metallic paper: Paper Adventures
Vellum: Paper Adventures
Mulberry paper: PrintWorks
Computer fonts: Berliner (title), downloaded from the Internet; Doodle Basic, "PagePrintables" CD Vol. 1, Cock-A-Doodle Design, Inc.
Punches: McGill (hole), Family Treasures (oval)
Scissors: Mini-Scallop edge, Fiskars
Pens: Zig Writer, EK Success; Metallic Gelly Roll, Sakura
Watch: Kathleen's own design
Idea to note: To create the chain, Kathleen cut both sides of a strip of cardstock with scallop-edged scissors. Then she punched along the inside of the chain with a hole punch.

"Roosevelt's Tree Army"
by Kerri Bradford
Orem, UT
SUPPLIES
Patterned paper: Scrap-Ease
Vellum: The Paper Company
Computer fonts: Rapier and Nicolas
CocTreg, downloaded from the Internet;
CK Chunky Block, "The Art of Creative
Lettering" CD, *Creating Keepsakes*
Other: Ribbon

"Serving Canada"
by Sharon Whitehead
Vernon, BC, Canada
SUPPLIES
Computer fonts: Mickey (title) and Jungle
Juice (journaling), downloaded from the
Internet
Eyelets: Welkmart
Maple leaf punch: Marvy Uchida
Chalk: Craf-T Products

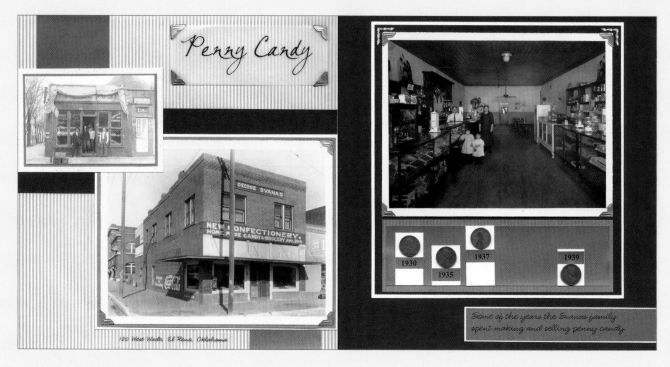

Penny Candy

120 West Wade, El Reno, Oklahoma

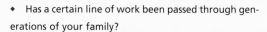
Some of the years the Svanas family spent making and selling penny candy.

"Penny Candy"

by Bettie Cross
Austin, TX
SUPPLIES
Metallic paper: Paper Adventures
Vellum: Paper Adventures
(clear), Pixie Press (striped)
Computer font: CK Bella,

"The Best of Creative Lettering"
CD Vol. 3, *Creating Keepsakes*
Photo corners: Canson
Idea to note: Bettie included
pennies from the 1930s, when
her family sold penny candy, on
her layout.

Journaling Starter:
The Family Business

❖ ❖ ❖ ❖ ❖

The entrepreneurial spirit seems to run in families. In fact, several of the successful businesses we enjoy today may have been started by the ancestors in your heritage photos. Take a moment to consider the career choices of your ancestors and family members, then record this information in your album. Here are a few ideas to get you started:

• Did any of your ancestors start a shop, service or business? What inspired them to do so, where was it located, and is it still there today? If so, have you been to visit it? Is it still owned by your family?

• Do the talents or skills needed to start the business run in the family? Have other family members started successful businesses as well?

• Has a certain line of work been passed through generations of your family?

• Were you ever involved in a family member's occupation as a child? Did you help out at your grandfather's store, or visit your dad's office on a regular basis? How did this affect your choice of careers?

• Do you wish you could be a part of a business or have a certain talent possessed by your ancestors?

As you scrapbook the lives of your ancestors, including their occupations, remember to include information about how that person's choice of career has affected his or her posterity—you'll be surprised at how many connections you can find!

"Dr. William Hale Siler"

by Lee Anne Russell
Brownsville, TN
SUPPLIES
Handmade paper: PrintWorks
Computer font: Harrington, Microsoft Word
Dried ferns: Nature's Pressed
Chalk: Craf-T Products
Fiber: On the Surface Fibers
Brads: American Pin & Fastener
Photo corners: Canson

"Textiles"

by Lisa Baker
Sayre, PA
SUPPLIES
Patterned paper: Amscan
Computer font: Freehand 591 BT and
Charlesworth, Microsoft Word
Letter accents: Pretty ABC,
Hot Off The Press
Antique paper dolls: Dover Publications

Dr. William Hale Siler

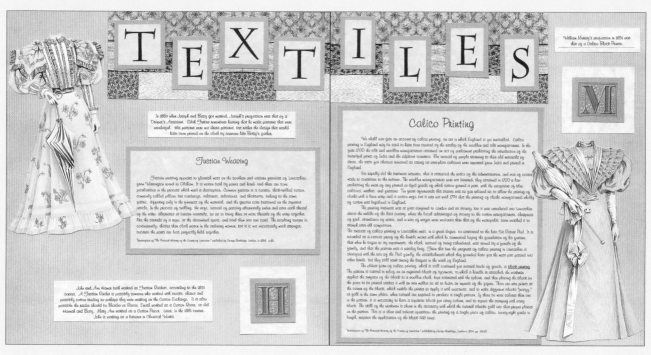

"New York's Finest"
by Anne Heyen
Glendale, NY
SUPPLIES
Vellum: Close To My Heart
Velveteen and metallic paper:
Paper Adventures
Computer fonts: Unknown (title);
CK Italic, "The Art of Creative
Lettering" CD, *Creating Keepsakes*
Letter stickers: Making Memories
Badge on pocket: Downloaded
from the Internet
Silver badge: Anne's own design
Idea to note: Anne included original
log sheets from her father's
logbook on her layout.

"M. J. Grogan II"
by Torrey Miller
Lafayette, CO
SUPPLIES
Patterned paper: Frances Meyer
Computer fonts: Blueprint and PP-HP20's,
packages unknown
Oil derrick: Torrey's own design
Corner punches: CARL Mfg. (corner),
Family Treasures (slot)

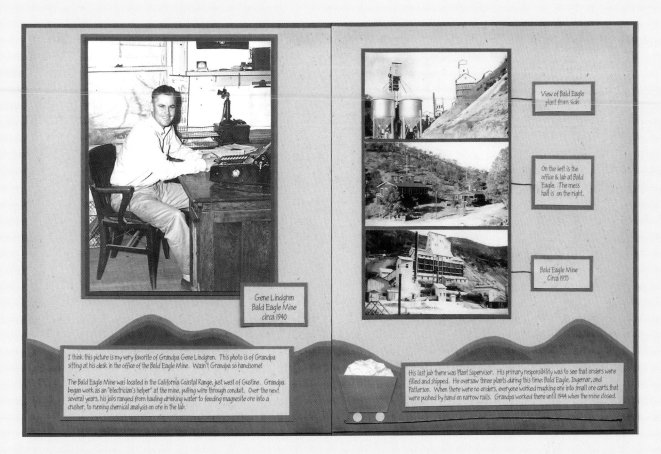

Gene Lindgren
Bald Eagle Mine
circa 1940

View of Bald Eagle plant from side.

On the left is the office & lab at Bald Eagle. The mess hall is on the right.

Bald Eagle Mine Circa 1935

I think this picture is my very favorite of Grandpa Gene Lindgren. This photo is of Grandpa sitting at his desk in the office of the Bald Eagle Mine. Wasn't Grandpa so handsome!

The Bald Eagle Mine was located in the California Coastal Range, just west of Gustine. Grandpa began work as an "electrician's helper" at the mine, pulling wire through conduit. Over the next several years, his jobs ranged from hauling drinking water to feeding magnesite ore into a crusher, to running chemical analysis on ore in the lab.

His last job there was Plant Supervisor. His primary responsibility was to see that orders were filled and shipped. He oversaw three plants during this time: Bald Eagle, Ingemar, and Patterson. When there were no orders, everyone worked mucking ore into small ore carts that were pushed by hand on narrow rails. Grandpa worked there until 1944 when the mine closed.

"Bald Eagle Mine"

by Brenée Williams
Boise, ID
SUPPLIES
Computer font: Source unknown
Craft wire: Artistic Wire Ltd.

Preservation 101: Choosing and Using Inks

Chances are you're creating a heritage album with the hope it will last for future generations to enjoy. If you want to ensure that your work will last through the years, use inks that will also stand the test of time to record information. Here are some guidelines on choosing and using ink in your heritage albums:

❶ Choose pens with permanent ink.

❷ When captioning and journaling important information, use black, permanent ink.

❸ When rubber stamping, seal the ink with clear embossing powder.

❹ Only use copy machines and computer printers that have powder toner or archival properties (you may have to call your printer company to find out if their inks are waterproof, light-fast and permanent).

❺ Don't use pens or markers that leave a bad chemical smell on the paper after the ink has dried.

I Will Never Forget the Day...

BY TERI ANDERSON

6 WAYS TO ADD HISTORICAL PERSPECTIVE TO YOUR PAGES

I will never forget the terrorist attacks on September 11, 2001. After waking up that morning, I turned on the TV and watched, stunned, as the second airliner flew into the World Trade Center. I still remember the overwhelming shock and sadness, and the hope that someone, anyone, would be found alive.

After the attacks, I realized the importance of scrapbooking the history I'd witnessed during my lifetime. I made a list of events, both historical and personal, that have shaped how I view the world around me. Answering the question "Where was I when …?" has given my pages an invaluable historical perspective. It's provided a look into the events that have defined the world for me.

It's not too late to get started on pages that reflect the climate of your world. By recording historical events and the life lessons you and others have learned from them, you'll provide a priceless snapshot of the world you live in—one that has personal meaning for you and your loved ones. Need help getting started? Read on to discover six ways to include a historical perspective in your scrapbook.

1. REFLECT ON A HISTORICAL EVENT.

Ask family members about World War II or the day Neil Armstrong walked on the moon. Ask them what they remember about the event, how old they were when it happened, and how it made them feel. Include their thoughts on a scrapbook page. My mother helped me chronicle my great-grandparents' lives during the Great Depression, painting a personal picture of a significant era in America and in their lives.

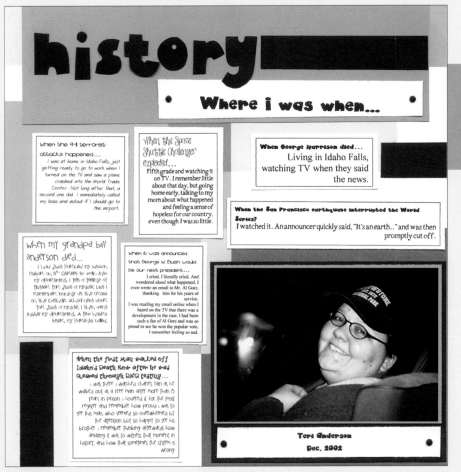

Focus on one event, or showcase several historical events and journal about what you saw and felt on each of those dates.

Page by Teri Anderson. **Supplies** *Patterned paper:* SEI; *Lettering template:* Watermelon, ScrapPagerz.com; *Brads:* Jest Charming; *Computer fonts:* 2Peas Blueberry, 2Peas Fairy Princess, 2Peas Unforgettable, 2Peas Drama Queen, 2Peas Beautiful and 2Peas Cherub, downloaded from *www.two-peasinabucket.com*; CK Print, "The Best of Creative Lettering" CD, *Creating Keepsakes*; CB Wednesday, Chatterbox; Times New Roman, Microsoft Word.

FINDING HISTORICAL INFORMATION

Want to include a bit of history on your pages? The following web sites will help you find historical information for dates that are important to your family.

dMarie
www.dmarie.com/timecap
Want to know what the cost of milk was the year you got married? Who was on TV and who was starring in the movies? This web site features news headlines and pop-culture trivia.

Scrapbook, Scrapbook
www.scrapbookscrapbook.com/dayinhistory/whathappenedwhen.html
Search here by date to get a general list of highlights of a certain day in history.

The History Channel
www.historychannel.com/tdih
Enter your birth date and find out what important historical events happened that day. I entered my mom's birthday and learned that the Cuban Missile Crisis ended on her thirteenth birthday.

On This Day
www.on-this-day.com
Want to know if you share a birthday with a historical figure? Find out by entering your birth date into this web site.

2. RECORD FAMILY MEMBERS' PERSPECTIVES OF A SIGNIFICANT EVENT.

Vanessa Reyes asked her family members to share their perspectives on the San Francisco Bay Area earthquake in 1989 (see below). What historical events has your family experienced? Perhaps you shed tears together when the Challenger space shuttle exploded. Maybe you rejoiced when Elizabeth Smart was found alive and was reunited with her family. Documenting family members' feelings will communicate their personalities and add meaning to your layouts.

Ask family members to share their perspectives on a significant event.

Pages by Vanessa Reyes. **Supplies** *Patterned papers:* American Crafts, Karen Foster Design and Li'l Davis Designs; *Vellum:* Paper Adventures; *Letter stamps:* Hero Arts; *Stamping ink:* StazOn (white), Tsukineko; ColorBox (black), Clearsnap; *Laser die cut:* Keepsakes; *Metal-rimmed tags and eyelet date:* Making Memories; *Beads:* Magic Scraps; *Vintage card:* me & my BIG ideas; *Other:* Pen, brads, ribbon, chalk and jute.

INTERVIEWING FAMILY MEMBERS

I've always marveled at the stories my older relatives tell. I like hearing what they remember about World War II, how our hometown has changed over the years, and what life was like in the 1960s.

Sometimes the most interesting aspects of historical events are the perspectives shared by loved ones. Next time you have the opportunity, sit down with an older relative and ask questions about his or her memories of an important day in history. The questions at right will get you started.

- How old were you when this event happened?
- Where were you living? What was your family life like at the time?
- How did you learn about the event? Who told you? What did he or she say? What went through your mind?
- In your opinion, why did this event happen?
- How did you feel before the event? How did you feel after?
- What did you learn from the event?
- Who did you talk to after the event? What did you talk about?
- Why is this an event people should remember?

3. DOCUMENT A PERSONAL PERSPECTIVE.

Catalina Luna documented the hour-by-hour progression of Hurricane Isabel's path, recording where she was during each hour of the storm (see below). Perhaps you could record the hour-by-hour progression of your wedding day, or your feelings as a loved one underwent surgery.

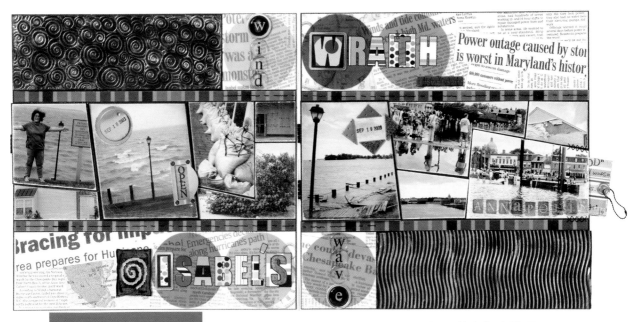

Document the hour-by-hour progression of a historical event.

Pages and photos by Catalina Luna. **Supplies** *Translucent black clouds:* The Paper Company; *Stripes and circle vellum, tags and letter stickers:* SEI; *Page pebbles, metal-rimmed tags, charmed alphabet circles, squares, frames, photo corners, eyelet phrases, clip, metallic eyelets, snaps and beaded chain:* Making Memories; *Square alphabet pebbles and poemstones:* Creative Imaginations; *Cracked glass letter and "Rule of Thumb" stickers and adhesive envelopes:* Sticko by EK Success; *Brass hinges:* Ives Schlage; *Metal sheet:* Paragona; *Letter stamps:* Hero Arts and PSX Design; *Rubber stamp:* Inkadinkadoo; *Embossing ink:* Amaco; *Chalks:* Stampendous!; *Pigment powder:* Perfect Pearls, Ranger Industries; *Pen:* Zig Writer, EK Success; *Other:* Newspaper articles and handmade paper.

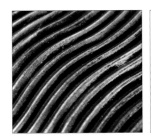

4. REMEMBER A SPECIAL DAY.

Take a special day in your family, such as the day you were married or the day your first child was born, and figure out what else happened on that date in history. What do you remember about those events? Combine the historical information and your feelings about them for a poignant layout.

On a more personal level, remember to record family members' memories and feelings about special days, too. How did your family react when the first grandchild was born? Although it's been 29 years, my Uncle Pat still remembers the joy of signing a Christmas tag "from Uncle Pat" to me.

5. REFLECT ON A WELL-KNOWN PERSON.

A scrapbook page is the perfect place to pay tribute to a notable figure who has personal meaning for you. On her layout below, Lisa Russo chronicled her feelings and thoughts on the day Princess Diana died. Ask your relatives to share their stories about the day President John F. Kennedy was assassinated or the day a sports legend passed away.

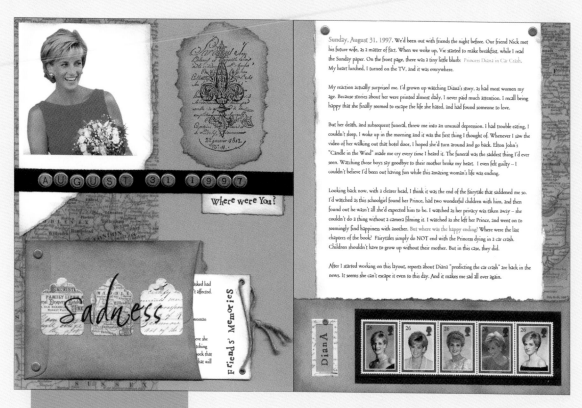

Chronicle your thoughts and feelings about someone special who has passed away.

Pages by Lisa Russo. **Supplies** *Patterned vellum, typewriter key letters, tag and frame:* K & Company; *Letter stickers:* Creative Imaginations; *Rubber stamp:* Stampers Anonymous; *Letter stamps:* Hero Arts; *Stamping inks:* Memories, Stewart Superior Corp.; Ranger Industries; ColorBox, Clearsnap; *Embossing powder:* All Night Media; *Computer font:* Furor Scribendi, downloaded from the Internet; *Commemorative stamps:* Royal Mail Mint; *Snaps:* Making Memories.

Idea to note: For the photo in the upper left, Lisa scanned the image, changed it to grayscale, and printed it on textured cardstock to match the journaling block.

FINDING PHOTOS

Want to scrapbook a page about the explosion of the space shuttle Columbia but don't have any photographs? No problem. The following web sites offer stock photos you can download for free.

Free Stock Photos
www.free-stock-photos.com
Find pictures of former presidents, the Titanic and more.

NASA Newsroom
www1.msfc.nasa.gov/NEWSROOM/photos/photopage.html
Find pictures of space shuttles, outer space and hurricanes.

Memory
www.memory.loc.gov
Find pictures of Alexander Graham Bell, Civil War soldiers and more.

If you can't find relevant photos, create a layout without them. Write a letter about the event, or journal on tags for visual interest. Use color and embellishments to create an appropriate mood.

Where I was

The year was 1996 and Rudy and I were celebrating our first anniversary. We had the entire evening planned out. The best were with their dad and we had reservations to spend a rare night alone at the Alexis Hotel - arguably one of the coolest hotels in town - located just above the waterfront between downtown Seattle and Pioneer Square. Our plans were to eat dinner at The Painted Table a romantic and artsy restaurant adjacent to the hotel, and then head over to Pioneer Square where we would dance the night away. It had been a long and difficult year for us and, though we were clearly in love with each other, there were a handful of times when we both wondered if we had made the right choice. It had taken Rudy much longer than either of us had imagined finding work and, after the honeymoon period when we adored each other's accents, his struggle with the English language was a constant source of frustration for both of us. We seemed to understand each other's hearts, but there were times we had no clue what the other was saying! And though our hearts were always in the right place, there were days when we both wondered if we would make it. So this felt like a huge milestone for us and we were both ready to celebrate!

We had a wonderful dinner at The Painted Table and were a little giddy when we headed hand-in-hand down the street toward Pioneer Square. It was a cool November night but it wasn't raining so we were looking forward to the walk. No more than five minutes later, we could hear a classic rock band playing inside one of the clubs. And then we met Robert. Though he looked much older, we guessed he was in his fifties and for some odd reason, he struck us both as a very kind soul when he asked if we could spare some change. On another evening we might have looked right through him but he was sober and there was something about him that gave us both pause. We told him that we could not give him any money but that, if he was hungry, we would buy him some food. We walked the few blocks with him to a small market and stayed with him as he picked some canned goods off the shelves. Our plan was to pay his bill and then wish him well. But Robert had other plans. He told us there was a Subway restaurant a few blocks away and asked if we could walk with him there to get a sandwich. Maybe it was the contrast between our situations - with him so alone and us so together - that made it difficult for us to say no. But whatever it was, we agreed, figuring we'd get him a sandwich and then be on our way. But again, Robert had other plans.

He was so polite when he asked if we could sit with him while he ate. Who was this guy, anyway? Little did we know, we were about to find out, as five minutes became ten, and then hours passed as he shared his life story with us. And it became more and more clear that it wasn't food that he wanted but company. He told us about mistakes he had made, and places he had been, and about the wife and children he had not seen in years. And right there in the middle of Subway, in between parts of his story, he broke into songs so quiet we had to struggle to hear him. And our hearts went out to him.

when I learned the true meaning of
How can I help?

When Robert finally finished telling his story and it was clearly time to go, he thanked us. And this may be what makes this story so memorable. Because when he thanked us, he said "I really want to thank you. From the bottom of my heart I want to thank you. Not just for the food, but for spending time with me. I'll never forget you." And it's no surprise that we haven't forgotten him either. Because there, at the most unexpected time and place, Rudy and I learned so much about the true meaning of generosity, compassion and love. The streets are a cold and lonely and dangerous place to live. We see it every time we're in the city, but reaching out can be scary, so we typically keep our distance and take the easy way out. Yet that night, feeling safer than we might have felt alone, we learned to look outside ourselves a little bit, and to help simply by being there and listening. Sure, we could have placed some coins in his hand and been done with him, but we were taught over the years not to do that. Nevertheless, it's a tough choice sometimes. This time we put our fears down and connected with him as we might a friend. And maybe it was a lucky break because the time we spent with him was priceless. And now we make a point of connecting in some small way every time we're in the city. Nobody, regardless of circumstance, deserves to be invisible. There's always something we can do, even if it's just making eye contact and sincerely wishing someone well. And there's a payback, too. Because sometimes we find lessons in the most unexpected places, you know? I feel so blessed.

- all photos taken in Pioneer Square in October of 2003 -

An unconventional first anniversary
November 11, 1996 • Pioneer Square • Seattle

Memorialize an event that changed your perspective on life.

Pages by Maya Opavska. **Supplies** *Textured cardstock:* Bazzill Basics; *Rubber stamps:* Art Impressions; *Stamping ink:* Stampin' Up!; *Pen:* Pigma Micron, Sakura; *Computer fonts:* Tomthumb (title), downloaded from the Internet; 2Peas Squish (journaling), downloaded from *www.two-peasinabucket.com; Snaps and eyelets:* Making Memories; *Elastic:* 7 Gypsies.

Ideas to note: Maya used the character-spacing feature in a word processing program to stretch the title and subtitle to fit the space. The middle photo at the top of the right-hand page is the top photo in a two-sided fanfold book that Maya designed herself.

---

6. RECALL AN EVENT THAT CHANGED HOW YOU THINK OR FEEL.

Maya Opavska created the layout above to capture the day she learned the true meaning of the question "How can I help?" Her layout recalls her unconventional first anniversary, which she and her husband spent listening to a homeless man named Robert tell them about his life. The conversation taught Maya the importance of connecting with other people. What historical and personal events have changed how you think or feel?

History happens all around us every day. By sharing your memories of these events, you can make history come alive for your children and grandchildren. You can teach them that history is more than just a day in a book—it's something real that affects real people. What's more, you can provide insight into what's meaningful to you and those around you.

Your perspectives will be an invaluable gift for generations to come.

Editor's note: Founding editor Lisa Bearnson was so inspired by this idea that she did her own page on the topic. See her layout on page 181.

days we'll never forget

Record where you were when major events happened

MARCH 12, 2003 was a day I'll never forget. Until that day, I'd been traumatized by the shocking news that nine months earlier Elizabeth Smart had been taken at gunpoint from her home in Salt Lake City, Utah. That was only 40 minutes from my home!

Most of us had given up hope that Elizabeth was still alive. Still, her family kept their faith and in March police found Elizabeth walking down a busy street in a Salt Lake City suburb. I was at a business lunch when my husband called with the good news, and I started jumping up and down and screaming. What a happy, happy day!

April 6, 1979 was another day I'll never forget. I was in junior high and wondered why my mother had unexpectedly checked me out of school early. When I got in the car, Mom told me that my beloved Grandma Downs had passed away just hours earlier. I cried and cried and thought my heart would break.

Where were you when you heard about the terrorist attacks on 9/11? When you experienced a natural disaster? When you went into labor?

During a crop in Idaho Falls, Idaho, last summer, I saw Teri Anderson's "Where I Was When" layout (see page 176). I loved the idea so much that I presented it to our editorial staff, and we decided to publish an entire article on the concept. What a unique way to record those snippets of time we think we'll remember forever. By creating a "Where I Was When . . ." layout, you'll help others—and you—remember those important and often sacred moments forever.

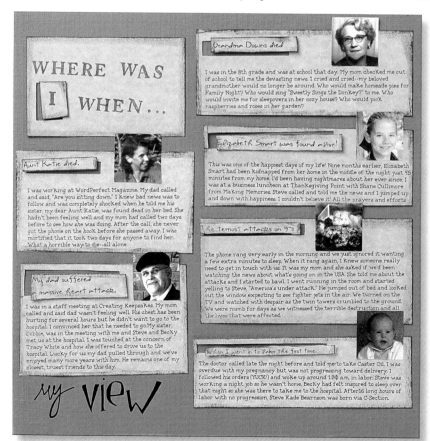

Page by Lisa Bearnson. **Supplies** *Alphabet stamps:* Rubber Stampede; *Stamping ink:* Stampin' Up; *Computer fonts:* CK Sloppy and CK Keystroke, Becky Higgins' "Creative Clips & Fonts" CD, *Creating Keepsakes; Word rub-ons:* Simply Stated, Making Memories.

Lisa

making the
connection

Where did you get that **Red** hair?

If my two beautiful red-haired daughters had a dime for every time they got asked that question, they would be millionaires! It is a legitimate question since both parents and their brother have decidedly ordinary brown hair. However, a closer inspection of the family tree reveals a few more "chestnut-haired beauties"!

AUNT JOYLYNN
(DAD'S SISTER)

GREAT AUNT PAT
(MOM'S AUNT)

AUNT CINDY
(MOM'S SISTER)

UNCLE FLINN
(MOM'S BROTHER)

DORIS ISABELLE ELLIOTT
HUCKINS
1902-1996
GREAT-GRANDMOTHER

LAURA LEISHMAN
CHRISTENSEN
1891-1987
GREAT-GRANDMOTHER

MARTHA SOPHIA PRICE
FAGG
1884-1966
GREAT-GRANDMOTHER

QUOTABLE QUOTE:

"A family without a storyteller or two has no way to make sense out of their past and no way to get a sense of themselves."

—FRANK PITTMAN

"Red Hair"
by Darcy Christensen
Tucson, AZ
SUPPLIES
Vellum: Paper Adventures
Computer fonts: Goudy (journaling) and Copperplate (tags), Microsoft Word
Lettering template: Blocky, Provo Craft
Tags: Darcy's own designs
Craft wire: Darice
Chalk: Craf-T Products
Embroidery floss: DMC
Photo corners: Canson

"Pamela Cordes Kopka"

by Pamela Kopka
New Galilee, PA

SUPPLIES

Patterned paper: Paper Patch
(dark brown), source unknown
(floral lace)
Computer font: Commercial Script
BT, package unknown
Embroidery floss: DMC

"She Got My Cheeks"

by Denise Pauley
La Palma, CA

SUPPLIES

Vellum: The Paper Company
Computer fonts: Emmascript, Adobe
Systems; Garamouche, downloaded
from the Internet
Hole punch: Fiskars
Chalk: Craf-T Products
Flowers: Denise's own designs

Though taken during different
seasons, in different decades, these
pictures reveal an aspect of Erin's
appearance that she definitely
inherited from me – chubby cheeks!
(I could never tease her about being
plump during her babyhood,
because…well, just look at me!)
Other similarities that you can't see
in our pictures (hers taken when she
was about four months and mine at a
year old, sitting on Grandma's lap)
are our stubborn streaks, silly sides, a
love of laughter, food, sleep,
shopping and books…Erin is
absolutely her mother's daughter!

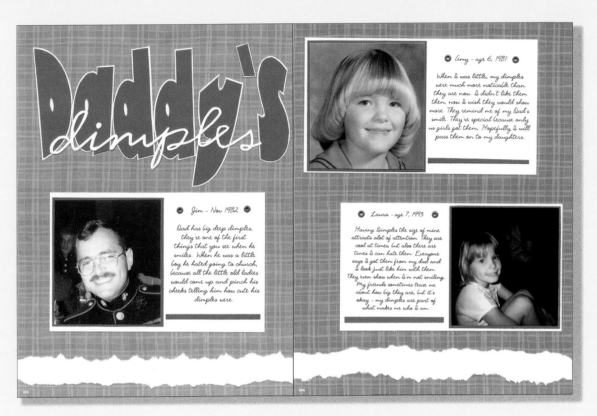

"Daddy's Dimples"

by Amy Grendell
Silverdale, WA
SUPPLIES
Patterned paper: Keeping
Memories Alive
Computer font: Doodle Super

Fat, "PagePrintables" CD Vol. 2,
Cock-A-Doodle Design, Inc.;
Scrap Script, "Lettering
Delights" CD Vol. 2, Inspire
Graphics
Eyelets: Impress Rubber Stamps

Journaling Starter:
What We Have in Common

❖ ❖ ❖ ❖ ❖

Looking at black-and-white photos of our ancestors taken long ago makes it easy to fall into the trap of thinking we couldn't possibly have anything in common with them. After all, they lived without the Internet, microwaves and cell phones! But, you'd be surprised at how many things you *do* have in common. Consider the following questions and start a running list of commonalities you share with your ancestors:

◆ What physical characteristics have been passed down through your family? Does red hair run in your family, or curly hair, or dimples, or double-jointed thumbs? How far back can you trace the trait?

◆ Do you see glimpses of your mother or father, grandmother or grandfather in your own children?

Have certain phrases been passed down through your family, or do you catch yourself "sounding like your mother"?

◆ What personality traits have been passed through the generations? Is your family a bunch of comedians, are they extremely shy, or do they have a soft spot in their heart for animals?

◆ What talents and abilities do family members share? Is your family famous for its artistic ability, or did several members study the same field in college?

Making generational connections like these will add meaning to your heritage album. Plus, future generations will love discovering where their freckles and love for reading came from!

"What's in a Name?"
by Allison Strine
Atlanta, GA
SUPPLIES
Corrugated paper: DMD Industries
Computer font: Mordred, downloaded
from the Internet
Pen: Milky Gel Roller, Pentel
Other: Wire
Idea to note: To add a Celtic touch to
the layout, Allison created a Celtic
Teardrop design with wire. She found
the design at *www. wigjig.com.*

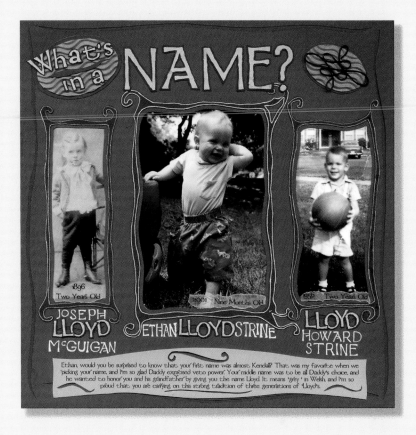

"Sharing the Name . . . Brina"
by Brenée Williams
Boise, ID
SUPPLIES
Patterned paper: The Robin's Nest Press
Vellum and velvet paper: Paper
Adventures
Computer font: Source unknown
Other: Ribbon and heart studs

"Our Heritage of Humor"
by Laura Bowden
Cedar Falls, IA
SUPPLIES
Computer fonts: Currency (title) and Castellar, One Scrappy Site; Garamond (subtitles), Microsoft Word
Medallion stickers: me & my BIG ideas
Pen: Zig Writer, EK Success
Chalk: Craf-T Products
Embroidery floss: DMC
Laser-cut accent: Scherenschnitte Designs
Eyelets: Dritz
Other: Brads

Accent Idea: Monograms

❖ ❖ ❖ ❖

The sophisticated, classic look of a monogram makes it a perfect accent for heritage pages. Just think of the monogrammed handkerchiefs, towels, pillowcases and shirt pockets you used to see at your grandmother's house!

You can find ideas for creating monograms in clothing catalogs, at printing stores or on the Internet. Simply type "monogram ideas" into any search engine, then browse the different monograms it pulls up. Monograms are so versatile, you can sketch them by hand (see our Monogram Alphabet on page 282) or create them using a computer font, rubber stamps or alphabet stickers.

An Introduction

Dad's mom died before I was born, but although I never knew her, I've always felt an affinity for her. I grew up hearing stories about her, the things she appreciated in life, and the way she raised my dad. As I've grown older, I've come to appreciate the tidbits I do know about her and the pieces of herself she left behind. This layout is a collection of some of those pieces that are most meaningful to me.

Music

My childhood memories involve a lot of classical music, and I have come to discover that my dad's love for classical music came from his mother. Helen had a great appreciation for classical artists, such as Bach and Mozart, and every time I play classical music I think not only of my dad, but also of his mother, who taught him to appreciate this art.

Moments

I always take it as a sincere compliment when Dad tells me I remind him of his mother. I remember walking to church one Sunday while Dad was visiting me at college. We walked past a store window, and I snuck a glance at the window to check my appearance. When I turned back, my dad was staring at me. He said, "You just made the same face my mother used to make when she looked at herself in the mirror." Unaware that I had made a face, I asked what it looked like. "Scrutinizing and almost critical," he replied. "She always liked things to be perfect, including her appearance." At moments like these, I can only hope that pieces of Helen live on in her son's daughter, and that my children will also continue to benefit from the legacies she has left.

Photographs

I don't have many photographs of Helen, but we have always had a very serious portrait of her hanging up in our home. One summer when I was home from college, I came across Dad's boxes of photos and items from his childhood. In the box I found several pictures of Helen I had never seen before. One quickly became my favorite, as it shows her radiance and happiness very vividly. Now when I think of Helen, the serious portrait I used to picture in my mind has been replaced by this sophisticated yet joyous snapshot.

Mary Helen Lawson Weber

Letters

In addition to the letters my dad wrote home from military school and college, which reveal much about his relationship with his mom, I received a special letter during a church activity that I have treasured ever since. Although it wasn't written directly by Helen, it contains much information that my dad wanted me to know about his mother. As a young teenager, I admired Helen because of the things I had learned in this letter.

My Dearest Catherine:

I was born on December 30, 1907, to George Franklin Lawson and Lottie Lawson Farnsworth Lawson, in Ravenswood, West Virginia. You have never met me in this life, but I know you once. You know me better as Helen Weber, your father's mother.

I am a small town girl. I grew up in small towns in West Virginia, Missouri and Texas. There is a story in the family that I first saw your grandfather at Rehoboth Beach, Delaware, and fell in love with his legs. Actually, there was a lot more about your grandfather to fall in love with besides his legs!

I want to tell you a little bit about me, and some of the important things in my life. First, I loved children. I gave birth to your father three years after we were married. I almost died in the process. But I had another two children—your Aunt Diana and your Uncle Charles. Our family was the most important thing in the world to me. Even though your father was a very difficult child!

All of my learning and studies were devoted to raising my children. Although I enrolled in schools, colleges and universities, wherever we lived, to further educate myself, it was always secondary to raising my family. I finally earned my college degree in the 1950s.

I was especially interested in learning and children all of my life, and I tried to make games for my children to play so they might be excited by all the amazing and beautiful things in this world—poetry, art, music, beautiful writing, nature—so many exciting things around us all the time. Sunsets, the sound of gentle rain, the ocean, puffy clouds, a field of wheat rippling in the wind. You know many of these things. I know you love them too.

Poetry

Each of the children in our family received when we were little a book of poems written by Helen. As a young child (and an avid reader), I tried to read the poems but found them very difficult to understand. Now that I am older, I have come to understand and love the poetry Helen wrote and published. Through her poetry I can feel her love for God, nature, her family, music, and life.

"Mary Helen Lawson Weber"
by Catherine Scott
Salt Lake City, UT
SUPPLIES
Handmade paper: The Natural Paper Co.
Computer font: Calligraph421 BT, WordPerfect
Border sticker: Class-A-Peels, Mark Enterprises

Embroidery was one of my favorite things to do with Grandma Zimmerman. She would rummage through her fabrics until she found just the right scrap for me to stitch. Then I would watch with anticipation as she ironed on the pattern I had carefully selected. After finding the perfect color of thread, we would sit side-by-side in the chair by the window and embroider. I don't remember a lot of conversation, I just remember how much fun it was to be together -- just Grandma and me. I wish she was still here so I could thank her for never being too busy to spend time with me. I felt very loved.

The photo on this page is the only one I have of just Grandma and me. It was taken on our farm in North Dakota, in 1953, when I was five years old and Grandma was 74.

Grandma gave me her little sewing scissors. The time we spent together must have been special to her too. The scissors remind me to not be too busy to spend time with my own children. Thank you Grandma.

The background is a collage of some of Grandma's iron-on transfers. She mail ordered them from Dakota Farmer magazine.

Thank You Grandma
for teaching me how to embroider

"Grandma's Scissors"

by Julie Turner
Gilbert, AZ
SUPPLIES
Computer font: Garamouche, package unknown; CK Primary, "The Art of Creative lettering" CD, *Creating Keepsakes*
Ribbon: Midori

Embroidery floss: DMC
Other: Buttons, scissors and needle
Idea to note: To create the background paper, Julie used her grandmother's vintage iron-on embroidery transfers to design a collage.

"Great-grandma's Sewing Machine"

by Leslie Watkins
Mesa, AZ
SUPPLIES
Patterned paper: Hot Off The Press
Computer fonts: CK Wedding and CK Cursive,

"The Best of Creative Lettering" CD Vol. 2, *Creating Keepsakes*
Photo corners: Canson
Poem: Downloaded from the Internet
Other: Buttons

Great Grandma's Sewing Machine

Our family quilt was started generations in the past. Designed with love, it's patterns rich in values that will last. Each person sews another square of memories that endure. While challenges add strength that makes our family life secure. And stitching it together- threads of closeness, warmth, and caring Make it cozy and more comforting with every year of sharing.

Clara Elizabeth Harkey
Born 1884   Married 12 Dec 1912 to Edgar William Stauden Jr.   Died

"It's Time"

by Jyl Read

American Fork, UT

SUPPLIES

Patterned paper: Hot Off The Press (brown)
Lettering stencil: Lil' Buster, D.J. Inkers
Computer font: Bernhard, WordPerfect
Clock and hand arrows: Jyl's own designs
Circle punch: Family Treasures

Colored pencils: Memory Pencils, EK Success
Idea to note: Jyl created background paper using various fonts downloaded from the Internet. The background paper reads "Tempus Fugit," which is a latin phrase meaning "Time Flies." This phrase was on the face of many of the clocks in the house Jyl grew up in.

Page Idea: Timeline Pages

❖ ❖ ❖ ❖ ❖

We all remember timelines from history class, but they're sure a lot more fun when you're designing your own to use on scrapbook pages! Timelines are a terrific option for including information in an interesting, useful way. Here are some fun ways to use timelines on your pages:

♦ Create a timeline of the major events in a family's (or ancestor's) life to use as a title page for an album.

♦ Plot the events directly before and after the birth of an ancestor on a timeline.

♦ Merge personal, historic and fun information onto the same timeline to give the big picture of what the world was like during a certain time period.

♦ Make a fun timeline of the events that happened in two ancestors' lives up to the point when they met and got married (you could scrapbook the events in the woman's life on the top of the timeline, and the events in the man's life below the timeline).

♦ Compare your life to an ancestor's by marking the kinds of activities and responsibilities you had at certain ages.

"This Little Piggy"

by Carolyn Gray
Shawnee, KS
SUPPLIES
Patterned paper: Keeping Memories Alive
(green plaid), Imaginations! (flower)
Lettering template: Chunky Block, Provo Craft
Computer font: Apple Chancery,
Microsoft Word
Piggy bank: Adapted idea from a die cut,
source unknown
Chalk: Craf-T Products
Pen: Creative Memories

When Darlene was a child during the Second World War, her brother Earl Burwell was in the army. While he was stationed in Italy, he bought presents for his mother and young sisters. He sent Darlene a piggy bank with red flowers, Dolores a piggy bank with brown spots, and his mother a packet of silk handkerchiefs. In September 2000, Darlene gave the piggy bank to her grandson Aaron. He loves the bank and calls it his World War II souvenir.

"Grandma's China"

by Brenée Williams
Boise, ID
SUPPLIES
Velvet paper: Paper Adventures
Vellum: Paper Cuts
Computer font: Unknown
Ribbon: Offray

This plate is part of
the set of China that now is
displayed on my dining room shelf.
Grandma and Grandpa gave the china
to me after Kelly and I were married.

Grandma and Grandpa Lindgren
bought this set of china in San
Francisco on their wedding
day in 1934.

Grandma Twin & Grandpa Gene decided to elope to get married in San Francisco. They borrowed Grandma's father's car and drove to S.F. to be married by a Justice of the Peace. They didn't know at the time that Grandpa's sister Ida and her boyfriend Tommy had also decided to elope on the very same day in Porterville, CA! These photos were actually taken before Grandma and Grandpa were married. They were both in their early 20's at the time.

"The Bread of Life"
by Jennifer Urich
Tempe, AZ

SUPPLIES

Patterned paper: Making Memories
Vellum: The Paper Company
Mulberry paper: PSX Design
Computer font: CK Calligraphy,
"The Best of Creative Lettering" CD
Vol. 1, *Creating Keepsakes*
Punches: EK Success (hole),
The Punch Bunch (corner)
Pen: Pigma Micron, Sakura
Corner template: Nouveau Corner
Designs, Design A Card

"Priceless Treasure"
by Taunya Dismond
Lee's Summit, MO

SUPPLIES

Specialty paper: Solum World Paper
Computer fonts: Brandy's Hand and Adorable,
downloaded from the Internet
Jute: Darice
Chalk: Craf-T Products
Photo corners: Canson
Memorabilia pocket: Creative Memories
Other: Dried leaves
Idea to note: To safely preserve the fragile bill,
Taunya placed it in a memorabilia pocket.

The Apron

I gaze at my modern kitchen, appliances by the score,
stand in every corner, but nary a one as handy

AS THE APRON THAT GRANDMA WORE

Huge, made of sturdy cotton, drab colored so spots would not show,
Held secure by a waistband, and tied with a ribbon and bow.
The best multipurpose appliance the world would ever know.

A supporter for the toddlers first steps, a hider for childish fears.
A wrapper on chilly evenings, a remover of childish tears.
A basket for every collection – grain, eggs or baby chicks.
The flowers for the mantel, cobs, kindling or buffalo chips.
The vegetables from the garden or sweet corn from the field.
A protector from hot pans or dishes, at the stove a good heat shield.

A communication signal to the workers on the farm.
To say that it is meal time, or to carry an alarm.

A driver of foul from the garden or flies from an opening door.
The dust from the parlor table, or crumbs to the kitchen floor.
A curtain for shadeless windows, a frost guard for tender plants.
A cradle for sleeping babies, a tanner for impish scamps.
These are some of the uses of that implement of yore, that best
of all types of equipment ---- the apron that Grandma wore.

So I gaze at my modern kitchen, a gadget for every chore, and
ADMIT that they are not as convenient as that apron that Grandma wore.

"The Apron"
by Chris Holmer
Elmwood Park, IL
SUPPLIES
Patterned paper: Susan Branch, Colorbök
(pink stripe), Minigraphics (green floral)
Stickers: Susan Branch, Colorbök
Computer fonts: CK Leafy Capitals (title),
"The Art of Creative Lettering" CD and
CK Journaling (journaling), "The Best
of Creative Lettering" CD Vol. 2,
Creating Keepsakes
Poem: Downloaded from the Internet

"Randall Family Farm"
by Shannon Wolz
Salt Lake City, UT
SUPPLIES
Patterned paper: Colors By Design
Mulberry paper: Black Ink
Computer font: Unknown
Other: Ribbon

Journaling Starter:
Stream-of-Consciousness Writing

❖ ❖ ❖ ❖

Do you ever look at a photograph, start journaling and find yourself "wandering" from the facts? Instead of erasing what you've written, recognize that you're actually utilizing a very helpful process: stream-of-consciousness writing. Stream of consciousness simply means that one thought logically leads to the next, which leads to the next, and soon you've got a whole paragraph of thoughts that are connected in different ways!

Shannon Wolz, of Salt Lake City, Utah, used this writing technique on her layout "Randall Family Farm." Notice how she begins talking about the little girl's grumpy face in the photograph, then mentions that the little girl is a flower girl for a dance. That information leads to the fact that the little girl's mother was in charge of the ball because she was president of a women's organization. Already there is much more information in the journaling than there would have been had Shannon limited herself to just the date and event.

Next time you're journaling and realize your thoughts have strayed, don't erase your work! Polish it up and put it on your page—future generations will thank you for it!

WHEN HER FIRST DAUGHTER,
MARGARET, WAS BORN
ELIZABETH GUTEKUNST MADE A
BEAUTIFUL EMBROIDERED
BABY BLANKET FOR THE CARRIAGE.
YEARS LATER WHEN MARGARET
AND WALTER BROWN HAD THEIR
SONS, WALLY AND BILL, THEY
USED THE SAME BLANKET. BY THE
TIME WALLY AND HIS WIFE, PAM,
HAD THEIR DAUGHTERS, LISA
AND MELISSA, THE BLANKET WAS
TOO FRAGILE TO USE BUT IT
REMAINS A TREASURED HEIRLOOM.

"Baby Blanket"
by Lisa Brown
Berkeley, CA
SUPPLIES
Patterned paper: K & Company
Vellum: PrintWorks
Rubber stamp: Rubber Baby Buggy Bumpers
Stamping ink: Source unknown
Pen: Zig Writer, EK Success
Lettering idea: Lisa's own design

"Legacy in the Lilacs"
by Noralee Peterson
Orem, UT
SUPPLIES
Patterned paper: I Design Greetings, Inc.
Vellum: Paper Adventures
Mulberry paper: PrintWorks
Title and dress: Noralee's own designs
Computer font: CK Script, "The Best of Creative
Lettering" CD Vol. 1, *Creating Keepsakes*
Clothes hanger: Provo Craft
Lace stickers: Mrs. Grossman's
Flower punch: EK Success
Chalk: Craf-T Products
Pen: The Ultimate Gel Pen, American Crafts
Idea to note: Noralee used a vellum copy of her
black-and-white photo to make the
picture look faint, "like a memory."

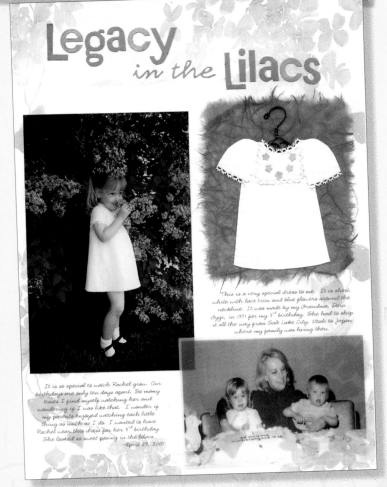

"Unspoken Words of Wisdom"
by Lisa Brown
Berkeley, CA
SUPPLIES
Vellum: Paper Adventures
Lettering template: Script, ScrapPagerz.com
Pens: Zig Writer, EK Success
Eyelets: Impress Rubber Stamps

"Great-grandma's Words of Yiddish Wisdom"
by Allison Landy
Phoenix, AZ
SUPPLIES
Vellum: Paper Adventures
Computer fonts: Unknown

Pens: Zig Writer, EK Success
Punches: McGill (star), Fiskars (hole)
Pop dots: All Night Media
Other: Silver studs

Nana's philosophy of life at age 90...

"Take what you got... and do the best you can with it!"

August 25, 2001

Dear Alisha Ann Kallunki,

    I tell you that you are my favorite and most precious granddaughter and you say that it is because you are my only granddaughter! Alisha you are precious to us all. Precious to your Mom and Dad, precious to your Grandmother and Grandfather Kallunki, to us, Grandmother and Grandfather Wilde, to Austin and to your Heavenly Father. Remember, you are a child of God.

    In these pictures Alisha, you are 7 years old. Your Grandmother, Gladys Judd Wilde is 90 — soon to be 91. The last year or so she keeps saying this statement: "Take what you got and do the best you can with it".

    The doily is from my mom's (Sabrina Cropper Ekins) sewing basket. Sabrina is your great grandmother who died in 1961. If she could speak to you Alisha, she would tell you to always look for the good or the positive in others, don't dwell on the negative. She always (always means very often) taught us as children to "Love one another" and we do!

    The hat is mine Alisha. I am Margaret Ekins Wilde, your mother's mother and I am 57 years old. Four months after you were born, in May of 1994, I was diagnosed with breast cancer. The drugs I took to kill the cancer left me without hair for 5 or 6 months so I got used to having a hat around. They are fun aren't they? You have always liked to try them on and wear them. As your Grandmother my message to you would come from the Book of Mormon, Helaman 5:12 —

    "And now, my daughter Alisha, remember, remember that it is upon the rock of our Redeemer, who is Christ, the Son of God, that you must build your foundation; that when the devil shall send forth his mighty winds, yea, his shafts in the whirlwind, yea, when all his hail and his mighty storm shall beat upon you, it shall have no power over you to drag you down to the gulf of misery and endless woe, because of the rock upon which ye are built, which is a sure foundation, a foundation whereon if men (and women) build they cannot fall."

    Alisha, remember who you are, where you are going and who you have always been. All your Grandmother's love you! You are precious to us!

"Grandmother's Legacies"

by Lisa Kallunki and Margaret Wilde
Orem, UT
SUPPLIES
Patterned papers: Frances Meyer,
Northern Spy, Scrappy Cat and Daisy D's
Vellum: The Paper Company

Computer font: Scrap Sister, "Lettering
Delights" CD Vol. 2, Inspire Graphics
Punches: McGill (micro and hole),
Family Treasures (daisy)
Other: Crocheted doily and crochet thread

Preservation 101:
Choosing and Using Adhesives

❖ ❖ ❖ ❖ ❖

While collecting supplies for your heritage album, be sure to select an adhesive that's safe to use with your valuable photos and memorabilia. The following tips will help you choose the right product and give you guidelines for using it in your album:

❶ Choose an adhesive that dries clear and doesn't have a strong odor.

❷ Use only as much adhesive as you need (this is generally a very small amount).

❸ For mounting photographs with tape, tape runner or squares, use a ¼" piece on the top and bottom of the photo.

❹ Never use glue or tape on valuable paper documents or on fiber-based black-and-white photographs. Use mounting corners or a corner-slot punch instead.

❺ Mount newspaper articles with a water-soluble glue stick, using only a dab in each corner.

❻ *Never* use magnetic albums.

❼ Make color copies of any photographs before trying to remove them from acidic or unsafe albums.

❽ Don't use adhesive labels to label the backs of photographs.

"Born in a Barn"

by Marsha Hudson
Seattle, WA
SUPPLIES
Vellum: Paper Adventures
Lettering template: Log
Cabin, ABC Tracers, Pebbles
for EK Success

Computer font: Gaze, down-
loaded from the Internet
Jute: Darice
Photo corners: Canson
Pen: Zig Writer, EK Success

"Fathers and Sons"

by Therese Boyd
Merriam, KS
SUPPLIES
Patterned paper: The Family Archives
Computer font: Tempus Sans, Microsoft Word
Stickers: me & my BIG ideas
Brads: American Pin & Fastener
Thread: On the Surface Fibers
Circle punch: Family Treasures

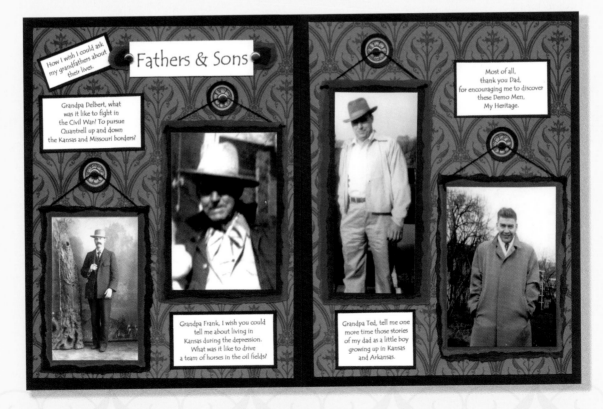

"Great-grandma"

by Heather Murray
Newbury Park, CA
SUPPLIES
Patterned paper: Pixie Press
Computer fonts: Kunstler Script (title)
and Garamond (journaling
and poem), Microsoft Word
Corner punch: Emagination Crafts

Accent Idea:
Store Bags and Boxes

❖   ❖   ❖   ❖   ❖

While sorting through items you've inherited from family members, take a look at what they're stored in. Many vintage store bags, boxes (such as hat boxes) and wrappings (like tissue paper) have designs that can be easily replicated on your scrapbook pages, giving you page accents that will perfectly match the time period you're scrapbooking.

Since the vintage look is back in vogue, many present-day store logos, bags, boxes and wrappings are a great source of ideas as well. Whether a men's suit store wraps its shirts in tissue paper and seals them with a monogrammed sticker, or the shopping bag at your favorite women's store uses the classic color combination of navy and off white, these items are sure to give you endless inspiration. Remember to keep your eyes open at all times for ideas to incorporate onto your pages, and jot them down in a notebook or sketchbook.

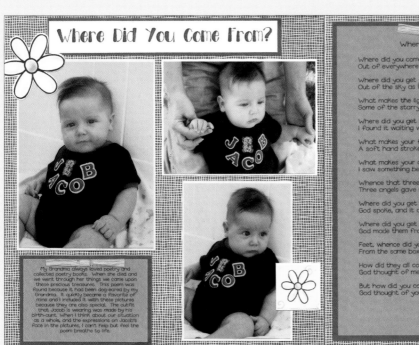

Where Did You Come From?

Where Did You Come From?

Where did you come from, Baby Dear?
Out of everywhere into here.

Where did you get your eyes so blue?
Out of the sky as I came through.

What makes the light in them sparkle and spin?
Some of the starry spikes left in.

Where did you get that little tear?
I found it waiting when I got here.

What makes your forehead so smooth and high?
A soft hand stroked it as I went by.

What makes your cheek like a warm white rose?
I saw something better than anyone knows.

Whence that three-corner'd smile of bliss?
Three angels gave me at once a kiss.

Where did you get this pearly ear?
God spoke, and it came out to hear.

Where did you get those arms and hands?
God made them from hooks and bands.

Feet, whence did you come you darling things?
From the same box as the cherub's wings.

How did they all come just to be you?
God thought of me, and so I grew.

But how did you come to us, you dear?
God thought of you, and so I am here.

-George MacDonald

My Grandma always loved poetry and collected poetry books. When she died and we went through her things we came upon these precious treasures. This poem was found because it had been dog-eared by my Grandma. It quickly became a favorite of mine and I included it with these pictures because they are also special. The outfit that Jacob is wearing was made by his birth-aunt. When I think about our situation as a whole, and the expressions on Jacob's face in the pictures, I can't help but feel the poem breathe to life.

"Where Did You Come From?"

by Emily Magleby
Springville, UT

SUPPLIES
Patterned paper: Provo Craft
Vellum: Paper Adventures
Computer fonts: CK Primary,

"The Art of Creative Lettering"
CD, *Creating Keepsakes*
Flowers: "The Art of Creative
Lettering" CD, *Creating
Keepsakes*
Other: Raffia

Journaling Starter:
Connecting the Generations

❖ ❖ ❖ ❖ ❖

How do you relate to past generations in your family? Have you had personal experiences that have helped you connect with relatives you never had the chance to meet? Recording your thoughts about ancestors of the past, even if you never knew them, can add meaning and insight to your albums. Consider the following questions to help you determine how you "connect" with your ancestors:

◆ Have you heard stories about ancestors that intrigued you or motivated you to look for more information?

◆ Have certain heirlooms or family items made you feel an affinity for a certain ancestor or relative?

◆ Have you drawn connections between your life and the life of an ancestor or family member?

◆ Have you made important decisions based on knowledge you have about an ancestor?

◆ Have you learned a new skill or talent because of the influence of a family member or a story about an ancestor?

◆ Have you grown to understand more about an ancestor as your life has progressed?

◆ Have you wished you could ask an ancestor for advice on a particular topic?

Consider including this information in your journaling. The personal connections you make will be of interest to future generations, and just may help someone in the future connect with you!

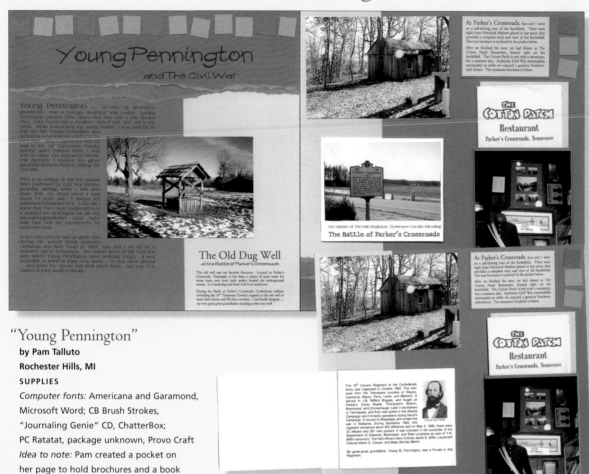

"Young Pennington"
by Pam Talluto
Rochester Hills, MI
SUPPLIES
Computer fonts: Americana and Garamond,
Microsoft Word; CB Brush Strokes,
"Journaling Genie" CD, ChatterBox;
PC Ratatat, package unknown, Provo Craft
Idea to note: Pam created a pocket on
her page to hold brochures and a book
to display additional information.

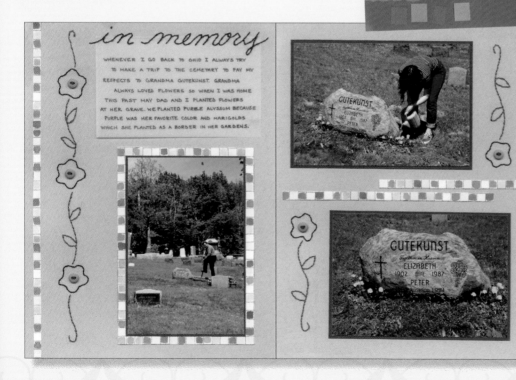

"In Memory"
by Lisa Brown
Berkeley, CA
SUPPLIES
Patterned paper:
Kathy Davis
Pen: Zig Writer,
EK Success
Embroidery floss: DMC
Buttons: Hillcreek Designs
Flowers and vines:
Lisa's own designs

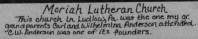

Moriah Lutheran Church
This church in Ludlow, Pa. was the one my gr. grandparents Carl and Wilhelmina Anderson attended. C.W. Anderson was one of its founders.

Dear Ancestor

Your tombstone stands among the rest;
Neglected and alone.
The name and date are chiseled out
On polished, marbled stone.
It reaches out to all who care
It is too late to mourn.
You did not know that I exist
You died and I was born.
Yet each of us are cells of you
In flesh, in blood, in bone.
Our blood contracts and beats a pulse
Entirely not our own.
Dear Ancestor, the place you filled
One hundred years ago
Spreads out among the ones you left
Who would have loved you so.
I wonder if you lived and loved,
I wonder if you knew
That someday I would find this spot,
And come to visit you.

"Finding Family"
by Gina Chesnes
Mt. Morris, NY
SUPPLIES
Vellum: Paper Adventures
Computer font: CK Italic, "The Art of Creative Lettering" CD, *Creating Keepsakes*
Pen: Gel Roller, Marvy Uchida
Poem: Downloaded from *www.dmarie.com*

I have been researching our family tree since high school. On this day, we all went to Warren and Ludlow to look for more information and visit the gravesites. At St. Joseph's, we found my gr. gr. grandparents Philip and Angelica Cappelletti and their son Angelo. His wife Rima was in another cemetery because she wasn't Catholic. In the Ludlow cemetery, we found my Anderson gr. grandparents - Carl and Wilhelmina. We also found a mystery stone - 2 little boys - Henry and Herbert. I think they are my grandmother's brothers who died before she was born. Hopefully I'll get back there again to do more research.

Journaling Starter:
Desire to Know

❖ ❖ ❖ ❖ ❖

Has heritage scrapbooking sparked a desire to find out as much as you can about your family's heritage? Has genealogy turned from a pastime into a passion? While you're creating your heritage scrapbooks, don't forget to document your efforts, travels, phone calls, and other information-gathering processes for others to learn from later. Your passion for family history will be an inspiration to others—and you'll have a fun documentation of a rewarding hobby!

"Ties That Bind"

by Amy Grendell
Silverdale, WA
SUPPLIES
Patterned paper: Colors By Design
Vellum: Paper Adventures
Computer font: Pristina,

downloaded from the Internet
Heart: Amy's own design
Chalk: Craf-T Products
Craft wire: Darice
Title: Downloaded from www.twopeasinabucket.com

"The Legend of Hannah Duston"

by Amy Williams
Old Town, ME
SUPPLIES
Patterned paper: Pages in a Snap, Karen Foster Design
Computer fonts: PC Wacky, package unknown, Provo Craft;

CK Journaling, "The Best of Creative Lettering" CD Vol. 2, *Creating Keepsakes*
Chalks: Craf-T Products
"A+" accent: Amy's own design
Other: Twine

My Great-Grandmother, Elizabeth Katharine Gutekunst, has always been my hero and always will be. Ever since I can remember my family would pile into our car after church on Sunday and make the forty-five minute drive out to Grandma G's farm in Leroy Township. Missy and I would spend the day playing with Grandma and helping Mom and Dad with chores when needed. We loved playing with Grandma because she loved playing with us. I wanted to be just like Grandma. She knew how to do everything wonderfully, from baking cookies to growing flowers. I even decided that my favorite color was purple because it was Grandma's favorite.

When I was in fourth grade Grandma came to live with us. I was really excited at first because I thought it was going to be a lot of fun to be able to play with Grandma all the time, not just on Sunday. Things didn't work out like I thought, however. Grandma was very sick so instead of playing, Missy and I helped Mom take care of her. Eventually Grandma had to go to the hospital where she passed away in the spring of 1987. I was absolutely devastated. I didn't go to school for a week and kept having dreams that Grandma was really alive, just someplace else for a while. Time passed and I grew to accepted her death, but I have always kept her close to my heart.

As I have become an adult my view of Grandma has grown. Not only do I see the amazing playmate of my youth, but I can also see the incredible woman she was. I've come to look back at Grandma's life in amazement. What kind of woman dares to leave behind her homeland for a distant country in hopes of a better future? What kind of woman has the fortitude to raise two children during the great depression? What kind of woman can keep her farm running while her husband is away working in the city? What kind of woman can carry on through severe health problems, such as epilepsy and several diagnoses of cancer? What kind of woman not only turns the other cheek, but gives of herself to those who have wronged her? The answer is a rare woman with the strength and courage of my Great-Grandmother. Her life was full of hardships, but no matter what misfortune befell her or how horribly people treated her, she never had anything but a smile on her face and a good word for all. I have never met anyone with such a giving heart. Now, even more than as a child, she is my role model. If I can even be half the woman my Great-Grandmother was, I will consider myself very successful in life.

Grandma
IS ALWAYS WITH ME...

...AS I Create

Grandma G was always busy making something. Her hands were never idle. One of her favorite things was to bake. Everything she made tasted wonderful, but her cinnamon rolls were legendary. When she wasn't baking you could be sure to find her crocheting. She made everything from afghans to pot holders. My favorite, however, were the little slippers, that Grandma would make for us to wear when we were at the farm. Every year she would take a piece of paper and trace our feet to use as a pattern for the bottom of the booties. Then she'd let Missy and I pick out what color yarn we wanted. My favorite were a purple pair she made me with little tassles.

Like Grandma I really enjoy making things. I may use an electric mixer and measuring cups instead of "eyeballing it", but the end result is the same–if you put a bit of love in it tastes great. I also love arts and crafts even though I don't crochet. I like to do needlework and sew like Grandma and I have a needlework that Grandma G. made for her daughter (my Grandmother) in 1929 hanging in my living room. My favorite craft, however, is working on my scrapbooks. Creative scrapbooking wasn't really around during her lifetime, but I know that she would have loved doing it because like all of her other pastimes, it is a labor of love.

As a little girl in Eastern Europe just after the turn of the century, Grandma G did not have a lot of educational opportunity. After she finished basic education her family needed her to help in their fields. One time Grandma's schoolteacher held her after class to work on writing the number three (she was writing it backwards) only to be punished when she came home for being late. I think that difficulties she experienced as a youngster made her realize the importance of nurturing children. Grandma G always had as much time to spend with me as I wanted. She spent countless hours playing with Missy and me. When I learned to read and was quite proud to show off my new skill, Grandma would sit with me as I read stories to her, correcting me as needed. One of my proudest days was when I came home from fourth grade with my report card and showed it to Grandma. She was bedridden by this time and very weak, but not too weak to tell me how proud she was of me. She made me feel like I could do anything.

When I packed up to go to Duke University in the fall of 1995 I made sure that I brought Grandma's desk-calendar. Ever since, I have always placed the calendar in the place I work, whether it be my dormitory desk, summer job cubicles, or more recently, my grad school office. Not only is it a beautiful antique, it also serves as a little reminder of the faith Grandma had in me.

...AS I Learn

...AS I Grow

One of the most striking features about Grandma G's farm was her amazing gardens. She didn't just have a green thumb, she had a green hand. She grew everything from vegetables to flowers and even had a huge number of various types of berry bushes. As a child I loved watching her make barren ground come to life as winter passed into spring each year. She even let Missy and I "help" her garden and sometimes she would let us make our own bouquets to take home with us.

Despite spending the previous five years in dormitories and apartments my desire to help things grow was still strong. As I was moving into my new apartment I spied a triangular patch of land covered with weeds in front of the building. After receiving permission from my landlord I transformed the little piece of land into a vibrant herb garden. Following Grandma's advice I even put in a border of marigolds (which she termed "stinky flowers") to keep the bugs away. I can't leave my apartment anymore without stopping by my little garden just to check out what new buds or leaves have appeared. I think that Grandma would approve.

One of the reasons that Grandma G's house was so fun to visit was because she had so many knick knacks and treasures for Missy and I to look at and (if we were careful) play with. The best part was her jewelry. Grandma had tons of costume jewelry and best of all she had clip on earrings. This made playing dress up so much fun. Missy and I would pin pieces of fabric together to make beautiful gowns. The "gowns" together with the jewelry made quite a statement. Dad used to refer to us as the little fruit fairies when we dressed up. Once we were in our full regalia Grandma, Missy, and I would have tea parties with Kool-Aid and Grandma's homemade cookies.

Before Grandma passed away she gave Missy and I her jewelry. Being costume jewelry isn't worth much money, but it has infinite value to us. When I graduated from high school I wore Grandma's white faux mother of pearl earrings as a tribute to her and I hope to wear them again when I get married someday. Grandma also gave Missy and I a lot of her knick knacks which I have scattered here and there around my apartment. When Dad helped me move into my apartment before he went back to Ohio he told me, "You know, Grandma would have really liked that you have made her treasures such a part of your daily life. It would have been really special to her."

...AS I **Dream**

...AS I **Live**

As a baby I loved to be rocked to sleep. No one was more obliging than Grandma G. She had a big rocking recliner in the corner of her living room and she would "rocker me to sleep" as she called it. As we grew older Missy and I got to sleep over at Grandma G's farm on special occasions. Nothing could have been more fun. We could stay up late playing with Grandma and in the morning we got to eat sugar cereal, which was strictly forbidden at home. The best part, however, was that at night Grandma would let us sleep with her in her huge feather bed and tell us stories. Grandma's bed wasn't just for sleeping, however. It was a prime place for jumping, pillow fighting, and wrestling with Missy and sometimes even our cousins, Kathy and Karen.

After Grandma passed away, my family inherited her bedroom set, which was later passed on to me. When I decided to go to graduate school in California, Dad and I somehow managed to fit the bed and two dressers in his van. Every night as I fall asleep in her old bed, I know that my Grandma is looking down on me wishing me sweet dreams and watching over me as I sleep.

"Grandma Is ..."
by Lisa Brown
Berkeley, CA
SUPPLIES
Mulberry paper: PrintWorks
Lettering template: Brush Stencil, The C-Thru Ruler Co.
Pen: The Ultimate Gel Pen, American Crafts

Journaling Idea:
A Note to the Future

❖ ❖ ❖ ❖ ❖

With all the work you've put into scrapbooking your heritage, you'll want to make sure that the album communicates your purpose and hopes for the future. When you reach the end of the album, consider closing with a personal letter or statement of your hopes and desires for the album. Here are a few things to consider mentioning:

- How you came to possess the photographs and items included in the album
- How long it took you to complete the album
- Who the album was created for—whether it's as specific as a certain relative or your own children, or as general as your posterity or community
- Why you started the album in the first place
- Any fun, touching or humorous experiences you had while creating the album
- Your hopes for the people who will be enjoying the album in years to come
- Your wishes for the future

A current picture of yourself included with this letter to the future will add the perfect finishing touch!

Dear Hailey,

As I am putting together this page about my third birthday, I am thinking about you. Your third birthday was the last birthday you celebrated and with your fourth one just around the corner, I'm thinking about how big you are getting! I'm also thinking about what a great kid you are and how fun it is to have you as a daughter. On this "occasion" of birthdays past and present, I thought I'd write out three birthday wishes that I have for you.

I wish:

*that you'll always look forward to your birthday with the excitement that you feel now (and not worry about getting older.)

*that you'll take pleasure in small blessings-like the wonder you find in the sights (and smells!) of tiny plastic dolls!

*that when you blow out your candles, you do it with all your heart, mess up someone's hairdo even, and never (ever!) worry about how you look!

This picture is a family favourite. We always said that it looked like Grandma was holding her hairdo from being blown away from my huge birthday blow!

Love Mom

I remember being so excited over this little doll in the plastic case. It was so cute and the case had pictures on the back of it that I found very interesting. I remember the smell of "new doll plastic" when I opened it. That is a smell that still evokes happiness for me and brings back lots of memories.

(Nov. 17, 1967)

"Janet Turns 3"

by Janet MacLeod
Dundas, ON, Canada

SUPPLIES
Clay: Creative Paperclay Co., Inc.
Lettering template: Block, ABC Tracers, Pebbles for EK Success
Computer fonts: Whipper Basic and Holly Edwards Bliss, packages unknown; CK Handprint, "The Best of Creative Lettering" CD Combo, *Creating Keepsakes*
Punches: McGill (mini flower), NanKong (jumbo flower), Marvy Uchida (hole)
Cake: Janet's own design
Paint: Delta Technical Coatings
Stickers: Making Memories
Pen: Pigma Micron, Sakura

Preservation 101:
Choosing an Album

❖   ❖   ❖   ❖   ❖

You've no doubt spent countless hours scrapbooking your heritage photos and memorabilia. Make sure they're safe for generations to come with these storage guidelines:

❶ Choose sheet protectors made of polyester, polypropylene or polyethylene—not vinyl or acetate.

❷ Select a binder made with acid-free board, glue and covering. If you use three-ring binders, look for one with heavy-duty rings.

❸ Make sure your binder has a slipcase to ensure your one-of-a-kind photographs are stored in the dark and are protected from dust and acid in the air.

No matter what kind of album style you choose, keep it away from eating and drinking areas. By following these guidelines, you'll help ensure your hard work isn't destroyed by harmful chemicals and acids.

This picture was taken on Grandma's parents' wedding day.

William Montgomery
and
Helen Collins

September 22, 1930
Norwalk, Connecticut

"William Montgomery and Helen Collins"

by Sue Schneider
Farmington, CT
SUPPLIES
Patterned paper and bow: Anna Griffin
Vellum: Paper Adventures
Computer font: Sheer Beauty, downloaded from the Internet
Beads: Bead It by Nicole
Craft wire: Artistic Wire Ltd.
Other: Brads

Dear Hailey and Morgan,

Remember how we go to the Sugar Bush every year before all the snow melts, to see maple syrup being made and to take walks through the woods? Well, when Mom was a little girl, she used to go on trips to the sugar bush, too! In this picture she is standing next to the place where they would put fresh snow and then pour out hot maple syrup to make "Taffy on Snow." I remember loving these trips to the woods in the last snow of winter. I hope you girls always love going, too!

Love Mom

1968

LAST SNOW

"Last Snow"
by Janet MacLeod
Dundas, ON, Canada
S U P P L I E S
Patterned paper: Debbie Mumm, Creative Imaginations
Charms: Impress Rubber Stamps
Stickers: Debbie Mumm, Creative Imaginations
Computer font: CK Handprint, "The Best of Creative Lettering" CD Combo, *Creating Keepsakes*
Craft wire: Westrim Crafts
Chalk: Craf-T Products

"Precious Picture"
by Anita Matejka
Bakersfield, CA
S U P P L I E S
Patterned paper and embossed vellum: K & Company
Letter stickers: K & Company; David Walker (on tags), Colorbök
Computer font: Hans Hand, downloaded from the Internet
Fibers: Source unknown
Metal-rimmed tags: Avery Dennison
Buttons: Favorite Findings

"A Grandmother's Gift"

by Teresa Snyder
Orem, UT
SUPPLIES
Vellum: Close To My Heart
Computer font: CK Sketch,

"The Art of Creative Lettering"
CD, *Creating Keepsakes*
Embroidery floss: DMC
Chalk: Craf-T Products
Other: Buttons

Journaling Ideas: Helpful Hindsight
by Denise Pauley

My mother-in-law (who would probably kill me if she knew I was talking about her in the context of "heritage" layouts) loves to travel. A couple of times each year, she embarks with her friends on an excursion to Europe, sets sail on a cruise, or even heads across the country on a road trip. Because of this, I was thrilled to discover some photos of her as a teenager taking one of her very first trips with friends … was this the journey that started it all?

One of the most wonderful aspects of scrapbooking heritage photos is that you have hindsight. There's so much more to write when you find a photo of a great-great-grandmother who has the same, lopsided smile as you; a long-lost relative holding an heirloom that was passed down to your family; or a grandfather playing baseball … holding the bat just like your son does!

Whenever you're journaling on heritage pages, try to make connections. See if there's an aspect that links past to present, present to future. In many cases, you may not have much more information for a photo than a name and date. But including details that uncover family ties and trans-generational traits can help give your writing much more depth and texture.

Take advantage of hindsight when journaling on heritage layouts. *Page by Denise Pauley.* **Supplies** *Vellum:* Paper Adventures; *Patterned papers:* Carolee's Creations (dark brown); Paper Pizazz, Hot Off The Press (compass and globe); *Gold paper:* Books by Hand; *Computer font:* Garamouche, Impress Rubber Stamps; *Alphabet stamps:* Good Alphabet, Hero Arts; *Stamping ink:* Dauber Duos, Tsukineko; *Tag:* Hot Off The Press; *Twine:* The Robin's Nest; *Eyelet and brad:* American Pin & Fastener.

"Jordana"

by Darcy Christensen
Tucson, AZ

SUPPLIES

Patterned paper: Anna Griffin
Vellum: Colorbök
Computer fonts: Garamond and
Academy Engraved, Microsoft Word
Charms: Source unknown
Ribbon: C.M Offray & Son
Photo corners: Canson

"Love-Ai"

by G-Marie Miyata
Shoreline, WA

SUPPLIES

Patterned paper: Scrap-Ease
Vellum: Paper Adventures
Computer font: Tempus Sans ITC,
Microsoft Word
Metallic rub-ons: Provo Craft
Chalk: Craf-T Products
Cherry blossoms: G-Marie's own designs
Ideas to note: To create the cherry blos-
soms, G-Marie crumpled cardstock, then
tore and rolled the edges. To create the
Kanji character, G-Marie did traditional
Sumi-e brushwork on rice paper, then
copied the image onto vellum. Then she
copied a letter from Japan onto an
overhead transparency and layered it
behind the Kanji character.

"Center Stage"

by Lynne Montgomery
Gilbert, AZ
SUPPLIES
Patterned paper: Source unknown
Glitter: Mark Enterprises
Computer font: Unknown
Double-stick adhesive: Wonder Tape,
Suze Weinberg
Other: Buttons

"Home Sweet Home"

by Cheri Thieleke
Ames, IA
SUPPLIES
Patterned paper: Anna Griffin
Vellum: Bazzill Basics
Flower and frame die cuts: K &
Company
Laser die cuts: Deluxe Cuts
Buggy clip art: Downloaded from
oldfashionclipart.com
Computer font: Unknown, "Print

Shop Premier Edition 5.0" CD,
Broderbund
Chalk: Craf-T Products
Grass punch: McGill
Embroidery floss: DMC
Ideas to note: Cheri used a needle-
work stitch to create the illusion of
photo corners on the mat, echoing
the gingerbread trim on her great-
grandparents' home.

BY JULIA COURT

Preserving the Past

Often, we're so busy looking to the future—to where we'll be and what we'll do—that we forget to think about the past. Just the other day, I was cleaning out a little-used closet when I discovered a sealed box. Inside was a picture of my grandfather, whittling a piece of wood as my grandmother embroidered nearby.

The moment I saw the picture, I remembered my family's visit each summer, and how Grandma taught me to put up peaches and Grandpa beat me at marbles. Times seemed simpler then, and I knew that I was part of something larger, something real.

Creating a heritage layout is a great way to feel that same connection. Here, talented scrapbookers show the lovely ways they've preserved the past on their pages. Note the special touches that help rekindle the memories. →

Rekindle the memories

FAMILY TIES

❖━━━◆❖◆━━━❖

by Lori Houk
Lawrence, KS

SUPPLIES
Patterned paper: Anna Griffin
Computer fonts: Birmingham ("Family"), down-
loaded from the Internet; CK Cursive ("Ties")
and CK Bella (journaling), "The Best of
Creative Lettering" CD, *Creating Keepsakes*
Other: Ribbon and twine

THE "OLDER" KIDS

❖━━━◆❖◆━━━❖

by Alannah Jurgensmeyer
Rogers, AR

SUPPLIES
Patterned paper: Solum World Papers
Punches: All Night Media (negative
pieces from "Baroque" punch,
Emagination Crafts (grape leaf)
Leaf die cuts: Gina Bear, Ltd.
Computer fonts: CK Anything Goes
(title), "The Best of Creative
Lettering" CD Combo, *Creating
Keepsakes*; Diskus Dmed (journaling),
Corel Draw
Colored pencils: Prismacolor, Sanford
Chalk: Stampin' Up!
Idea to note: Alannah scanned the
photographer's description on
the back of the photograph, then
printed it on cardstock so she could
include it on her layout.

NATURAL POSE

— ❖ —

by Shimelle Laine
Stanford-le-Hope, Essex, England

SUPPLIES
Leaf punch: The Punch Bunch
Pen: Zig Writer, EK Success
Lettering: Inspired by Becky Higgins'
Crooked Classic alphabet,
The Art of Creative Lettering
(Creating Keepsakes Books)
Torn frame: Technique by Heidi Swapp
(see step-by-step instructions on page 38)

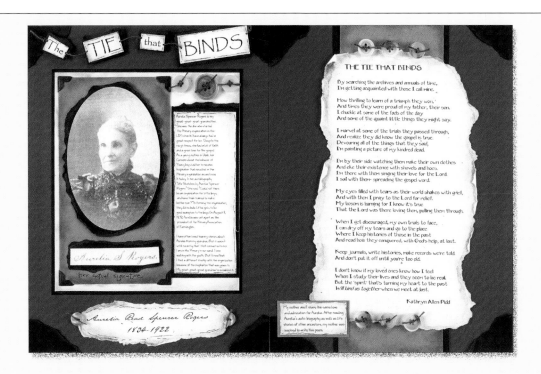

THE TIE THAT BINDS

— ❖ —

by Eva Flake
Mesa, AZ

SUPPLIES
Photo corners: Canson
Computer fonts: Papyrus (title),
Microsoft Word; Texas Hero
(name), downloaded from the
Internet; DJ Classic (poem),
"Super Fontastic!" CD, D.J. Inkers;
CK Penman (journaling), "The
Best of Creative Lettering" CD
Vol.3, *Creating Keepsakes*
Pen: Zig Writer, EK Success
Pop dots: All Night Media
Chalk: Craf-T Products
Other: Buttons and twine

SNOWDEN

by Nicole Keller
Rio Hondo, TX

SUPPLIES
Computer fonts: CK Script (journaling),
"The Best of Creative Lettering" CD,
Creating Keepsakes; Moonpie a la mode
(title), Emerald City Fontworks
Leaf punch: Emagination Crafts
Pen: Pigma Micron, Sakura
Photo corners: Deluxecraft
Charms: Boutique Trims
Chalk: Craf-T Products
Pop dots: All Night Media
Other: Organza ribbon

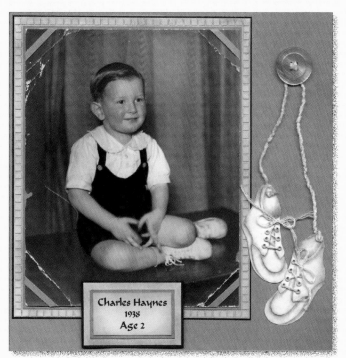

CHARLES HAYNES

by Lee Anne Russell
Brownsville, TN

SUPPLIES
Computer font: Calligrapher,
Microsoft Word
Grommets: Impress Rubber Stamps
Square punch: Family Treasures
Pop dots: All Night Media
Chalk: Craf-T Products
Fiber: On the Surface
Embroidery floss: DMC
Other: Button
Ideas to note: The paper-pieced shoes
were inspired by a Creative Memories
sticker. Lee Anne chalked them with
black and brown chalk to create a
scuffed look. ♥

circa 1931 Grandma Opal and her twin sister in the family orchard.

THE TWINS

by Julie Turner
Gilbert, AZ

SUPPLIES
Background paper: Shabby Shades and handmade paper by Memory Lane
Stamping ink: VersaColor, Tsukineko; Clear Emboss It, Ranger Industries
Clear embossing powder: Gary M. Burlin and Company
White ultra-thick embossing enamel: Suze Weinberg
Flower punch: All Night Media
Pen: Gel X-Treme, Y & C
Chalk: Craf-T Products
Crochet thread: DMC
Other: Pearls
Note: The techniques on this page are part of a class Julie teaches at Memory Lane in Mesa, Arizona.

STEP BY STEP

1 For the top portion, select a handmade paper with an embossed flower pattern.

2 Lightly rub the surface of the paper with a yellow ink pad (or chalk) to highlight the flowers.

3 For the bottom portion, create texture on yellow cardstock by heat embossing clear and white embossing powders over a clear embossing ink. A similar effect can be achieved by lightly splattering the surface with white paint.

4 Punch small flowers, curl the petals up a bit, lightly chalk the center of each with yellow chalk, then tie the flowers to your page with crochet thread and small pearls.

5 Get a duplicate photo made. Prepunch holes in your paper, then sew a frame around your photo with the same type of thread and pearls used for the flowers.

BETTY JANE

by Kris Stanger
St. George, UT

SUPPLIES
Floral patterned paper: Colors By Design
Computer font for title: Dauphin, Microsoft Word
Pen: Pigma Micron, Sakura
Beads: Mill Hill

"The Parlour"
by Violet Burgess
The Family Archives
Mission, British Columbia, Canada

SUPPLIES

Flower and filigree die cuts: The Family Archives
Patterned paper: The Family Archives
Scissors: Scallop edge, Fiskars
Gold paint pen: Hybrid, Pentel
Lettering: Violet got the idea for her title
from the Raphael font in Adobe Photoshop 5.
Idea to note: Violet ripped a piece of black
cardstock to create the antique look on her layout.

Great Aunt Kate and Uncle Jake. Their girls from left to right... Sarah Ann & Jessie.

The Parlour

Charlotte, Dennis & Jim with Pete's Chevy.

"Pete's Chevy"
by Laurie Carley
Centralia, Washington

SUPPLIES

Patterned paper: NRN Designs
Scissors: Deckle edge, Fiskars
Photo corners: Stamp by Stamp Craft
Computer font: DJ Serif,
Dazzle Daze, D.J. Inkers

"Fitzgerald Family Heritage"
by Jana Francis
Provo, Utah

SUPPLIES

Pressed flowers:
Distinctions in Nature
Patterned paper: Frances Meyer
Velvet paper: DMD Industries
Pens: Zig Writers, EK Success
Colored pencil:
Prismacolor, Sanford

Fitzgerald Family Heritage
LaDawn, Scott, Edna 1941

"Kent and Linda Scott"
by Jodi Olson
Kaysville, Utah
SUPPLIES
Leaf punch: Family Treasures
Pen: Milky Gel Roller, Pentel

"Neill and Nell Patterson"
by Carol Banks
Newhall, California
SUPPLIES
Laser-cut frame: Simply Scherenschnitte, Accu-Cut Systems
Punches: Family Treasures (small maple leaf);
McGill (mini maple leaf)
Chalk (on bow): Craf-T Products
Idea to note: Carol made the vines by following the
instructions in the "Playful Paper Wisps" article in
the May/June 1999 issue of *Creating Keepsakes*.

"Clint and Lona Hayes"
by Pam Talluto
Rochester Hills, Michigan
SUPPLIES
Scissors: Deckle edge, Fiskars
Computer font: DJ Fancy, Fontastic!, D.J. Inkers
Pens: Tombow
Paper-lace border: D.O.T.S.
Lettering template: Block, Pebble Tracers, Pebbles in my Pocket
Idea to note: Pam sewed actual buttons on her layout.

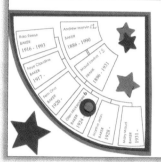

Glen McKendree Baker, born September 13, 1924 in Sullivan, Missouri. Glen was the fourth child in a family of six (one brother and four sisters). His mother died when he was only six and Glen spent the rest of his youth in foster homes in Missouri, as did his other siblings. He enlisted in the Navy when he was 17 and served in W.W.II doing aircraft maintenance. Glen married Charlotte Marie Reid on April 4, 1945 and had six children (two boys and four girls). He left the Navy in 1945 and in 1948 enlisted in the AirForce. While in the USAF, Glen served in the Korean War and the Vietnam War. On June 1st, 1972, he retired as a Master Sergeant and settled in Dixon, Missouri on a farm with several acres of land.

St. Louis, Missouri ·1945·

Glen's first suit after the Navy.

·Charlotte Marie & Glen McKendree·

·St. Louis· 1944

Glen Baker, 1944
Naval Petty Officer First Class
Aircraft Maintenance
SanDiego, CA

"Glen McKendree Baker"

by Alycia Alvarez
Jacksonville, North Carolina
SUPPLIES
Computer fonts: CK Fill In, "The Best of Creative Lettering" CD Vol. 1, *Creating Keepsakes* (title); CAC Camelot, Create-A-Card (journaling)
Punches: Family Treasures (large star and circle); Marvy Uchida (small star)
Colored pencils: Memory Pencils, EK Success
Pen: Zig Millennium, EK Success
Hole punch: Punchline, McGill
Other: Alycia scanned the large photo of Glen into her computer and printed it on Kodak Ink Jet paper.
Idea to note: Alycia included a portion of the genealogy chart on her layout, marking Glen's lineage.

"Room for Rent"

by Linda Milligan
El Paso, Texas
SUPPLIES
Photo corners: Moments
Scissors: Stamp, Ripple and Victorian edges, Fiskars
Pens: Micron Pigma, Sakura; Le Plume II, Marvy Uchida
Colored pencils: Prismacolor, Sanford
Plastic photo-mounting sleeve (on wedding proposal): Creative Memories
Flowers and fence: Linda's own designs
Idea to note: Linda used pressed flowers on her layout.

ROOM FOR RENT

∞Lulu's Story∞

When I was sixteen, my family had a boarding house.
I saw many a boarder come in and go out.
When the rooms were full, we were sent to retire,
in the parlor on pallets so there were rooms for hire.
One night as I lay on the floor, I recall,
I saw a gentleman in a top hat come to call.
Just as he walked up the stairs to his room,
My heart sent a flutter, my love did bloom.
At the moment I knew I would be his wife,
to love and to hold for the rest of my life.

Lulu's Story is a verbal history that was retold here in poetry written by her 2nd great granddaughter. Leah Suzanne Kennedy

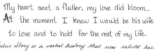

The Boarding House   Everest, Kansas

···born··· ·27 November 1869·   ···born··· ·11 October 1880·

John Hartley Dinkle   ···married··· 13 January 1898 Kansas City, Kansas   Louella "Lulu" Walter

"Glen L. Murdock, Iowa Farm Boy"

by Joanne DaPrato
Vancouver, Washington

SUPPLIES
Patterned paper: NRN Designs

"Royal Canadian Air Force"

by Beth Wakulsky
Haslett, Michigan

SUPPLIES
Patterned paper: Keeping Memories Alive
Corner slot punch: Family Treasures
Canadian flag: Beth's own design
Maple leaves: Beth adapted the maple leaves from
Print Artist clip art. She printed them in color, traced them
onto cardstock that matched the red flag, and cut them out.

1953
Freshman
14 years old

1955
Junior
16 years old

1954
Sophomore
15 years old

1956
Senior
17 years old

"Freshman, Sophomore, Junior, Senior"

by Shauna Fassett
Price, Utah

SUPPLIES

Scissors: Mini-Scallop edge, Fiskars
Corner edger: Nostalgia, Fiskars
Stickers: Mrs. Grossman's
Computer font: Garamond Italic, Microsoft Word

"Vallon Sperry Vickers"

by Jenny Jackson
Arlington, Virginia

SUPPLIES

Horseshoe stamp: D.O.T.S.
Photo corners: D.O.T.S.
Scissors: Deckle edge, Fiskars

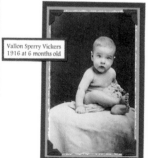

Vallon Sperry Vickers
1916 at 6 months old

Vallon Sperry Vickers

Vallon Sperry Vickers graduated from
Utah State University in Accounting
1939

Vallon S. Vickers pitching horseshoes
with his father, Wallace J. Vickers

College Family - Jane, Dr. Wallace J.
Vickers, back row, Ruth V. Clayton,
Verdena V. Purcell & Mrs. Vickers

Five members of the Vickers family climb the
hill every day to Utah State. Dr. Wallace J.
Vickers is head of the English Department
there and is remembered by many former
students for his classes in college grammar,
and the Bible as English Literature, to name
just two. Mrs. Vickers has been interested in
photography and painting and usually takes
classes each quarter. The painting in the
background is one of Mrs. Vickers'. Jane is a
sophomore, Ruth is taking her master's degree
in clothing and allied arts and Verdena is
doing graduate work while her husband,
Major Arthur Lake Purcell is in Korea.

Val Vickers &
Ruth Klomp
walking down
the streets
of downtown
Salt Lake City
1940

Wallace J., Eva Pearl, & Vallon S.
Vickers in Salt Lake City at Dee Ray
Apartments.

On The Home Front...
August 13, 1944

"Dad posed this one especially for you, Johnnie. Doesn't he look well & as fat as ever? Love Helen."

"Mom, Bobbie & I & 'Skippy.' Isn't he cute in this snap beside me? He follows me all over. Doesn't Mom & Bobbie look well? Love Helen."

"Mother. Taken Aug. 13, 1944. Doesn't she look well? Love Helen."

"Mom and Dad. Good eh Johnnie? I had quite a time coaxing them to have them taken. See Dads specs? Love Helen."

"The Gang. Note Dads new pipe I got him. Wanted to show you it. Have you noticed Fords new home in background? Nice eh? Across from ours. Love Sister Helen."

"To Jack. Taken Sun. Aug. 13, 1944. Isn't the kiddies big & cute? Love Helen."

During World War II, John Shickluna was in the Royal Canadian Air Force and stationed in Europe. His sister Helen wrote to him regularly and sent him many photographs of his family back home. She kept him up on all the happenings from his hometown of Port Colborne, Ontario. These photos were taken on August 13, 1944. Helen always wrote details on the backs of each photograph. Her words are reprinted in the captions of each photo.

"On the Home Front"
by Beth Wakulsky
Haslett, Michigan
SUPPLIES
Patterned paper: Hallmark
Flowers: Beth got the idea for the flowers from a ScrapEase die cut.
Computer font: DJ Classic, Fontastic!, D.J. Inkers
Pens (flower edges): Tombow

"My Great Grandmother"
by Debbie Snell
Gilroy, California
SUPPLIES
Laser-cut lace: Paper Pizazz, Hot Off The Press
Stickers: Heritage Collection, Creative Memories
Patterned paper: Source unknown
Computer font: Source unknown

My Great Grandmother

W. Y. Wright

Cambridge, Nebraska

Susan Rebecca Peters
1888-1932

Charlie Peters

Susie Peters

The Family Mystery

This note has set us to wondering. It was found in the front of and old album belonging to Susan Rebecca. The content of the note is quite curious. First of all, her name is spelled incorrectly. Secondly, her birthday was in March, not October, and thirdly, her father was Charley Peters not Bryan Day. They did, however, live near a small town called Indianola. Susie would have been around 11 years old when she read this note.

Who was Bryan Day? Was he a real person or a made up character? Perhaps a joke between father and daughter? But why would he give her a birthday gift six months after her birthday? Was Susan adopted? How could that have been kept a secret for so long? And why?

Mystery Man
This man's picture was found in Susie's and her mother's photo album. Could he be Bryan Day?

"Mildred and Betty at Ocean Park"
by Jana Francis
Provo, Utah

SUPPLIES

Laser-cut designs: Victory Springs
Computer font: CK Calligraphy, "The Best of Creative Lettering" CD Vol. 1, *Creating Keepsakes*
Idea to note: Jana used torn paper to represent the sand at the beach.

Mildred and Betty Brown at Ocean Park, California
Circa 1917

"Around the Table"
by Pam Talluto
Rochester Hills, Michigan

SUPPLIES

Scissors: Deckle edge, Fiskars
Pens: Zig Writer and Zig Fine & Chisel, EK Success
Idea to note: Pam drew a floor plan of the home to illustrate the memories of the family home.

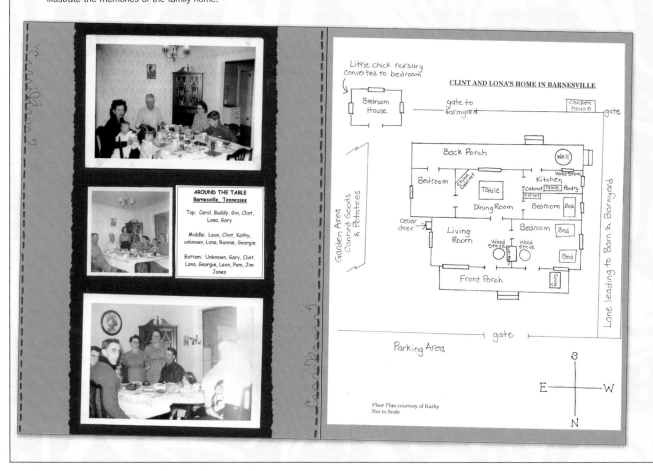

AROUND THE TABLE
Barnesville, Tennessee

Top: Carol, Buddy, Gin, Clint, Lona, Gary

Middle: Leon, Clint, Kathy, unknown, Lona, Ronnie, Georgie

Bottom: Unknown, Gary, Clint, Lona, Georgie, Leon, Pam, Jim Jones

CLINT AND LONA'S HOME IN BARNESVILLE

Little chick nursery converted to bedroom

Bedroom House

gate to farmyard

Chicken house

gate

Back Porch

Well

Bedroom

China Cabinet

Wood Stove

Kitchen

Table

Cabinet

Table

Pantry

closet

Dining Room

Bedroom

Bed

Garden Area Canned Goods & Potatoes

cellar door

Living Room

Bedroom

Bed

Wood Stove

Wood Stove

Bed

Lane leading to Barn & Barnyard

Front Porch

pans

Parking Area

gate

Floor Plan courtesy of Kathy
Not to Scale

S
E — W
N

Family - that miraculous group of folks who note our imperfections but accept us just the same.

A home is filled with mementos that mark the beginnings of great times to come.

"Family Wall Portraits"
by Janae Goerz
Past and Present
Maple Grove, Minnesota

SUPPLIES
Patterned paper: Design Originals (wallpaper); Keeping Memories Alive (plaid chair cushion)
Frame stickers: Frances Meyer
Computer font: Calligraphy, Microsoft Works
Pens: Tombow
Plant and chair clip-art images: Home Publisher
Idea to note: Janae made color copies of the frame stickers, enlarging or shrinking them to fit her photos.

Edith Joseph goldsmith
John and Sue goldsmith (Mimi)

Rolinda Joseph
John and Sue goldsmith

"The Goldsmith Family"
by Karen Glenn
Orem, Utah

SUPPLIES
Photo corners and accents: Karen's own designs
Pen: Zig Writer, EK Success

"Marion Palfry"
by Amber Blakesley
Provo, Utah
SUPPLIES
Stationery: Mara-Mi

Marion Palfry
circa 1926

"Diane and Bill"
by Janette Clayton
Sandy, Utah
SUPPLIES
Patterned paper: Keeping Memories Alive
Patterned vellum: Paper Adventures
Corner punches: Family Treasures (slot); McGill (heart)
Pens: Gelly Roll, Sakura; Pilot
Scissors: Deckle edge, Fiskars
Stickers: Class A'Peels, Mark Enterprises

"Brick Union Cemetery"
by Linda Milligan
El Paso, Texas
SUPPLIES
Rubber stamps: D.O.T.S.
Pens: Le Plume, Tombow; Micron Pigma
and Callipen, Sakura

Scissors: Provincial edge, Fiskars
Corner punch: Source unknown
Idea to note: To remember some of her
more distant relatives, Linda took photos
of her ancestors' grave sites and included
them on her layout along with a portion of
her genealogy chart.

THERE WAS SOMETHING SPECIAL ABOUT

Grandma's Buttons

VIRGINIA WAGSTAFF BUSHMAN

Whenever Janie and I went to Grandma's house, we always loved playing with Grandma's buttons. They were in an old film reel tin box. It always smelled the same! We would sort them, count them, imagine who once wore them, etc. We played with them for hours! Grandma didn't have many toys for us, but we never minded. We felt the buttons were treasures!

My Mother

My mother died when I was only nine years old and unfortunately I remember very little of my time with her. I have, however, been very lucky to have had others share their stories and memories of her with me. The more I learn of her the more I miss her in my life. She was considered a true friend by many and could relate well with others. She was confident and strong willed. She loved learning and believed in the power of education. She had the ability to put her thoughts into written words and blessed many with her talent to teach. She had compassion and taught her children to have compassion. She carried a sense of peace about her and could see beauty in all things. She truly was an amazing woman and was everything that I want to become

Beatrice Lewis Checketts

Born: July 2 1940
Died: February 4 1983

"Grandma's Buttons"

by Robin Johnson
Memory Lane
Chandler, Arizona

SUPPLIES

Paper-lace border: D.O.T.S.
Pen: Zig Writer, EK Success
Colored pencil: Prismacolor, Sanford
Idea to note: Robin used Grandma's actual buttons on the layout.

"Beatrice Lewis Checketts"

by Amy Williams
Ogden, Utah

SUPPLIES

Patterned paper: Source unknown
Leaf punch: Family Treasures
Vine stencil: Plaid Enterprises
Scissors: Colonial edge, Fiskars
Computer fonts: Delphin, Adobe (title);
Bergell, Letraset (journaling)
Pen: Zig Writer, EK Success
Other: Amy used vellum for the yellow leaves and journaling box.

"Linda Susan Schellschmidt"
by Amber Blakesley
Provo, Utah

SUPPLIES

Patterned paper: Keeping Memories Alive (burgundy);
The Paper Company (leaves)
Idea to note: Amber printed the journaling on vellum to
create a soft look and included a ribbon on her layout.

"Kirkwood Apartments"
by Nancy Church
Augusta, Georgia

SUPPLIES

Patterned paper: Keeping
Memories Alive
Cloud die cuts: Pebbles in my
Pocket

Punches: Family Treasures
(circles, triangle); All Night
Media (spiral, flower)
Grass stickers: Frances Meyer
House: Nancy's own design
Pen: Zig Writer, EK Success

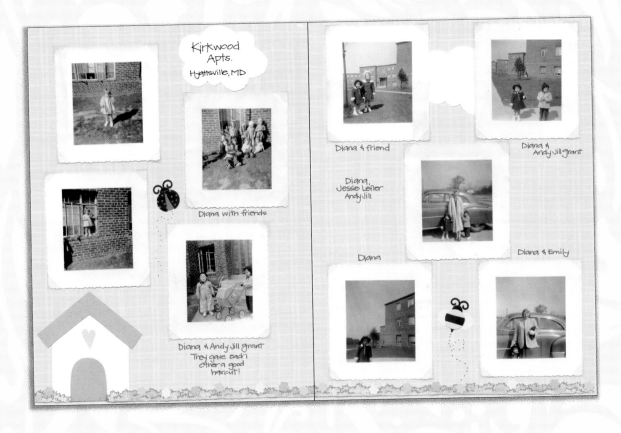

"And They Grew, 2 by 2"

by Gayle Holdman
American Fork, Utah

SUPPLIES

Scissors: Scallop and
Mini-Scallop edges, Fiskars
Patterned paper: Keeping Memories Alive
Flower stamps: D.O.T.S.
Corner-slot punch: Family Treasures
Photo corners: D.O.T.S.
Hole punch: Punchline, McGill

Computer fonts: CK Anything Goes, "The
Best of Creative Lettering" CD Vol. 1,
Creating Keepsakes (title); Graphite Light,
Microsoft Word (journaling)
Colored pencils: Prismacolor, Sanford
Ideas to note: Gayle used scallop-edged
scissors and a hole punch to create a lacy
effect on some of the borders. She also
colored white photo corners with a
D.O.T.S. ink pad and sponge.

"Phyllis Abbott"

by Angelyn Bryce
West Chester, Pennsylvania

SUPPLIES

Computer font: CK Anything Goes, "The
Best of Creative Lettering" CD Vol. 1,
Creating Keepsakes (title); Font unknown,
Microsoft Word (journaling)
Pen: Le Plume II, Marvy Uchida
Car: Angelyn's own design

Sara Doherty, Sally's Great-Great Aunt, was born on December 17, 1874 in Saginaw, Michigan. She was the youngest of Peter and Margaret Wright Malcolm's six children. Aunt Sara lived much of her life on Mackinac Island with her husband Frank, and dog "Blackie." Frank and Sara moved to the Island in hopes that its clean, pure air would improve Frank's poor health. The couple lived on Market Street, next to the Beaumont Memorial Museum. Aunt Sara was very patriotic and always had an American Flag flying. She was proud of her home, and kept its white exterior freshly painted.

Aunt Sara had a large, beautiful backyard garden. She would carry bouquets of the flowers she loved in a special basket (facing page). Sara was a lovely, happy-go-lucky lady. She would often invite friends and relatives up to the Island to enjoy her warm hospitality. Aunt Sara was fond of traveling as well, throughout both the United States and Europe.

Aunt Sara passed away on April 29, 1960 in a nursing home in Dewitt, Michigan after a long and fulfilling life.

Sara R. Malcolm Doherty
Mackinac Island, 1940's

"Sara R. Malcolm Doherty"

by Sally Garrod
East Lansing, Michigan

SUPPLIES
Computer font: DJ Classic, Fontastic!, D.J. Inkers
Stickers: The Gifted Line, Michel & Co.

"Rachel Coombs Larson"

by Valerie Duffy
Washington, Utah

SUPPLIES
Rubber stamps: Stampin' Up! (stripes and flowers)
Pen: Stampin' Write, Stampin' Up!

Rachel Coombs Larson

At the Temple Motel which she owned

Manti, Utah

PATRICK JOSEPH SAVAGE, 2

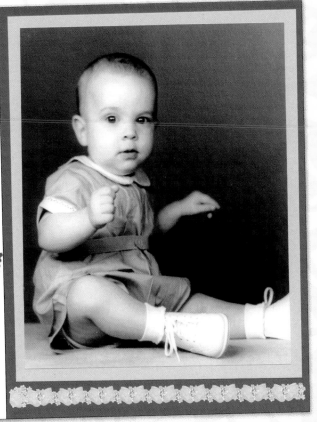

Patrick Joseph Savage, born January 21, 1949 in Detroit, Michigan. The second son in a family of five, three brothers and one sister, Patrick was an "Air Force brat" and lived in several different places, including Paris, France. He graduated highschool in California and went on to obtain a Bachelors of Arts in Zoology from the University of Missouri, Columbia, Missouri in 1971. Shortly after, he married his highschool sweetheart, Mary Louise Baker, on July 3, 1971. Patrick also received a Doctor of Medicine from the Medical College of Virginia in Richmond, Virginia specializing in Internal Medicine and Pulmonology after graduation. Pat served in the Air Force for 15 years, after which he went into private practice. He and Mary raised three children; Alycia, Patrick, and Caitie. In addition to pulmonology, Pat is also certified in Addictionology and Hyperbaric Medicine.

·· PATRICK JOSEPH ··

· AUGUST 1957 ·

Patrick Joseph Savage
1949

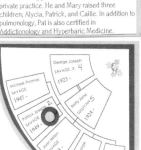

"Patrick Joseph Savage"

by Alycia Alvarez
Jacksonville,
North Carolina
SUPPLIES
Scissors: Stamp edge, Fiskars
Computer fonts: CK Fill In, "The Best of Creative Lettering" CD Vol. 1, *Creating Keepsakes* (title); CAC Camelot, Create-A-Card (journaling)
Stickers: The Gifted Line, Michel & Co.
Colored pencils: Memory Pencils, EK Success
Pen: Milky Gel Roller, Pentel
Circle punch: Family Treasures
Hole punch: Punchline, McGill
Other: Alycia scanned the large photo of Patrick into her computer and printed it on Kodak Ink Jet paper.
Idea to note: Alycia included a portion of the genealogy chart on her layout, marking Patrick's lineage.

Hazel Roxie Irwin
Graduation day 1913.
The locket she is wearing was given to her niece Helen.
July 1998 Helen gave the locket
To her granddaughter Denise Helen, when she left home to go to law school.
The gold locket is engraved with an H.
(photo copy of original locket)

"Hazel Roxie Irwin"
by Kathy Stott
Mom and Me Scrapbooking
Salt Lake City, Utah
SUPPLIES
Stationery: NRN Designs
Computer font: Scrap Calligraphy, Lettering Delights Vol. 2, Inspire Graphics
Idea to note: Kathy included a photo copy of Hazel's locket on her layout.

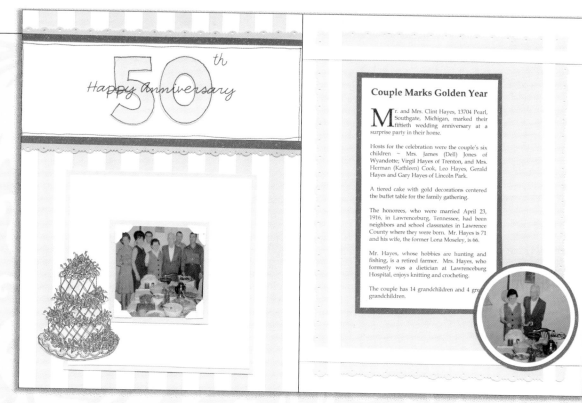

Couple Marks Golden Year

Mr. and Mrs. Clint Hayes, 13704 Pearl, Southgate, Michigan, marked their fiftieth wedding anniversary at a surprise party in their home.

Hosts for the celebration were the couple's six children ~ Mrs. James (Dell) Jones of Wyandotte; Virgil Hayes of Trenton, and Mrs. Herman (Kathleen) Cook, Leo Hayes, Gerald Hayes and Gary Hayes of Lincoln Park.

A tiered cake with gold decorations centered the buffet table for the family gathering.

The honorees, who were married April 23, 1916, in Lawrenceburg, Tennessee, had been neighbors and school classmates in Lawrence County where they were born. Mr. Hayes is 71 and his wife, the former Lona Moseley, is 66.

Mr. Hayes, whose hobbies are hunting and fishing, is a retired farmer. Mrs. Hayes, who formerly was a dietician at Lawrenceburg Hospital, enjoys knitting and crocheting.

The couple has 14 grandchildren and 4 great grandchildren.

"Hayes' 50th Anniversary"

by Pam Talluto

Rochester Hills, Michigan

SUPPLIES

Pens: Zig Writers, EK Success
Lettering template: Block, Pebble Tracers, Pebbles in my Pocket
Patterned paper: Keeping Memories Alive
Scissors: Bounce edge, Provo Craft
Hole punch (⅟₁₆"): Punchline, McGill
Cake cutout: Keeping Memories Alive
Ideas to note: Pam made her own striped paper by adding white strips to tan cardstock. She made the lacy border with scallop-edged scissors and a hole punch.

"The Hayes"

by Pam Talluto

Rochester Hills, Michigan

SUPPLIES

Scissors: Scallop edge, Fiskars
Hole punch: Punchline, McGill
Pens: Zig Writer and Zig Fine & Chisel, EK Success
Hearts: Pam's own design
Other: Pam included a copy of the Hayes' marriage certificate on her layout.

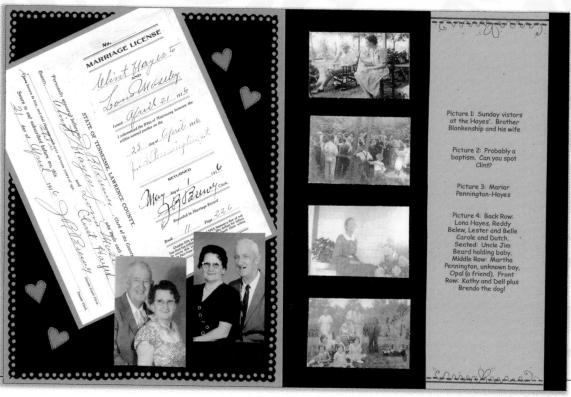

Picture 1: Sunday vistors at the Hayes'. Brother Blankenship and his wife

Picture 2: Probably a baptism. Can you spot Clint?

Picture 3: Mariar Pennington-Hayes

Picture 4: Back Row: Lona Hayes, Reddy Belew, Lester and Belle Carole and Dutch. Seated: Uncle Jim Beard holding baby. Middle Row: Martha Pennington, unknown boy, Opal (a friend). Front Row: Kathy and Dell plus Brendo the dog!

"Linda May Scott"
by Jodi Olson
Kaysville, Utah
SUPPLIES
Vellum: Paper Adventures
Pens: Zig Writer, EK Success; Milky Gel Roller, Pentel
Colored pencil: Prismacolor, Sanford
Clip art: "Cute Things," Amy Wilson
Idea to note: Jodi printed the clip art from her computer and traced it onto vellum paper to create the frame.

"High School Sweethearts"
by Jennifer McLaughlin
Backdoor Friends
Azusa, California
SUPPLIES
Patterned paper: Paperbilities, MPR
Heart embossed paper: Frances Meyer
Hearts: Jennifer's own designs
Pen: Zig Writer, EK Success
Colored pencils: Memory Pencils, EK Success
Other: Jennifer got the idea for the title from the CK Anything Goes font from "The Best of Creative Lettering" CD Vol. 1, *Creating Keepsakes.*

"My Mom"
by Violet Burgess
The Family Archives
Mission, British Columbia, Canada
SUPPLIES
Flower die cuts: The Family Archives
Patterned paper: The Family Archives
Scissors: Colonial edge, Fiskars
Photo corners: Class A'Peels, Mark Enterprises
Computer font: Claren, Adobe Photoshop 5

HIS
HERS

Parents of Thomas Holdman
William Floyd Holdman
Ann Evelyn Speisser Holdman
June 19, 1965

Parents of Gayle Terry Holdman
Jay Dewitt Terry
Joan Marilyn Curtis Terry
September 2, 1958

"His and Hers"
by Gayle Holdman
American Fork, Utah

SUPPLIES

Rubber stamps: D.O.T.S. (patterned paper, hearts);
Hero Arts (alphabet)
Corner slot punch: Family Treasures
Computer font: Dauphin, Microsoft Word
Pen: Legacy Writer, Close to my Heart

"A Lifetime of Love"
by Brenda Bennett
Morenci, Arizona

SUPPLIES

Vellum paper: The Paper Company
Embossing template: Lasting Impressions
Colored pencils and blender: Prismacolor, Sanford
Pen: Zig Writer, EK Success

My maternal grandparents,
Genevieve Farr of Provo, Utah,
& Gail S. Lee of Salt Lake City, Utah,
met at Hill Air Force Base in 1944.
Genevieve was an upholsterer and
Gail was a mechanic on the
flight line. They became
engaged on February 14, 1945, and
were married in the Salt Lake
Temple on May 11, 1945.

1945

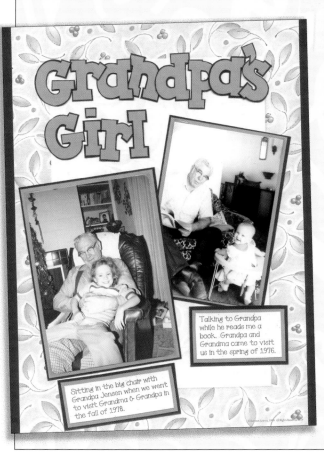

"Betty Brown"
by Jana Francis
Provo, Utah
SUPPLIES
Pressed flowers: Distinctions in Nature
Idea to note: Jana made a "peek-a-boo" page—simply untie the ribbon to reveal the photo inside.

"Grandpa's Girl"
by Tamara Wheeler
Hurricane, Utah
SUPPLIES
Lettering template: Block Serif, Pebble Tracers, Pebbles in my Pocket
Stationery: Autumn Leaves
Computer font: DJ Squared, Fontastic!, D.J. Inkers

"Nita Lou"
by Kerri Bradford
Orem, Utah
SUPPLIES
Stickers (lace): Paper Whispers, Mrs. Grossman's
Scissors: Deckle edge, Fiskars
Pen: Zig Opaque Writer, EK Success
Patterned paper: Paper Pizazz, Hot Off The Press

"Virginia Was Born"
by Violet Burgess
The Family Archives
Mission, British Columbia, Canada
SUPPLIES
Embossed rose die cuts: The Family Archives
Scissors: Scallop edge, Fiskars
Pen: Micron Pigma, Sakura
Computer font: Claren, Adobe Photoshop 5
Vine: Violet's own design

Growing up in Burley, Idaho

"Growing Up in Burley, Idaho"
by Barbie Jarvis
Wheat Ridge, Colorado
SUPPLIES
Corner punches: Starburst and Corner Frame, Family Treasures
Corner edger: Nostalgia, Fiskars
Pen: Zig Writer, EK Success

"Gone Fishin'"
by Lori Berry
Coquitlam, British Columbia, Canada
SUPPLIES
Patterned paper: Design Originals
Scissors: Stamp edge, Fiskars; Deckle edge, Creative Memories
Stickers: Creative Memories
Pen: Zig Writer, EK Success
Hearts: Lori's own designs

"Brothers 'n Sisters"
by Pam Talluto
Rochester Hills, Michigan
SUPPLIES
Mulberry paper: Personal Stamp Exchange
Computer fonts: DJ Classic and DJ Squared, Fontastic!, D.J. Inkers
Pen: Zig Writer, EK Success
Puppy sticker: The Gifted Line, Michel & Co.
Heart punch: Family Treasures
Lettering template: Block, Pebble Tracers, Pebbles in my Pocket

BETTY JANE SULLIVAN

Betty Jane Sullivan, born October 11, 1924 in Detroit, Michigan. She was the youngest of six; two brothers and three sisters. Betty received a teaching degree and married George Joseph Savage, Jr. on February 22, 1947. While raising five children, four sons and one daughter, she enjoyed the life of a military wife. After George retired from the Air Force in 1974 they settled down in Aledo, Texas, where they have been for several years.

Betty Jane, 1945
Betty had this picture taken after she and George were engaged. She sent this photograph to him when he was "safely over in the Pacific". Her father was distraught that she sent such a "suggestive" picture.

Betty Jane Sullivan
Summer, 1943

"Betty Jane Sullivan"
by Alycia Alvarez
Jacksonville, North Carolina
SUPPLIES
Scissors: Victorian edge, Fiskars
Punches: Family Treasures (flower, spiral, leaf and circle)
Hole punch: Punchline, McGill
Corner slot punch: Family Treasures
Computer fonts: CK Fill In, "The Best of Creative Lettering" CD Vol. 1, *Creating Keepsakes* (title); CAC Camelot, Create-A-Card (journaling)
Colored pencils: Memory Pencils, EK Success
Other: Alycia scanned the photo of Betty on the left page into her computer and printed it on Kodak Ink Jet paper.
Idea to note: Alycia included a portion of the genealogy chart on her layout, marking Betty's lineage.

"Diana"
by Nancy Church
Augusta, Georgia
SUPPLIES
Corner rounder (flowers): Family Treasures
Teardrop and hole punches: Punchline, McGill
Scissors: Deckle edge, Fiskars
Lettering template: Classic, Pebble Tracers, Pebbles in my Pocket
Computer font: Scrap Rhapsody, Lettering Delights Vol. 2, Inspire Graphics

Sugar and Spice and everything nice That's what little girls are made of!
Diana Lee Barrick
February 25, 1951

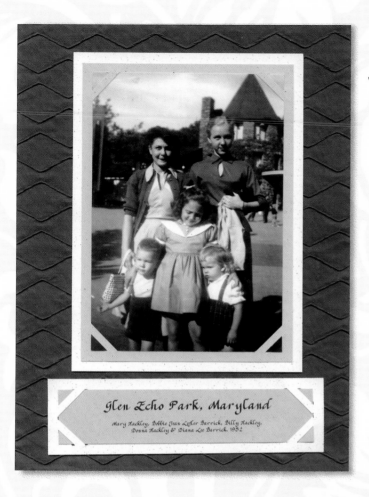

Glen Echo Park, Maryland

Mary Hackley, Bobbie Jean Lefler Barrick, Billy Hackley,
Donna Hackley & Diana Lee Barrick, 1952

"Glen Echo Park"
by Valerie Dellastatious
Orem, Utah

SUPPLIES

Handmade background paper: Solum World Paper
Corner slot punch: Family Treasures
Computer font: CK Calligraphy, "The Best of Creative
Lettering" CD Vol. 1, *Creating Keepsakes*
Other: Valerie used the Kodak Picture Maker's "Color
Restoration", "Picture Zoom" and "Enlarge" features to
enhance the photo on her layout.

"The Klomp Family"
by Jenny Jackson
Arlington, Virginia

SUPPLIES

Patterned paper: Close to my Heart
Ivy stamps: D.O.T.S.
Corner slot punch: Family Treasures
Scissors: Pinking edge, Fiskars

The Klomp Family
Back: Spencer & Katie Klomp, Betty Klomp,
Ruth & Val Vickers. Front: Gerard Sr. & Zina Geneva Klomp,
Dorothy, Nancy, & Gerard Jr. Klomp.

Preserve your family history with accents that perfectly enhance a loved one's portrait, an old-time family photograph or a cherished memento. With the accents here, you can celebrate the past while creating a legacy for the future.

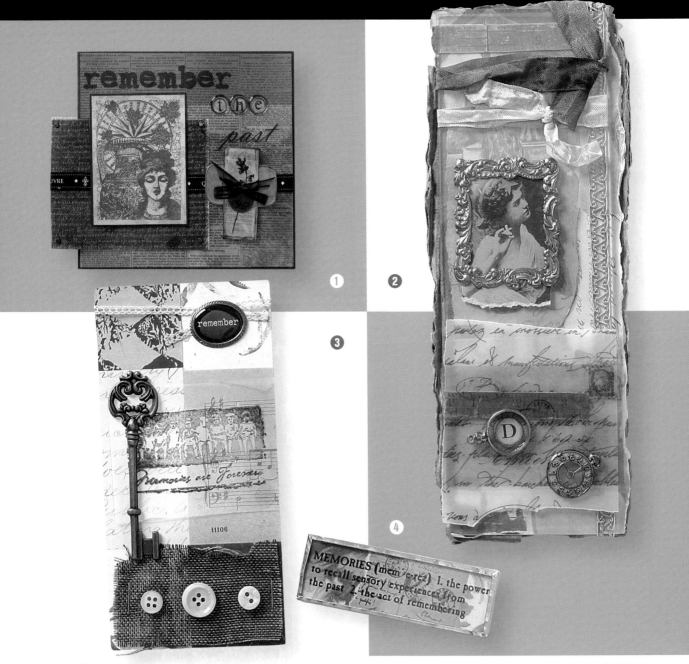

❶ **"REMEMBER" by Lilac Chang, San Mateo, CA. Supplies** *Patterned papers:* Doodlebug Design (yellow), Creative Imaginations (beige), 7 Gypsies (black), K & Company (maroon); *"Remember" and transparencies:* Narratives, Creative Imaginations; *Alphabet pebbles:* Making Memories; *Letter stickers:* Nostalgiques, EK Success; *Brads:* Lost Art Treasures; *Rubber stamp:* Inkadinkado; *Other:* Stamping ink, ribbon and mesh. ❷ **"HERITAGE ACCENT" by Kelly Anderson, Tempe, AZ. Supplies** *Patterned paper:* Design Originals; *Travel transparency image:* ARTchix Studio; *Gold frame, antique ruler and vintage ribbon:* Memory Lane; *Other:* Cardboard, glass and buttons. ❸ **"YEARS GONE BY" by Renee Camacho, Nashville, TN. Supplies** *Patterned paper:* Anna Griffin (flower), 7 Gypsies (word and brown); *Walnut ink:* Postmodern Design; *Stamping ink:* Ranger Industries; *Mica:* Manto Fev; *Eyelet word:* Making Memories; *Square punch:* EK Success. ❹ **"MEMORIES" by Lynne Montgomery, Gilbert, AZ. Supplies** *Patterned paper:* Anna Griffin; *Foil tape:* USArtQuest; *Definition:* Making Memories; *Other:* Microscope slides, sticker and postcard.

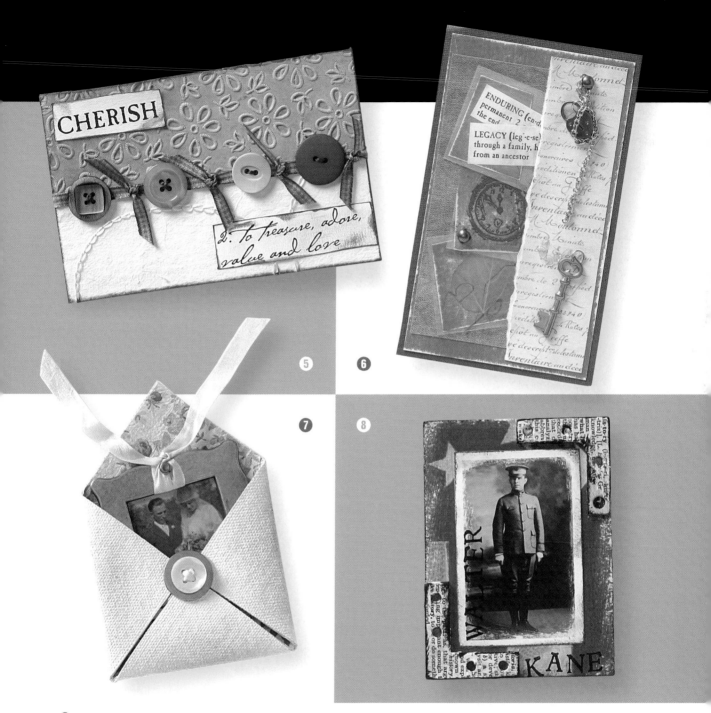

⑤ **"CHERISH" by Shannon Jones, Mesa, AZ. Supplies** *Specialty papers:* Source unknown; *Buttons:* La Mode and Making Memories; *Ribbon:* Michaels; *"Cherish" word strip:* Making Memories; *Stamping ink:* Ancient Page; *Embroidery floss:* DMC. ⑥ **"LEGACY" by Denise Pauley, La Palma, CA. Supplies** *Patterned papers:* SEI (brown), 7 Gypsies (word); *Definitions:* Making Memories; *Leaf:* Nature's Pressed; *Rubber stamp:* Rubber Stampede; *Stamping ink:* Tsukineko; *Embossing powder:* Ranger Industries; *Transparency:* Stampendous!; *Studs:* Prym-Dritz: *Other:* Gold chains and charms. *Ideas to note:* To create "slides," adhere pieces of sanded cardstock and accents to transparency rectangles and decoupage with a light coat of adhesive before applying another piece of transparency over the top. ⑦ **"ENVELOPE POCKET" by Julie Turner, Gilbert, AZ. Supplies** *Patterned paper:* Anna Griffin; *Canvas fabric:* Joanne's; *Paint:* Liquitex Gesso; *Adhesive:* Perfect Paper, USArtQuest; *Frame:* Making Memories; *Ribbon:* Bucilla; *Stamping ink:* Ranger Industries; *Other:* Button. *Ideas to note:* Julie made the envelope by gluing a piece of canvas fabric to the back of patterned paper, then when dry, trimming it to a four-inch square and folding it into an envelope. She joined the envelope with a button and stippled the canvas with ink to give it an aged look. ⑧ **"WALTER KANE" by Karen Russell, Grants Pass, OR. Supplies** *Patterned paper:* K & Company; *Letter stamps:* PSX Design; *Stamping ink:* Stampin' Up!; *Other:* Metal L brackets. *Ideas to note:* Karen scanned and printed a definition from the dictionary, adhered it onto the L brackets, then sanded it.

Very Vintage

Products with an old-time feel

My dad's family loved to take pictures. When my grandfather died, Dad inherited thousands of candid and portrait photographs dating from the mid 1800s through the present. Grandpa stored most of the beautiful pictures in old boxes and manila envelopes. Despite the disarray, the blessing in having this many pictures is that almost all of them are labeled.

While searching for a specific photo a few months ago, I couldn't help but wonder how many other people have photos from bygone eras. And for those of us who scrapbook, are there products that can do justice to these nostalgic treasures?

The answer is a resounding yes! So, dust off the Irving Berlin LP, crank up the old phonograph, and read on for some favorite vintage finds.

by Lanna Wilson

Tag Art
HOT OFF THE PRESS

Looking for a quick, 3-D accent for your layout or card? Consider Tag Art by Paper Pizazz. These artistically designed tags capture the mood of yesteryear for the contemporary on-the-go scrapbooker. Simply cut the tags out and attach them with foam tape or pop dots.

Web site: . . . .*www.paperpizazz.com*
Phone: *800/227-9595*

Add a pre-made tag to your layout for dimensional flair. *Card by Hot Off The Press.* **Supplies** *Patterned paper, specialty paper, cutouts and lace paper:* Paper Pizazz, Hot Off The Press; *Card:* Paper Flair; *Gold pen:* Gelly Roll, Sakura; *Mounting tape:* Scotch; *Gold cord:* Hirschberg Schutz & Co.; *Computer font:* CK Cursive, "The Best of Creative Lettering" CD Combo, *Creating Keepsakes.*

7 Gypsies

The colorful tags, albums and papers by 7 Gypsies are enchanting and will add a vintage feel to any layout. Create a serendipity tag from the colorful papers, or customize your vintage album with one of the company's spiral-bound books.

Web site: *www.7gypsies.com*
Phone: . . . . .480/325-3358 (wholesale only)

Add an old-time feel to your layouts with vintage labels. *Page by Lori Houk.*
Supplies *Embossed paper, patterned paper and die cuts:* K & Company; *Textured paper and brads:* Sources unknown; *Sticker label:* Heart and Home Collectables; *Computer font:* Spring, downloaded from the Internet; *Other:* Foam tape.

Heart and Home Collectables
MELISSA FRANCES

New on the scrapbook scene, the Vintage Peel and Stick labels by Melissa Frances add vintage flair to scrapbook layouts (or even your own jam jars). You'll love the charming, realistic artwork created in beautiful watercolors.

Web site: . . . .*www.melissafrances.com*
Phone: . . . . .888/616-6166 (wholesale only)

EMBELLISHMENTS

Use a combination of buttons, fiber, mesh and more to dress up a vintage layout. *Page by Kerri Bradford.* **Supplies** *Patterned paper:* Provo Craft; *Buttons, fiber, mesh, ribbon and coin:* Magic Scraps; *Eyelet:* Making Memories; *Chalk:* Craf-T Products; *Computer font:* PaletteD, downloaded from the Internet; *Lettering stamps:* PSX Design; *Stamping ink:* Clearsnap; *Tag:* Kerri's own design.

Magic Scraps

If you think the early decades of the 1900s were filled with drab colors, think again! Add life, color and shimmer to your layouts with fiber, buttons, glitter, ribbon, eyelets, brads, raffia, mesh and more from Magic Scraps.

Web site: ....*www.magicscraps.com*
Phone: 972/238-1838

Blumenthal Lansing

Sorting through an assortment of baubles by Blumenthal Lansing brings back memories of Grandma's button collection. You'll find one-of-a-kind buttons in a variety of shapes, colors and sizes. Can't remove the shank from the button? Try a pair of wire cutters. Or, check out Blumenthal Lansing's button shank remover.

Web site: ....*www.buttonsplus.com*
Phone: 800/553-4158

Rummage through your button collection for great embellishment ideas. *Page by Ashley Gull.* **Supplies** *Patterned paper:* Close To My Heart; *Buttons:* Favorite Findings, Blumenthal Lansing; *Photo corners:* 3L Corp.; *Photo ribbon:* Anna Griffin; *String pearls:* Magic Scraps; *Computer font:* Lucida Calligraphy, downloaded from the Internet; *Other:* Wire ribbon.

Merry Christmas!

Here are Annie and William Gierisch enjoying their Christmas at home in the old yellow house in Burley, Idaho. Unfortunately, no one knows much about this photo, but it is a family favorite because of how happy they are. It was taken around 1950.

Add charm to your layout with a period accent, such as a bauble or trinket. *Page by Kerri Bradford.* **Supplies** *Patterned paper:* Anna Griffin; *Key charm:* Freckle Press; *Fiber:* Magic Scraps.

Freckle Press

In a word, the charms and baubles by Freckle Press are charming. The company's line of handmade ribbon and beaded flowers are colorful and add a touch of homespun craft to your pages.

Web site: . . . .*www.frecklepress.com*
Phone: 877/4FRECKL

RUBBER STAMPS

Oscar McCunn
Seattle, Washington
Circa 1901

PSX Design

PSX Design touts a wide variety of detailed, vintage-style stamps. The company recently released a "Passport" paper line that includes vintage patterns and colors.

Web site: ....*www.psxdesign.com*
Phone: 800/782-6748

Re-create the look of time gone by with vintage-themed rubber stamps. *Page by Laura Gaillard.* **Supplies** *Leather paper:* XPedX; *Watch stamp:* PSX Design; *Craft wire:* Artistic Wire Ltd.; *Beads:* Magic Scraps; *Embossing powder:* Stampendous!; *Stamping ink:* Clearsnap; *Brads:* Boxer Productions.

many thanks

Stampin' Up!

Whether it's photos from the world wars or your parents' 1933 trip to Kitty Hawk, the vintage stamps from Stampin' Up! feature memorable sketched details for your layouts.

Web site: ....*www.stampinup.com*
Phone: 800/stamp-up

There's nothing like a Model T to add vintage character to your card or scrapbook page. *Card by Stampin' Up!* **Supplies** *Patterned paper, mulberry paper, rubber stamps and stamping ink:* Stampin' Up!; *Other:* Hemp.

Protect-A-Page
DOLPHIN ENTERPRISES

While page protectors aren't a thing of the past, they are a product for the future. Protect-A-Page was designed specifically for scrapbookers who want to include 3-D objects in their layouts without puncturing their page protectors or damaging other layouts.

Web site: . . . .*www.protectapage.com*
Phone: 877/910-3306

Include bulkier memorabilia on your layouts without damaging your album. *Pages by LaRayne Stuber.* **Supplies** *Page protector:* Dolphin Enterprises; *Patterned paper:* Frances Meyer; *Metallic paper:* Paper Adventures; *Mulberry paper:* PrintWorks; *Computer font:* Kaufmann BT, WordPerfect; *Other:* Lace frame, pressed flowers, pickle forks, handkerchief, gloves and fan.

"Age" It Yourself

Want your page to have a worn, weathered look? Consider running a wire brush back and forth over your decorative paper and accents.

Supplies *Patterned paper:* Pixie Press; *Wire brush:* Magic Scraps

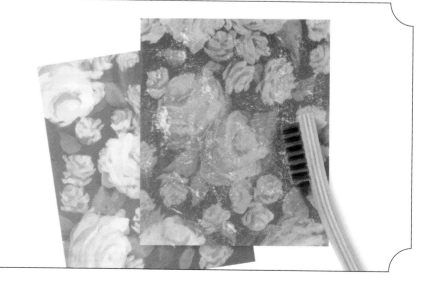

Create a memorial for your loved ones with vintage art and drawings. *Page by Mary Larson.* **Supplies** *Crimped and textured paper*: Memory Lane; *Computer font*: New Yorker, downloaded from the Internet; *Flag clip art*: Celebrate America; "the vintage workshop" CD, Indygo Junction; *Chalk*: Craf-T Products; *Fiber*: Fibersbytheyard.com; *Other*: Star nailheads.

the vintage workshop
INDYGO JUNCTION

For the computer-savvy scrapbooker, the Click-n-Craft CD-ROM collection by Indygo Junction offers a selection of beautifully illustrated vintage images to ornament your layouts. Each CD features 17 images and 20 project ideas.

Web site: . . . .*www.thevintageworkshop.com*
Phone: 913/341-5559

A Stroll Down Memory Lane

For more vintage ideas, check out the following products:

K & Company

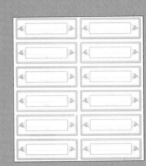

Mrs. Grossman's

SRM Press

Karen Foster Design

The Family Archives

Tumblebeasts

Colorbök

journaling life's chapters

Record the events you planned—or didn't

Figure 1. Sure, lots of couples start a family. But isn't it funny how it's different when it happens to you? *Page by Rebecca Sower.* **Supplies** *Embossed cardstock:* Frances Meyer; *Pen:* Zig Writer, EK Success; *Tag:* EK Success; *Other:* Ribbon and vintage button.

JOURNALING SPOTLIGHT

"I determined I would go back to work after you were born. But that was before I saw you. I did go back. I sat in those business meetings that before were so important. But I couldn't help but notice how trite it all seemed. All I could think about was you. So I quit. No, I didn't quit you. I quit my job. I'll never quit you."

Whether it's planned and expected or whether it feels like your feet were just knocked out from beneath you, we all face new life chapters now and again.

I READ A LOT. Every time I take a trip, I buy a new book at the airport and am usually finished by the time my plane lands back home in Nashville. I love stories that pull me into the plot, that make me temporarily

ARTICLE BY REBECCA SOWER

Figure 2. When life throws you a curve, document the emotions you and your family experience. They're part of your history. *Pages by Heidi Stepanova.* **Supplies** *Metal mesh, screw snaps and date stamp:* Making Memories; *Patterned paper:* Design Originals; *Computer fonts:* Times New Roman, Microsoft Word; Antique Type, downloaded from the Internet; *Stamping ink:* StazOn, Tsukineko; *Alphabet stamps:* Rubber Stampede; *Copper flakes:* Arnold Grummer.

JOURNALING SPOTLIGHT

"In May 2003, Alexy was finishing his PhD and teaching statistics, while I was teaching calculus. We spent our days working, and our nights and weekends together as a family. Life was good.

". . . And then came change. Governor Granholm cut the funding for higher education statewide. In only three days, we became a family of four with no jobs, scrambling to find work. We weren't prepared. We had excellent references and resumes, and no place to send them.

". . . Alexy got a new job, but it meant relocating. The house was not finished in time, so we had no hot water, no bathroom, no kitchen, no laundry hook-ups and no closets. The boys' preschool was cancelled at the last minute. My toilet was sitting in the front yard, a fitting symbol of the chaos in our lives.

. . . "As time has passed, some of the problems have been resolved, and new ones have come. But as I look at our lives, still in many ways chaotic, this move has been a true blessing. . . . I think there has been a plan for us all along. The three days that started the chaos have refocused our lives. And just like our toilet, we've found our home."

lose track of the real world that's still tripping by around me. I'm always intrigued by the authors who have me believe all is unraveling, then—bam!—the chapter ends and a new one begins with an unexpected new twist. But wait, isn't life a little like that?

Turning the Page

Whether you call them "chapters," "new beginnings" or "the next phase," certain events, planned or unplanned, cause us to turn a new page and begin each day with a different set of rules. Some chapters won't be a surprise at all, but others may. In any regard, the importance of documenting the events leading up to these chapters and our feelings toward them doesn't wane. And scrapbooking the events can be therapeutic and help us gain perspective (see facing page).

Figure 3. Journal through life's changing chapters. It's great therapy. *Page by Kim Mattina.* **Supplies** *Patterned paper and letter tag stickers* ("Memories"): Rusty Pickle; *Fibers:* Fibers By The Yard; *Beads:* Wal-Mart; *Paper yarn, pewter brads and disc letters, Scrabble tile letters:* Making Memories; *Letter stickers* ("OF" and "Time"): All My Memories ("Another") and Creative Imaginations ("OF" and "Time"); *Slide mount:* Scrapworks; *Tag stickers:* Karen Foster Design; *Key sticker:* Nostalgiques, Sticko by EK Success. *Ideas to note:* Kim hid her journaling behind the focal-point photo. She sewed the string of beads to the journaling page so the stitching wouldn't show on the photo mat.

JOURNALING SPOTLIGHT

"Days come, and days go. Time passes, and as I look back, I can see the changes more clearly. We had been married about a month when these photographs were taken in Brindisi, Italy. In October of 1989, we were so in love. Newlyweds setting out on a new adventure called marriage. This was the beginning of a life that we thought we would share forever.

"Then the days began passing. And the days became years. We both tried to share the moments, though the shared moments became fewer and fewer until we were living two separate lives. The one bond that we still had was our love for our son. That is something that we still each have a part of, though we're no longer sharing a life together as one family.

"As I approach the fourteen-year anniversary of our marriage and the one-year mark of our divorce, I'm finally able to see things more clearly. I can see where mistakes were made by us both. I can see where more time could have been shared. But I can also see a future that I could not have imagined a year ago. I'm stronger. I'm independent. And I'm the mother that I've always known I could be, to the most amazing segment of my life, our son Michael. At thirteen years old, he has been a rock for me. Michael has been my only priority, the motivation for everything I have done in the last year.

"So now, I see that these photos are memories of another time and another place. Something I don't want to forget, but memories nonetheless."

Usual Life Chapters

Life chapters can include:

- Leaving your childhood home to begin life on your own
- Getting married
- Beginning a family
- Getting divorced
- Losing a close family member
- Beginning a new career
- Moving to a new place
- Buying a home
- Becoming a grandparent
- Retiring from a job
- Becoming a person of faith

But what about the following situations? Don't they involve turnarounds, too?

- Discovery of personal illness
- Extensive weight loss
- An event (see layout on page 253) that suddenly changes your outlook on life
- Discovery of a new hobby
- A near-death experience such as a bad car accident
- Anything that causes you to about-face and look at life differently

If you're already including issues like these in your scrapbooks, job well done! Just make sure you're incorporating the significant points surrounding these issues, such as: your feelings while going through the situation, how the new chapter affected those around you, why the change took place, whether or not it was planned, and the events leading up to and taking place after the new chapter.

How Did I End Up Here?

Have you ever noticed how daily life can be a lot like sleepwalking? We engross ourselves in the nitty-gritty, just trying to keep our heads above water, and suddenly we wake up and wonder how we got where we are. Sometimes we find we've actually turned the page to a new chapter in life without ever realizing we've done so.

No one plans to divorce at the time they're getting married. But sometimes life catches us off guard. Kim Mattina's optimistic attitude toward her husband, the birth of their child and ultimately their divorce is an amazingly poignant piece of her personal history (see layout on page 251). An event as traumatic as divorce should certainly be journaled through, whether in the pages of your scrapbook or in a private journal.

Many times, our changing life chapters aren't expected, pleasant or welcomed. Journaling through our emotions, good and bad, helps capture real life. And we are scrapbooking about real life, right? Remember, no one lives a fairy tale.

Heidi Stepanova created a captivating layout that illustrates the major life chapters of new home and new job (see layout on page 250). She tells it all—the good, the bad and the toilet. I love how she took one small element of her situation (the toilet sitting in the yard) and let it epitomize all the

No one lives a fairy tale.

chaos that she and her family endured during the beginning of a new life chapter.

And then come times when fate is kind enough to give you a small heads-up that a new chapter is about to begin. My husband and I had been married for four years when we found out we were expecting our first child. Although it certainly wasn't a planned pregnancy, we weren't devastated by the news either.

A baby? For us? Did someone possibly make a mistake? How could we be parents? At the time I discovered this piece of news, I was very involved in my career. I assumed I would go back to work at the earliest possible opportunity after I'd had my baby. The layout on page 249 illustrates the rest of the story.

It Happens to the Best of Us

No person who's ever lived can say his or her life was uneventful. Events happen! Sure, some people experience more drastic levels of change, but we all turn the page over to a new chapter once in a while. Bring those new chapters to life on the pages of your albums. Remember, we're documenting our personal histories. Don't leave out one little piece of that history. ❤

We all turn the page over to a new chapter once in a while. Bring those new chapters to life on the pages of your albums.

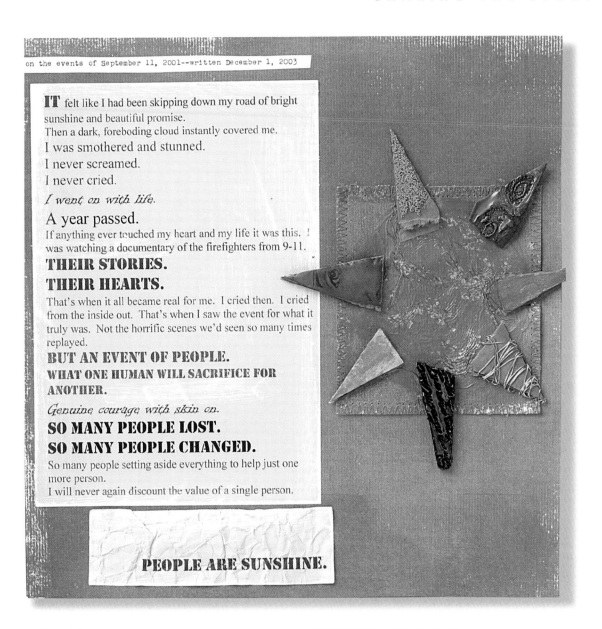

on the events of September 11, 2001—written December 1, 2003

IT felt like I had been skipping down my road of bright sunshine and beautiful promise.
Then a dark, foreboding cloud instantly covered me.
I was smothered and stunned.
I never screamed.
I never cried.
I went on with life.
A year passed.
If anything ever touched my heart and my life it was this. I was watching a documentary of the firefighters from 9-11.
THEIR STORIES.
THEIR HEARTS.
That's when it all became real for me. I cried then. I cried from the inside out. That's when I saw the event for what it truly was. Not the horrific scenes we'd seen so many times replayed.
BUT AN EVENT OF PEOPLE.
WHAT ONE HUMAN WILL SACRIFICE FOR ANOTHER.
Genuine courage with skin on.
SO MANY PEOPLE LOST.
SO MANY PEOPLE CHANGED.
So many people setting aside everything to help just one more person.
I will never again discount the value of a single person.

PEOPLE ARE SUNSHINE.

Figure 4. Share which events, large or small, have completely changed your outlook on life. *Page by Rebecca Sower.* **Supplies** *Acrylic paints:* Jacquard Products; *Computer fonts:* Times New Roman, Microsoft Word; Informal Roman and Stencil, downloaded from the Internet; *Embossing enamel:* Suze Weinberg; *Micro beads:* Provo Craft; *Craft wire:* Darice; *Rubber stamps:* All Night Media (eyes), EK Success (script) and Uptown Design Company (eye); *Double-coated cardstock:* Making Memories; *Metallic rub-ons:* Craf-T Products; *Stamping ink:* Brilliance, Tsukineko.

JOURNALING SPOTLIGHT

On the events of September 11, 2001, written December 1, 2003:

"It felt like I had been skipping down my road of bright sunshine and beautiful promise. Then a dark, foreboding cloud instantly covered me. I was smothered and stunned. I never screamed. I never cried. I went on with life.

"A year passed. If anything touched my heart and my life it was this. I was watching a documentary of the firefighters from 9-11. Their stories. Their hearts. That's when it all became real for me. I cried then. I cried from the inside out.

"That's when I saw the event for what it truly was. Not the horrific scenes we'd seen so many times replayed. But an event of people. What one human will sacrifice for another. Genuine courage with skin on. So many people lost. So many people changed. So many people setting aside everything to help just one more person.

"I will never again discount the value of a single person. People are sunshine."

Mother's Letters, Mother's Love

MOTHER'S LETTERS, MOTHER'S LOVE
by Robin Benjamin Bock
Dallas, TX

Supplies
Patterned paper: K & Company
Eyelets and eyelet letters:
Making Memories
Computer fonts: Scriptina, downloaded
from the Internet; CK Carefree,
"Creative Clips and Fonts for Girls" CD,
Creating Keepsakes
Embossing enamel: Suze Weinberg
Nailheads: Jest Charming
Key charm: Jolee's By You
Hinges: National Hardware
Metallic card frames: Tonertex Foils
Other: Cotton fabric and embroidery floss

Robin's mother, an avid letter
writer, wrote letters nearly
every day that Robin was
away from home. Robin was
happy to have these precious
letters when her mother passed
away. She preserved these priceless
memories on a page to keep her
mother's voice alive.

when someone dies ...

Let scrapbooking help heal a broken heart

Figure 1. If you could go back in time, what would you most like to do with your loved one? *Page by Rebecca Sower.* **Supplies** *Fabric:* Nouveau Fabrics; *Definition stickers:* Making Memories; *Photo corners and vintage trim:* EK Success; *Writing ink:* Sanford; *Fabric paint:* Lumiere, Jacquard Products; *Other:* Vellum, vintage jewelry piece, old typewriter and ribbon. *Idea to note:* Rebecca printed a scanned photo of her grandmother on vellum, then layered it over a definition sticker sheet.

"Strange, isn't it, how a man's life touches so many other lives? When he isn't around, he leaves an awful hole, doesn't he?"

— CLARENCE THE ANGEL, "IT'S A WONDERFUL LIFE"

MY SON IS ON THE VERGE of losing his first tooth. This morning I lost (once again) my car keys. And there are days when I think I'm losing my mind—ha! If you think about it, we all experience losses virtually every day. But no loss cuts so deep and stops our world from spinning like the loss of a person we love (Figure 1).

Many people enter our lives, stake their claims on our hearts, and are still with us. This is a blessing. But there are those to whom we give and receive love, then one day they are gone from us. We call this heartache

ARTICLE BY REBECCA SOWER

JOURNALING EXCERPT:

"When Emma's birth mother decided she wanted our precious girl back, we were devastated. It's amazing how such a small child can impact your life on such a large scale. We didn't realize it until she was gone. My heart will always have a spot for Emma. I will always love her."

Figure 2. Soothe a devastating loss with a lovely layout that expresses your love. *Pages by Catherine Matthews-Scanlon.* **Supplies** *Patterned paper and letter stickers:* K & Company; *Chalk:* Stampin' Up!; *Tags:* Avery; *Sequins:* Darice; *Embroidery floss:* DMC; *Gingham ribbon:* C.M. Offray & Son; *Computer fonts:* Garamond ("Treasure"), Microsoft Word; Clear Typewriter (journaling) and Hannibal Lecter ("American"), downloaded from the Internet; *Other:* Brads, felt and silver charm.

and pain. And, like many deep emotions that run straight to our hearts, pain can be made easier with therapeutic journaling. Let me and a few talented scrapbookers walk you through some suggestions on how to help heal your broken heart through scrapbooking.

Take Your Time

Many people who suffer loss sim- ply cannot put into words what they are experiencing, at least not right away. That's okay. If it helps, just start scribbling on a notepad and get down whatever surfaces— it could be anything from rage to fear to sorrow. That's okay, too. Then throw those notes away if you want. When the time comes to create a meaningful memorial for your loved one, you'll have sifted through all the negative feelings you may have experienced early on.

I experienced the above scenario just a few months ago when a dear uncle passed away. I was angry that he was taken so early in life, at age 58. I thought it unfair that my grandmother had to watch her son die. I felt fear for the brevity of life—when would it

No loss cuts so deep and stops our world from spinning like the loss of a person we love.

Figure 3. Frame a special photo with journaling that tells what you'd do if you had one more day with someone. *Pages by Sande Krieger.* **Supplies** *Patterned paper:* Scrap-Ease; *Tab:* 7 Gypsies; *Ribbon charm, brads, eyelets and "Love" and "Cherish" charms:* Making Memories; *Nailheads:* Lost Art Treasures; *Computer fonts:* Fine Hand (title) and Shelman (journaling), downloaded from the Internet.

JOURNALING EXCERPT:

"If I had one more day with you, I would . . . play canasta with you as my partner, buy a whole box of hand-picked See's Candy and eat it with you, take pictures of you with each of my boys, and ask you to tell me about your life, especially your childhood."

be my turn to experience this?

One evening, after returning home from the hospice, I pulled out a notepad and started scrawling out negative emotions. Soon, when I create a memorial for my uncle, I'll be able to focus clearly on him and my positive memories of his life.

Speaking of heartbreak, scrapbook artist Catherine Matthews-Scanlon had prayed and dreamed of a baby daughter her entire life. The day finally came when she and her husband got the call that they could adopt little Emma. Imagine Catherine's grief when Emma was taken back by her birth mother a few months later.

How does one create a memorial for something so devastating? Catherine gathered the courage and strength to write down what Emma meant to her. She scrapbooked her photos of Emma (Figure 2). This brought Catherine peace, which is what memorials are all about.

Turning Back Time

Sande Krieger and I took a similar approach to our memorial journaling. What would we do if we had just a bit more time with the one we loved? Sande's layout in Figure 3 showcases her close relationship with her dad and highlights precious memories of her life with him.

What is this doing? Lots of things! It's putting on paper for Sande's children and their children some of the pieces of her dad's story that might otherwise never be known. It's solidifying in her heart just how much this man meant to her. And it's reminding her that she still has time now to appreciate the people she loves.

Anyone who has followed my work knows that my maternal grandmother played an irreplaceable role in my life, especially as a child. When I got older, she would ask me repeatedly to come see her. But I thought she would live forever. I was busy, and it wasn't convenient.

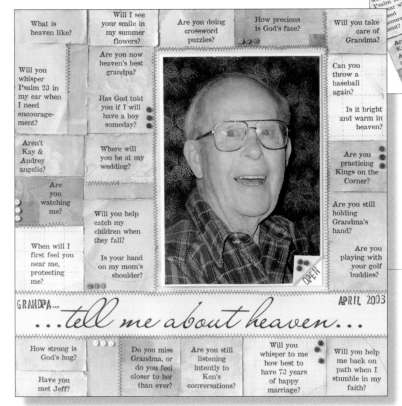

JOURNALING EXCERPT:

"What is heaven like? Are you watching me? Will you help catch my children when they fall? Will you whisper to me how best to have 73 years of happy marriage? Will you help me back on the path when I stumble in my faith?"

Figure 4. Pose questions about "what heaven is like" and include a personal letter to a loved one who has passed on. *Page by Jennifer McGuire.* **Supplies** *Patterned papers:* Autumn Leaves, Creative Imaginations, Daisy D's, K & Company and KI Memories; *Buttons and rubber stamps:* Hero Arts; *Computer fonts:* Attic and Lainie Days, downloaded from the Internet; *Other:* Thread. *Idea to note:* A few days after her grandfather died, Jennifer jotted down some thoughts. Months later, when she felt strong enough to scrapbook her thoughts, she pulled the layout together. "It was wonderful therapy," says Jennifer.

Figure 5. Tuck favorite pet memories on tags in vellum pockets. Highlight favorite traits in slide holders. *Page by Deena Hopkins.* **Supplies** *Vellum, heart photo corners, ribbon and ribbon charm:* Making Memories; *Slide mounts:* Jest Charming; *Brads:* Club Scrap; *Computer fonts:* 2Peas Beautiful (text on tag and behind slide holders) and 2Peas Think Small ("of Kandy"), downloaded from *www.twopeasinabucket.com*; Times New Roman (journaling), Microsoft Word.

JOURNALING EXCERPT:

"I spent the whole thirteen years laughing at, playing with and loving Kandy. When I think of her, I don't remember the cancer. I remember her lying in her favorite corner of the yard. I remember her poking her nose in every grocery bag. I remember her 'abu' in the middle of the night to be let out. . . ."

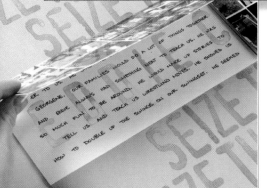

Figure 6. Remind yourself and others that now is the time to "seize the day." Showcase a life with a line-up of photos that have journaling displayed discreetly beneath. *Pages by Lisa Brown.* **Supplies** *Textured cardstock:* Bazzill Basics; *Letter stamps:* Ma Vinci's Reliquary; *Stamping ink:* ColorBox, Clearsnap; *Pen:* Zig Writer, EK Success.

JOURNALING EXCERPT:

"When Missy and I were growing up, Eddie was like an older brother. He would teach us wrestling moves. He showed us how to double up on the swings. . . . Eddie was born with a heart defect and was not expected to live. He defied the odds, and passed away during his last year of college. His time on earth was too short, but I'll always cherish the memories."

How much larger a message did she need to send to me? Why didn't I just make the time to go? So many regrets. So, to bring myself a little peace and to somehow let her know I'm sorry, I created an "If I Could" page about tender moments I would spend with her if I could (see page 255).

Time to Fly

Nowhere have I seen such an endearing, bittersweet approach as Jennifer McGuire's "Grandpa, Tell Me About Heaven" page (Figure 4). Just looking at the photograph of this sweet man makes me smile. And Jennifer's journaling warms my heart and puts a lump in my throat.

No one has to wonder how much Jennifer's grandfather meant to her. Forevermore, her future generations will have (and no doubt cherish) her beautiful memorial to him. I have a very

special grandfather who's passed away as well. I can't wait to create this type of page for him.

Memorials aren't just about human loss. Many people (that includes me) develop strong bonds with special pets. Animals bring so much joy, and it's down-right painful when we lose them.

If you've experienced the loss of a pet, create a memorial about it. An ideal example? Deena Hopkins' page in Figure 5 is a

JOURNALING EXCERPT:

"We are trying to honor Shannon's memory by making more time for our friends, encircling his family with love and support, and really savoring the things in life that matter: family, friends, faith and love."

touching tribute to her little dog, Kandy. Also, if your child or grandchild was especially close to a pet that died, encourage them to talk about their feelings and memories—get that down on paper, too.

Times of Their Lives

Spend some time focusing on the living years of your loved ones. What did they accomplish? Whose hearts did they touch? What were they known for? Did they live their lives to their fullest? Tell how they affected your life while they

were here. Lisa Brown's "Seize the Day" layout (Figure 6) and Stacy Hackett's "True Blue" layout (Figure 7) are wonderful examples of focusing your memorial on a person's living years.

I've always said scrapbooking is therapeutic, and I believe it is in so many ways, especially when you lose someone you love. Bring closure and peace to your heart by creating a memorial page for someone you've lost but want to hold on to forever. ♥

Figure 7. Share friends' or family members' thoughts with journaling pieces clipped to the layout. A mini-tag, attached with a jump ring, identifies the person who expressed the thought. *Pages by Stacy Hackett.* **Supplies** *Patterned papers:* Carolee's Creations (words and definitions) and Pebbles Inc. (blue checked); *Textured cardstock:* Club Scrap; *Book plates, java weave and triangle clips:* Jest Charming; *Micro eyelets:* Making Memories; *Jump rings:* Darice; *Jewelry tags:* Avery; *Pen:* Pigma Micron, Sakura; *Chalk:* Craf-T Products; *Foam tape:* 3M; *Photo-editing software:* PhotoStudio 3000; *Computer font:* Carbonated Gothic, downloaded from the Internet.

journaling your beliefs

Chronicle your values for your posterity

Figure 1. Be sure your scrapbooks include your beliefs. *Page by Rebecca Sower.* **Supplies** *Patterned paper:* EK Success; *Fiber:* Adornaments, EK Success; *Fountain pen:* Sheaffer; *Other:* Beads.

Excerpts from Rebecca's journaling: "I believe every small, kind act will be returned to you. I believe true friends are rare and precious. I believe laughter can cure anything. I believe the best therapy in the world is wide open spaces, fresh air and sunshine. I believe in miracles and the power of prayer. And yes, I believe in Santa Claus."

"He does not believe that does not live according to his belief." —*Thomas Fuller*

WHEN I WAS VERY YOUNG, I believed vines would grow out my ears if I accidentally swallowed a watermelon seed. Where did I get such an idea? My uncle told me so. Why did I believe him? Because he was much older and wiser. Big deal, you say? Well, you weren't the little girl whose entire watermelon-eating experience was excruciatingly difficult. You weren't the one who looked longingly at watermelon at family outings and lived in fear of the horrible consequences of one stray seed. You weren't the one who watched

Figure 2. Share your strongest convictions in your scrapbook. *Page by Allison Strine.* **Supplies** *Specialty paper:* ArtisticScrapper.com; *Rubber stamps:* Zettiology (background on green paper), Hero Arts (alphabet), Rubber Baby Buggy Bumpers (frame); *Stamping ink:* Clearsnap and Ranger Industries; *Picture frames and tag:* Making Memories; *Round brass accent:* Anima Designs; *Computer fonts:* Eat Your Face, Fulton Artistamp; Emmascript, downloaded from the Internet; *Photographic images:* Microsoft Design Gallery Live; *Metallic rub-ons:* Craf-T Products; *Other:* Newspaper clipping (sprayed with Archival Mist), opthamologist lens, jump rings, polymer clay and beads. *Idea to note:* Allison created her stamped frame from white polymer clay, baked the frame, then painted it with metallic rub-ons.

the adults as they carelessly munched on their melon and wondered how they made it look so easy. That was *me.*

Why was my behavior so transformed because of something I believed? Because that's what *beliefs* do—they shape our actions. How we live is directly related to what we know to be true, what we *believe.*

If something is so important that you place your faith and trust in it, it's definitely in the belief category. If something has that much impact on you, be sure your

posterity knows about it.

Beliefs come in all sizes and varieties. Core beliefs, such as integrity and respect, are embraced by most of society. But, you also have more personal beliefs, too. Regardless of their significance, document your heartfelt beliefs in your scrapbooks.

Following are some beliefs categories to get you started. But don't stop here. Any time you recall an issue you feel passionately about, write it down. Then work it into your album pages, creating a legacy that will last for ages.

You and Only You

These are the issues that might be unique to you. You could call them your "soap box" beliefs. For example, I'm infuriated and confused by litterbugs. I believe that people who throw trash out their car windows don't value God's beautiful world. You should hear me preach about it! I've even gone so far as to follow a person to her destination and let her have a piece of my mind. Why? Because of what I *believe.*

And since that belief is part of who I am, I should record it in my

If you're like me, your faith is the single most important belief in your life.

Figure 3. Record your core beliefs for future generations to cherish. *Page by Faye Morrow Bell.* **Supplies** *Background paper:* Source unknown; AGC, Inc. (musical notes); *Cut-out accents:* FreshCuts, EK Success; *Pewter letter:* Two Peas in a Bucket; *Vellum:* The Write Stock; *Computer fonts:* 2Peas Rustic and 2Peas Falling Leaves, downloaded from *www.twopeasinabucket.com*; Ned's Hand and Perkin's Hand, downloaded from the Internet; *Clear pocket:* The Card Connection; *Rubber stamp:* Anita's; *Stamping ink:* Tsukineko (black) and Anita's (terra cotta); *Other:* Coin envelope. *Excerpts from Faye's journaling:* "Our core beliefs: God first. Learn the lesson. Always intend good."

scrapbooks. In Figure 1, I created a layout about some of my "smaller" beliefs. Now I have a record of some of my heart's beliefs for future generations to see.

Allison Strine created an entire page about a single belief (see Figure 2). She wanted to leave a legacy about something her heart knows for sure. What a terrific way to share your beliefs with others!

Shared with Others

What do you and your family and friends believe *together*? A perfect

Figure 4. Encourage your family members to document their beliefs by putting them on paper. *Pages by Rebecca Sower.* **Supplies** *Specialty paper:* ArtisticScrapper.com; *Printed vellum:* EK Success; *Ball chain:* Impress Rubber Stamps; *Pen:* Zig Writer, EK Success; *Fiber:* Adornaments, EK Success; *Sticker:* The Robin's Nest Press; *Other:* Eyelets, beads, wire and safety pin.

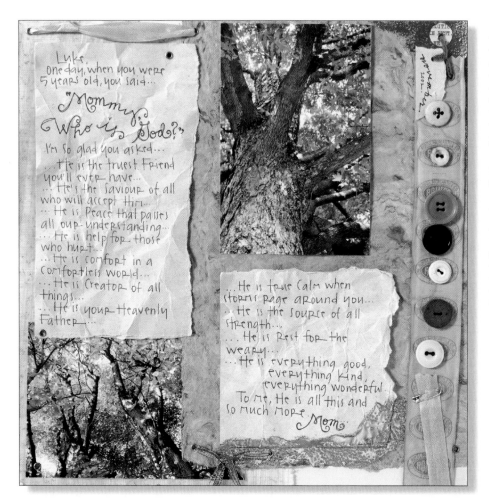

Figure 5. Create a layout that lets your faith take center stage. *Page by Rebecca Sower.* **Supplies** *Specialty paper:* ArtisticScrapper.com; *Fiber:* Adornaments, EK Success; *Eyelets:* Making Memories; *Pen:* Zig Writer, EK Success; *Embossing enamel:* Suze Weinberg; *Circle punch:* Family Treasures; *Other:* Safety pin, vintage trim, seam tape and vintage buttons. *Excerpts from Rebecca's journaling:* "Luke, one day when you were five, you said, 'Mommy, who is God?' I'm so glad you asked. He is the truest Friend you'll ever have. He is everything good, everything kind, everything wonderful. To me, he is all this and so much more. Mom."

example is Faye Morrow Bell's layout that documents the beliefs she and her husband had before their daughter was born (see Figure 3).

What about your relationships? What beliefs do you share? Whether they're shared between husband and wife, the entire family or a close friendship, your mutual beliefs are part of what hold you together. Have you documented them?

Hope for Tomorrow

You know how important it is to have beliefs and to stand up for those beliefs. But how do you encourage those over whom you have influence to determine and cherish their own beliefs? Whether we have children or not, we significantly influence the lives of young people—grandchildren,

nieces and nephews, students, neighbors and more.

I wanted my daughter to take time to clarify her beliefs now and for the future, so I created the layout in Figure 4. It includes space for her to write down the issues in life that her heart believes to be true.

Keep the Faith

If you're like me, your faith is the single most important belief in your life. Everything else revolves around your spiritual beliefs. Is this monumental part of your life included in your scrapbook pages? Will future generations have to wonder what your spiritual beliefs were?

Whether you share your beliefs through a journal, a scrapbook page (see Figure 5) or multiple pages woven throughout your

scrapbooks, please take time to record your beliefs now.

I haven't covered all the areas I could: political beliefs, work ethics, finances and more. The list goes on and on. Chances are, you can't sit down and write down *everything* you believe in one sitting. But I encourage you to start a list.

As issues come to mind, jot them down. Your beliefs can be the sole message of a layout like those featured here, or they may be incorporated along the way as you scrapbook. Either way, you and those you love will be glad you took the time to write them down. That's what *I* believe!

(Oh, by the way, by the time I was seven or so, I figured out my uncle was just a great, big *tease*!) ❤

7 steps to making a scrapbook page

HAVE YOU FOUND YOURSELF staring at a stack of photographs, wondering how to even begin creating a scrapbook page—let alone an entire album? Here are seven basic "how to's" that will make creating your first scrapbook page a snap:

❶ Select a group of photographs related in theme or event. In general, 5–7 photos fit on a two-page spread, and 3–5 photos fit on a single page. Remember, you don't have to scrapbook every photograph you have—choose the best photos to highlight the event,

feeling or memory you want to convey.

❷ Select 2–3 colors of archival paper that will complement colors found in your photographs. You may want to include patterned or decorative papers that support the theme of your pages.

❸ Choose a photograph to be your focal point. As a general rule, select a photo with sharp images, vivid colors and well-lit subjects.

❹ Shape and mat your photos. Add extra prominence to your

focal-point photo by matting it with a wider border than the others or double-matting it. Keep in mind that simple shapes (rectangles, circles, ovals and squares) are among the most eye-pleasing shapes.

❺ Add journaling. No page is complete without adding your thoughts, feelings and memories. Take a few minutes to write down not only the "who" and "when," but also the "what" and "why."

❻ Arrange your photos, journaling and title on your page. As you arrange these elements, pay close attention to the direction your eye naturally moves. In general, well-designed pages are balanced and follow a natural flow that mimics the letter Z. To check the balance, imagine that your layout is on a scale. Does one side tip the scale? Once you're pleased with the layout, adhere the elements to the page.

❼ Try a few extras. As you get more comfortable with scrapbooking, try your hand with some embellishments—stickers, die cuts, rubber stamps and punches are among the most popular page accents. Use these items sparingly; you don't want them to overpower your photos.

Congratulations! You've successfully completed your first scrapbook page. You'll find that as you scrapbook more and more, you'll develop your own style (Figure 1), but these tried-and-true basics will serve as a strong foundation. Happy scrapping! ♥

As you scrapbook more and more, you'll develop a style all your own! *Page by Shannon Wolz of Salt Lake City, Utah.* **Supplies** *Patterned papers:* Scrap-Ease; *Computer font:* Source unknown; *Rusted shape:* Provo Craft; *Eyelets:* Doodlebug Design.

by Souzzann Carroll

Uncover a Treasure

Ascrapbook is an excellent way to unlock the door to the past, and your family history album is no exception. By taking the time today to compile your photos and gather stories of days gone by, future generations will be able to enjoy the richness of their past. Whether you only have a few pictures from your grandparents' era or boxes full of antique photographs, you can make scrapbook pages that will pass on their stories. Read on for some helpful tips that will make your family history album complete and meaningful.

FINDING YOUR ROOTS

Before you get started gathering your family history, it's a good idea to identify your family roots. Filling in the simple details of your family tree (names, date and location of births and deaths), will be a great help as you begin to locate additional information about your roots. You can find family history sheets at your local genealogy store. If there's not one in your area, you can order family history sheets from Storbeck's Genealogy Supplies (www.storbecks.com) or make your own family history sheet (see Figure 1).

When searching for information on your family tree, look for photos, family Bibles, genealogy information and certificates, which frequently contain information that will help you identify your roots.

Once you've filled out your family tree, you may find that you're missing some information. Check with family members to help you fill in the blanks. Frequently, your best source for learning about both your lineage as well as your family history is your oldest living relative. If possible, sit down with your relative and show him or her the information you already have—your relative may be able to add missing names and information. If, after speaking to your relative, you're still missing information, check out the many Internet genealogy sites and books available (see the "Genealogy Resources" sidebar on page 267 for some great resources).

Unlock the door to your past

ADDING DIMENSION

It's nice to know the names of your great-grandparents, but wouldn't it be great if you could understand how they lived? What did they do to get by during the Depression? How much money did your grandfather spend on his first car? Or how did your grandmother know that your grandfather was "the one"? With the basic skeleton of your family tree complete, you're ready to begin flushing out the details of your ancestors' lives. The following tips will help you create a family history that's enjoyable to read.

Figure 1. Creating your own personalized family tree is easy. This one was created by typing the information on a word processor, then drawing the lines with a ruler. *Pages by Souzzann Carroll.* **Supplies** *Punches:* McGill (small heart); Family Treasures (oval, circle, flower, birch leaf, large heart); *Hole punches:* Punchline, McGill; *Punch-art design:* by Tracey L. Isidro.

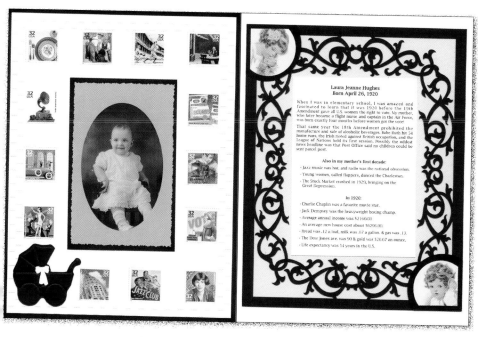

Figure 2. Adding vintage images, like these Celebrate the Century stamps, and historical details to your heritage layouts is a great way to bring your ancestor's era to life. *Pages by Souzzann Carroll.* **Supplies** *Embossed paper:* Lasting Impressions; *Embossing template:* Lasting Impressions, *Laser-cut frame:* Gina Bear, Ltd.; *Stickers:* Melissa Neufeld; *Scissors:* Deckle edge, Fiskars.

into your scrapbook because they're printed on photo-safe paper.

Research historical facts. Most people are fascinated by the historical contexts of their grandparents' and great-grandparents' lives. How did they travel? How much did they pay for a postage stamp? Although some of these details may come out in personal interviews, you can get this general information in other ways as well. (See the "Resources for Historical Background" sidebar on page 269 for web sites that provide information about specific years and dates.)

Frequently, magazine publishers publish a retrospective of the magazine's content over the years. For example, the *Journal of the Century*, covering 100 years of *Ladies Home Journal*, provided me with most of the historical color for my heritage album.

When it comes to defining an era, including images from that time is just as important as supplying written information. And vintage images are

Interview your relatives. You have several options when it comes to collecting your family history, but probably the most enjoyable (and thorough) way is to interview your relatives. Before interviewing family members, take some time beforehand to prepare questions and gather photos you'd like more information on. Frequently, these photos will serve as memory triggers, helping your relative recall stories or events.

As long as the person you're interviewing doesn't object, record your conversation with a tape recorder. You'll have a word-for-word account to refer to, and you'll preserve your relative's voice for posterity. (You may want to bring along a Voice Memory Button from Voice Express [*www.voice-express.com*]. The button is small enough to fit in your scrapbook and it allows you to record a person for 10 seconds then play it back anytime. It'll be a priceless addition to any heritage album.)

It's a good idea to take notes too. Often, the stories your relative tells will bring back memories from your own childhood, and your notes will help you capture them.

During the interview, relax and enjoy the process. Usually, all you need to do as an interviewer is give your subject a starting point, such as "Aunt Marion, tell me about your first year teaching," or "What was Halloween like when you were a child?" (See the "Discussion Starters" sidebar on page 270 for a list of topics that will help with your interview.)

If distance makes a personal visit impractical, send a note to your relative, asking him or her for *specific* information. This usually brings better results than a blanket request to "tell me all you know about the Jones family." Soleil Press (www.turningmemories.com/photoscribe.html) has their own line of "Mail-a-Memory" postcards that are great for getting handwritten memories from your family members. They can easily be slipped

Figure 3. Some photos just beg to be explained. Without the accompanying bit of journaling, the photo on the left half of this layout would have been a mystery. *Pages by Souzzann Carroll.* **Supplies** *Laser-cut numbers:* Gina Bear, Ltd; *Roses:* Secrets of the Heart; *Scissors:* Ripple edge, Fiskars; *Doily:* Brooklace; *Pen:* Zig Clean Color, EK Success; *Planes:* Souzzann traced the planes from an Air Force photo. *Idea to note:* Souzzann cut the center of the doily out and used it as the photo's frame.

Figure 4. "Story bits" capture the details of Sarah Kelly's history while breathing life into the photos. *Page by Souzzann Carroll.* **Supplies** *Patterned paper:* Paper Pizazz, Hot Off The Press; *Embossing template (on ivory frame):* Heritage Handcrafts; *Laser-cut frame, numbers and words:* Gina Bear, Ltd.; *Rose frame:* Secrets of the Heart; *Doily:* Brooklace; *Scissors:* Victorian and Deckle edges, Fiskars.

becoming easier for scrapbookers to find. Even the U.S. Post Office offers a series of stamps called Celebrate the Century. These stamps (which are archivally safe) are available for the decades from 1900 through the 1950s, with the rest of the century due out soon (Figure 2). Other stamps on topics such as the Civil War, the Irish Immigration, and vintage dolls are also available and can be used to add historical enhancements to heritage pages. (*Note:* If you're a stamp collector, never adhere stamps—it lessens their value.)

Start a family history jar. A family history isn't just about your grandparents and great-grandparents—it includes you, too! A family-history jar is a great way to get started writing your own family his-

tory. (*Note:* While you're making your own family history jar, why not make a few extra? It will make a great gift, and will help encourage your friends and family members to record their own memories.)

Making a family history jar is easy. Using the Internet, memory-jogger books and the ideas in the "Discussion Starters" sidebar, simply type out a series of questions (100 questions is a great start). Include questions that will gather basic information as well as questions that will get to the heart of a person's personality, such as "Tell me about the first fight you had with your best friend." Once you've typed the questions, print the lists out on different colors of paper, then cut each question out. (You'll end up with strips of questions.) Next, curl each strip (just wrap them around a pencil) and place them in a jar.

Now comes the fun part. Once a week, sit down with a permanent pen and acid- and lignin-free paper, and pull a question out of the jar. Spend some time answering the question. You'll be amazed at the memories that come to you. You may want to gather your family around and have each member write down his or her own answers, each of which can be included in your heritage album.

WRITING IT DOWN

Now that you've gathered the stories and anecdotes you want to include in your family history, you have several options for presenting the

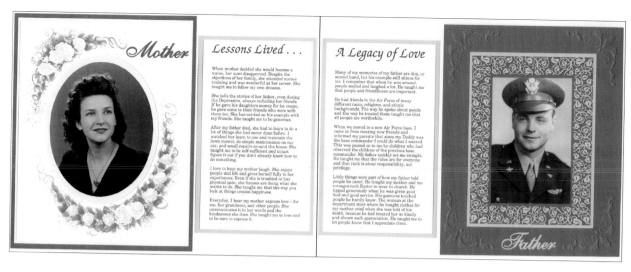

Figure 5. Use the "story bits" technique to recall your memories of a special person. *Pages by Souzzann Carroll.* **Supplies** *Laser-cut frame and words:* Gina Bear, Ltd.; *Rose frame:* Secrets of the Heart; *Stencil:* Heritage Time, Tapestry in Time.

information in your scrapbook. It's important to put the stories in your albums along with the photos. In some cases, without the story, a picture is actually a puzzle. Had I not included the story in Figure 3, for example, the photo of my parents outside the base chapel just following their marriage would have left someone with a lot of questions. With the story, the page becomes a touching insight into my father's life and his special friendship with the men of his squadron.

Let the information you found determine the format of your writing. Here are some suggestions:

Captions. For photos you know little about, simple captions that answer the who, what, where and when may be all you can add. As you review your captions, give as much information as possible. For example, the caption "Hockery family farm in Slater, Missouri, summer of 1940," gives

more history than just "Summer on the Farm."

Identify each person in the photos of an event, but don't force yourself to repeat the names in caption after caption. If, for example, the details of a wedding are included in a newspaper clipping or invitation that you've included on the page, don't duplicate the same facts in your captions. Take a moment to look at the photos with the eyes of someone who has never seen the people pictured there, and identify them if there might be any question. Finally, double check the facts in all your written information. You want to be sure you're passing on an accurate family history!

Story bits. If your information goes beyond a caption, but is just related bits and pieces about your ancestors, try bullet-type journaling, which I call "story bits." Although these "story bits" are just simple lists of information, they're sure to add fascinating tidbits about your ancestors (see Figure 4).

Sometimes the written word is the only tool you have to convey special aspects of your memories of your ancestors. Because I wanted to include insights into my parents' values and character, I listed some of their habits and what I learned from their examples on a scrapbook page (Figure 5.)

Narrative. If you have the skeleton of a story about your relative, consider writing it in the form of a narrative. This really isn't difficult, but it does take some practice to do it well. One trick that may help is to tell the story about a photo to a friend while you record your conversation. Then play back the tape and transcribe your stories for your album.

For step-by-step coaching in writing down your stories, check out *The Photo Scribe* by Denis Ledoux from Soleil Press [*www.turningmemories.com*]. This book is written just for scrapbookers and will help you include the details that will make your stories come alive.

PUTTING IT ALL TOGETHER

Once you've gathered your photographs, mementos, vintage images, genealogy data, personal stories and period information, you're ready to put your family history album together. Your first step is to choose the basic organization for your album. The amount of information you've gathered will probably determine whether you're creating one heritage album or several volumes. Your family tree is a great way to gather clues as to how to best organize your album. Since I like chronological organization and wanted photos of the same time period near each other in my album, I chose the following sequence (you can customize your album's sequence to fit your own needs):

- Family tree and/or photo family tree
- Grandparents and earlier ancestors, father's side
- Grandparents and earlier ancestors, mother's side
- Transition pages of several generations
- Father's childhood
- Father as an adult prior to meeting mother
- Transition page (memorial page or other)
- Mother's childhood
- Mother as an adult prior to meeting father
- Transition page (memorial page or other)
- Pictures of you and the generations after you

Here are some suggestions of layouts that may add depth to your family history album. (If you find you have more family history stories

Figure 6. Your heritage album is a wonderful place to connect generations. Be sure to include significant family heirlooms and document family connections in your heritage book. *Pages by Souzzann Carroll. Photo of Jared by Linda Boyd of Busath Photography.* **Supplies** *Embossing templates:* Heritage Handcrafts; *Scissors:* Mammoth Edge Accents, Paper Adventures; *Title:* Page Topper, Cock-A-Doodle Design, Inc. *Idea to note:* Souzzann made her own picture frame by cutting an oval out of a piece of embossed vellum.

than photos, consider how to use other items, such as vintage images and paper, to make the written information most attractive.)

Mark a place in history. Some events seem to define a generation—the Great Depression, the two World Wars, the assassination of President Kennedy and so on were major events in history. Although you may not have photos of particular events, those memories are vital to a person's view of life.

Discussion Starters

Interviewing family members is a great way to gather information for your heritage album. Use these ideas to jog your memory.

Day-to-Day Life:
- □ your city or town
- □ special toys
- □ best friends
- □ chores
- □ pillow and water fights
- □ pets
- □ picnics
- □ lessons
- □ practice time
- □ clubs
- □ church

- □ cooking and baking

Events:
- □ dances
- □ reunions
- □ weddings
- □ crises
- □ elections
- □ political events
- □ military or church service
- □ promotions

- □ awards
- □ injuries and accidents
- □ moves
- □ vacations
- □ camp
- □ graduations

Firsts:
- □ bike
- □ day of school
- □ job
- □ car

- □ home
- □ Christmas tree

Favorites:
- □ song
- □ joke
- □ TV show
- □ movie
- □ dinner
- □ dessert
- □ hobby
- □ book
- □ teacher

- □ subject
- □ poem
- □ toy
- □ game
- □ recipe
- □ fad
- □ hangout
- □ quotation
- □ saying
- □ entertainer
- □ author
- □ hero
- □ painting

- □ season
- □ flower
- □ color
- □ holiday
- □ sport
- □ animal
- □ restaurant

Other:
- □ goals
- □ prices of goods
- □ headlines of the day

Note: Chatterbox (208/286-9517) publishes *The Scrapbooker's Instant Interviews*, which is filled with questions to ask your relatives. For another great list, visit Rootsweb's web site at *www.rootsweb.com/~genepool/oralhist.htm. plus list].*

Following this same concept, I asked my mother to write the story of when she attended the premiere of *Gone with the Wind*. Her recollection of this event, combined with a portrait of my mother taken about the same time as the premiere and a publicity photo from the movie, not only recreates that time in her life, but also provides a sample of her beautiful flowing and uniform handwriting.

Connect the generations. Your heritage album is a wonderful way to span the years and connect different generations. If you find a remarkable family resemblance in different generations, create a layout with photos that illustrate this resemblance. Or, if a particular family heirloom is important to you or your children, take a photo of the item and include the photo along with the story of its importance (see Figure 6).

Include little details. When compiling your heritage album, include some of the everyday details that will add richness and depth to your layouts. If you're fortunate enough to have old drawings (or floor plans) of family homes, letters or other visuals that document your family history before the time of photography, include them in your album along with any stories you have about that period (see Figure 7).

Nothing can tell the story of your family quite the way a scrapbook does. By combining the stories and photos of your family and putting them in an album, you create something that will be enjoyed by generations to come. So far four generations have enjoyed the story of my father escaping from the POW camp during World War II and have smiled at his habit of referring to that time when he was "a guest of the German government" (see Figure 8). Save and write the stories of your family members' lives. Combine them with your photos and mementos to create a rich record that will be enjoyed by many generations. ♥

Souzzann is the author of A Lasting Legacy, *published by Living Vision Press, from which portions of this article were adapted.*

Figure 7. Add richness to your heritage album with drawings, sketches and even floor plans. *Page by Souzzann Carroll.* **Supplies** *Laser-cut frame:* Paper Lace; *Stickers:* The Gifted Line, Michel & Co.

Figure 8. Don't forget to include special mementos on your scrapbook pages. In this example, the newspaper articles, postcards and telegram tell the whole story. *Pages by Souzzann Carroll. Idea to note:* Souzzann sprayed the postcards and telegram with deacidification spray before placing them in her scrapbook. She also photocopied the newspaper articles on oatmeal-colored paper to keep the aged appearance.

Figure 1. Add dimension to heat-embossed letters by cutting them from foam tape. *Page and samples by Linda Beeson.* **Supplies** *Patterned paper:* Frances Meyer; *Tag:* Stamp in the Hand; *Number tags:* Hot Off The Press; *Diploma envelope:* Stamp Your Heart Out; *Lettering template:* Wordsworth; *Embossing enamel:* Suze Weinberg; *Square concho:* ScrapWorks; *Foam tape:* Scotch, 3M; *Other:* Buttons, fiber and velvet ribbon.

Embossed Foam Letters

While searching for another option for heat-embossed letters, I found that embossing powder will stick to foam tape and can be embossed with a heat gun without damaging the tape. Most foam tape is ½" wide, but I found a 1" roll at a discount store and it's perfect for many lettering templates. Here's how to create the embossed foam letters as shown in Figures 1 and 2:

❶ Remove a length of tape from the roll and place it on a non-stick surface (leftover sticker backing paper works well).

❷ Use a lettering template and permanent pen to trace your letters on the foam tape. The protective coating for the tape is slippery and hard to write on, so you'll need a pen like a Slick Writer or a Sharpie. Cut out the letters.

❸ Peel the letters from the sticker backing paper and arrange them on your layout or tag. After they're in place, remove the top piece of protective coating to expose the adhesive.

❹ Pour the embossing powder over the letters, lightly tap the powder into the adhesive, then turn your project over. Tap off the excess powder and return it to the jar.

❺ Using the heat gun, melt the embossing powder. You can quickly apply another coat of embossing powder while the image is still hot if you want a thicker, more complete covering.

Variation: Simple punches also work well with this technique. Note, however, that some punches have too much detail to punch through the tape. Other punches don't have an opening wide enough to fit the tape.

—*Linda Beeson, Ventura, CA*

Figure 2. Liven up tags with textured, embossed foam letters. *Page by Linda Beeson.* **Supplies** *Patterned paper:* EK Success (lace) and Frances Meyer (tan); *Square tag and number eyelets:* Making Memories; *Diploma envelope:* Stamp Your Heart Out; *Chalk:* Craf-T Products; *Lettering template:* Wordsworth; *Embossing enamel:* Suze Weinberg; *Foam tape:* Scotch, 3M; *Other:* Buttons, rubber stamps and stamping ink.

Quick Custom Roses

For rose accents that look dimensional, coil fiber to create your flower centers. You can use fiber for stem accents as well (Figure 3).

—*Eva Flake, Mesa, AZ*

Figure 3. Create a romantic rose bouquet with fiber, ribbon, chalk and paper. *Accent block by Eva Flake.* **Supplies** *Chalk:* Craf-T Products; *Pen:* Zig Writer, EK Success; *Glue pen:* Sailor.

Easy Letter Cutouts

If you have problems cutting out the insides of certain letters, such as the spaces in "R," "B" and "D," here's an easy solution. I don't cut out the inside of the letter. Instead, I trace it onto a scrap of paper that matches my background paper, then adhere it on top of the letter where the cutout should be.

—*Sher Miller, Bristol, TN*

As you both began your your life together, little did you know you what your future held in store for you. WW2 was the focus in everyone's lives in those days. But as the years passed and as your family grew from two to three, four, five, and finally six; so your love flourished.
You look so young and in love here. Fifty one years later, although there were a few more wrinkles - that glint was still in your eyes when you looked at one another. I hope I can say the same after 50 years in my marriage.

50th Anniversary 1994

mom & dad 1944

Life is the flower for which Love is the honey

Figure 4. Sanding copper foil creates a muted look that's perfect for accenting heritage pictures. *Page by Sharon Whitehead.* **Supplies** *Copper foil:* Scrapbook Essentials; *Green textured paper behind flower:* Victoria Art Supply Store; *Green vellum:* Paper Adventures; *Large flower punch:* EK Success; *Ink spritzer:* Inkworx; *Computer fonts:* Dragonfly, downloaded from *www.twopeasinabucket.com*; Brush Script and NewZurica, Microsoft Word; *Other:* Mesh and copper beads.

Brushed Copper Accents

Copper foil is such a versatile product, and it's easy to give it a muted look simply by sanding it. For my layout in Figure 4, I sanded the copper foil and used it to create a variety of accents. I punched it to create the flower, cut it to create the "Love" accent in my title (and the decorative strip behind the drop-cap "A" in my journaling), and twisted it to create swirly embellishments. As a finishing touch, I adhered a sprinkling of copper beads to the page.

—*Sharon Whitehead, Vernon, BC, Canada*

try our timeless alphabet

Create a look that will endure as long as the memories

Figure 1. The Timeless Alphabet will give your heritage pages a sophisticated look that will endure as long as the photos and stories you're preserving. *Pages by Karen Glenn.* **"Heritage Album" Supplies** *Patterned paper:* Scrap-Ease; *Pen:* Zig Writer, EK Success; *Colored pencils:* Prismacolor, Sanford. **"Edith Joseph" Supplies** *Patterned paper:* Source unknown; *Pen:* Pigma Micron, Sakura; *Colored pencil:* Prismacolor, Sanford; *Other:* Ribbon.

FOR CHRISTMAS A FEW YEARS AGO, my mother gave me a notebook filled with copies of old family photos from several generations. It was exactly what I'd been wanting. I've looked through those photographs numerous times, studying the faces of my ancestors and remembering the stories I've heard about them. I love to look for family resemblances and ponder on the other less tangible characteristics they may have passed down to me.

One by one those photos have been disappearing from the notebook my mother gave me and (with her approval, of course!) reappearing on scrapbook pages in what has now become my family's official Heritage Album. To kick off the album, I wanted a title page with a lettering style that would endure as long as the photos and memories I was trying to preserve. That's what inspired the Timeless Alphabet (Figure 1).

The Timeless Alphabet is classic at the core but has a touch of style all its own. (See the full alphabet in Figure 2.) A little on the formal side, it's perfect for old black-and-white portraits or for your most recent wedding photos. And it's simple to create. Just follow these four steps:

❶ **Start by lightly penciling in your base letters.** Keep the letters' curves rather full, so you'll have plenty of room to add secondary lines. (*Hint:* Drawing guidelines

Figure 2. The delicate Timeless Alphabet has a classic feel with a touch of flair. **Supplies** *Pen:* Zig Writer, EK Success.

STEP BY STEP

❶ Lightly pencil in your letters between horizontal guidelines.

❷ Add secondary lines parallel to the main vertical lines and curves.

❸ Add serifs and curls.

❹ Go over your final lines with pen. Erase your pencil marks and guidelines.

❸ Now add the serifs and the "curls" (note that the serifs on the tops of most of the lowercase letters are angled and slightly curved). Also, replace some of your original straight lines with curves, as in the letters "A," "E," "F," "H," "K," "L" and "N." Keep these curves soft to maintain the classic feel.

❹ Take a moment to look things over and make any needed adjustments. When your letters look just how you want them, go over them with a pen. Erase your pencil marks and guidelines when the ink is dry.

The Timeless Alphabet looks terrific left as an open-face type, as in Figure 3, and can also accommodate a variety of "fills." For a bold look, simply fill in the letters with the same color of marker you used on the outline (Figure 4). A brush pen is the easiest for filling. For a softer look, fill your letters in with colored pencils in one or more shades (Figure 5). You can even fill the letters in with a small pattern that complements your layout. Need more ideas? Try writing your titles in all capitals, enlarging the first and last letters (see Figure 1), or use the alphabet to create a monogram.

Next time you want to add a classic feel to your layouts, give the Timeless Alphabet a try. It's one lettering style that's sure to help your scrapbook pages stand the test of time! ♥

lightly in pencil will help you keep the height of your letters uniform.)

❷ Next, add secondary parallel lines to the main vertical lines of your letters, and secondary arcs to the curved parts of your letters. The space between lines should be narrow—about ⅛" or a little less.

Figure 4. For a bold look, fill in your letters with the same color you used for the outline. A brush pen makes it easy. *Title by Karen Glenn.* **Supplies** *Patterned paper:* Minigraphics; *Pens:* Zig Writer, EK Success.

Figure 3. Use the Timeless Alphabet as an open-faced lettering style for a simple, beautiful look on your scrapbook pages. *Pages and titles by Karen Glenn.* **"1943" Supplies** *Embossed sticker:* K & Company; *Pen:* Zig Writer, EK Success. **"Then and Now" Supplies** *Patterned vellum:* PrintWorks; *Pen:* Zig Writer, EK Success.

Figure 5. Create a soft look on your heritage pages by filling in the Timeless Alphabet with colored pencils. *Titles by Karen Glenn.* **Supplies** *Patterned paper:* Colors By Design; *Pen:* Zig Writer, EK Success; *Colored pencil:* Prismacolor, Sanford.

homespun accents

BY DARCY CHRISTENSEN

Add a vintage look to heritage pages

CREATING SCRAPBOOK PAGES with treasured photographs is a meaningful way to preserve your family heritage (Figure 1). Whether your photos were snapped decades ago or just last week, dress them up with these heritage-themed titles and accents, created by scrapbook artist Darcy Christensen.

Simply copy the titles and accents onto neutral-colored cardstock, reducing or enlarging the images as needed. For a vintage look, copy the designs onto vellum, then color them with colored pencils, watercolors, markers or chalks that coordinate with your layout's color scheme. You can add interesting details, such as charms, stitching, torn edges or ribbon, to make the look all your own, then mat the title or accent with cardstock (Figure 2). These homespun designs are sure to help you treasure your memories and your handiwork! ♥

Figure 1. Highlight the memories and photographs that have been passed down in your family using scrapbook-page titles and accents with an old-fashioned feel. *Page by Darcy Christensen.* **Supplies** *Patterned papers:* Susan Branch, Colorbök; *Mulberry paper:* PrintWorks; *Vellum:* Paper Adventures; *Computer font:* CK Curly, "The Best of Creative Lettering" CD Combo, *Creating Keepsakes; Heart fastener:* HyGlo; *Colored pencils:* Memory Pencils, EK Success; *Chalks:* Craf-T Products; *Other:* Buttons and gold thread.

Figure 2. Personalize your titles and accents with fun techniques, such as tearing, chalking, stitching and watercoloring. *Pages by Darcy Christensen.* **"POCKET WATCH" Supplies** *Vellum:* Paper Adventures; *Colored pencils:* Memory Pencils, EK Success; *Chalks:* Craf-T Products; *Chain and rings:* Westrim Crafts; *Other:* Thread. **"REMEMBER WHEN" Supplies** *Pens:* Zig Writer, EK Success; *Circle punch:* Family Treasures; *Tag:* Darcy's own design; *Other:* Crochet thread. **"FAMILY HEIRLOOMS" Supplies** *Pen:* Zig Writer, EK Success; *Colored pencils:* Memory Pencils, EK Success; *Chalks:* Craf-T Products; *Button:* Dress-It-Up, Cut-It-Up; *Other:* Thread and fishing lure (used to dangle the button from the title). **"FAMILY TREE" Supplies** *Patterned paper:* Scrap-Ease, *Pen:* Zig Writer, EK Success; *Chalks:* Craf-T Products; *Other:* Crochet thread.

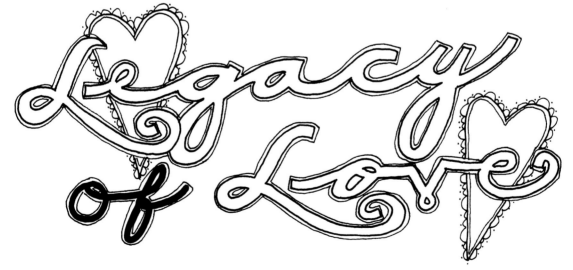

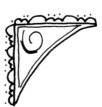

 Memories

generations

OUR FAMILY HERITAGE

Legacy of Love

Family Tree

Remember when

FAMILY HEIRLOOMS

Our Family portrait

Grandfather

Grandmother

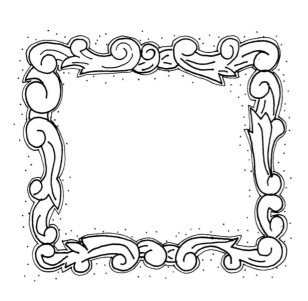

THE FAMILY HOMESTEAD

by Heather Holdaway Thatcher

Try our Monogram Alphabet

Have you been on the lookout for a creative lettering style that will enhance your old black-and-white photos? Our Monogram Alphabet is sure to offer just the perfect touch to any heritage layout. Whether you want to include your ancestors' initials or create a classic title for your layout, this alphabet can be custom designed to fit any style or era (Figure 1). "Initially" the Monogram Alphabet may seem intimidating, but it's not—simply follow these five easy steps to create your own timeless alphabet.

CREATING THE MONOGRAM ALPHABET

❶ Using a pencil and square template, trace a square onto a piece of paper. *Note:* You can alter the size of your alphabet by tracing a larger or smaller square. Inside the box, print the letter in pencil.

❷ Still using a pencil, enhance the letter by drawing serifs (short lines at the end of each stroke on the letter), then connect the serifs by drawing a line that curves in toward the middle. The result is a stroke that's wider at the ends and thin in the middle. Add decorative curls to the end of the letter (*Note:* Not all letters have curled ends).

❸ Once you've written the letter (or word) the way you like it, outline the

Figure 1. Add a patriotic flair to your military-service photos with the Monogram Alphabet. *Page by Heather Holdaway Thatcher.* **Supplies** *Pen:* Zig Writer, EK Success; *Colored pencils:* Prismacolor, Sanford; *Patterned paper:* Northern Spy; *Velvet paper:* Cache Junction.

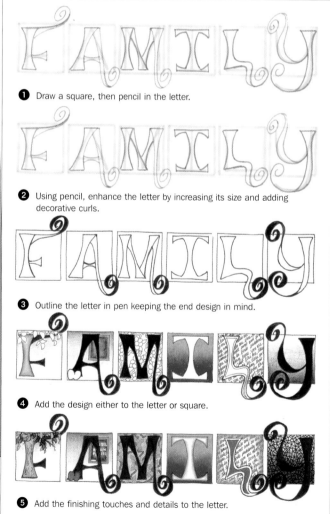

❶ Draw a square, then pencil in the letter.

❷ Using pencil, enhance the letter by increasing its size and adding decorative curls.

❸ Outline the letter in pen keeping the end design in mind.

❹ Add the design either to the letter or square.

❺ Add the finishing touches and details to the letter.

Figure 2. The Monogram Alphabet will go with any era—simply vary the design to complement your photos. **Supplies** *Pens:* Zig Writer and Zig Millennium, EK Success; Milky Gel Roller, Pentel; *Colored pencils:* Prismacolor, Sanford.

Figure 3. The Monogram Alphabet is a perfect way to enhance heritage layouts. *Page by Heather Holdaway Thatcher.* **Supplies** *Pen:* Zig Writer, EK Success; *Patterned paper:* Frances Meyer; *Colored pencils:* Prismacolor, Sanford.

Figure 4. Handmade paper is the perfect accent for the Monogram Alphabet. **Supplies** *Pens:* Zig Writer, EK Success; Milky Gel Roller, Pentel; *Colored pencils:* Prismacolor, Sanford; *Patterned paper:* Keeping Memories Alive.

letter with a marker, then erase the pencil lines. (*Note:* Keep the end design of the letter in mind before you outline the letter. For example, the leaves in the "tree" in the "F" (see alphabet on previous page) overlap onto the letter. If this is the case, add the design prior to outlining the letter in marker. See the next step for instructions on adding the design.)

Next color in the decorative curls, keeping in mind that some parts of the curls are thicker than others.

❹ Now you're ready to add the design to your letter. I recommend penciling in your design before using a marker. I've given you 26 different options in the full alphabet (see Figure 2). Remember that each design can be applied to any letter. Try coloring in the letter and decorating the background, or decorate the letter with a subtle design. The possibilities are practically endless.

❺ Add the final details to your design, such as the knots on the "trunk" in the letter "F," or the stained-glass design to the background of the letter "Y." I've found that colored pencils are great for shading and blending, while markers create bold letters

and lines. I also use opaque pens on the designs that need it—they're especially handy if you accidentally make a mistake.

Once you've finished your monogram, you have several options to complete your title. You can print the rest of the word, write it in cursive or use a computer font to finish the word. I've found that when you write the rest of the word out along the upper half of the square (see Figure 3), it gives the impression that you're reading a fairy tale.

A FEW IDEAS

Remember that you aren't limited to writing the Monogram Alphabet on solid paper. You can write your letter on patterned paper then back the letter with handmade paper (see Figure 4), or write the letter on patterned vellum (see Figure 5).

There you have it—a timeless alphabet that will perfectly enhance your heritage layouts. The Monogram Alphabet will help you leave your mark on your scrapbook pages, while preserving important information about your ancestors. ♥

Figure 5. For a different look, write your letters on patterned vellum. *Page by Heather Holdaway Thatcher.* **Supplies** *Pen:* Zig Writer, EK Success; *Colored pencils:* Prismacolor, Sanford; *Patterned paper:* Keeping Memories Alive; *Patterned vellum:* The Paper Company.

by Becky Higgins

Cut 'n Copy

Does your layout need one final enhancement? On the next two pages, you'll find a handful of great titles to enhance just about any heritage photos you have. Just copy the lettering on a copy machine, enlarging or decreasing the size to your desire. I recommend copying onto a neutral or light-colored paper, such as white, taupe, cream or gray (Figure 1). This will give you more flexibility when coloring in with pencils, chalks, pens or any other medium you choose. Once your title is colored, simply mat it with cardstock or decorative papers. These titles will add the finishing touch to your layouts! ♥

Figure 1. These titles will bring the "good ol' days" back to your scrapbook pages. **Supplies** *Leaves:* Wallies, McCall's; *Patterned paper:* Carolee's Creations; *Photo corners:* 3L Stationery Corp.; *Colored pencil:* Prismacolor, Sanford; *Pen:* Zig Writer, EK Success. *Idea to note:* To give the title block a rustic look, Becky shaded it with tan chalk. She also added gray shadowing lines around the letters in the title to add dimension.

A LASTING LEGACY

the good old days

MY HERITAGE

OUR Family

golden ANNIVERSARY

Traditions

WORLD WAR I

WORLD WAR II

FAMILY TREE

a living legend

the family HOMESTEAD

the heritage photographs of tomorrow

To us, heritage photographs are black-and-white, tattered photos taken decades or even a century ago—with serious-faced subjects standing on the wooden porch of their Victorian houses. What we don't realize is that in a hundred years, the photographs we're taking today will be considered "heritage photographs" by generations to come. While you're busy capturing great photos for your scrapbooks, remember to capture shots that provide a glimpse of what life is like for you. The following ideas will get you started:

- A family portrait (update as needed)
- The houses you've lived in (inside and out)
- Key aspects of your daily routines
- Favorite hobbies and activities
- How you get around (transportation, including your family car)
- The town you live in

- Places you enjoy visiting—every day and as a special treat
- Where you work and what you do
- The most technologically advanced items you own
- How you communicate with others
- Family traditions
- Your most valued possessions

- Foods you enjoy, and where you get them (garden, supermarket, favorite restaurant)
- Relationships between family members or friends
- How you and your family dress

ARTICLE BY CATHERINE SCOTT